DEDICATION

Again to Chris, Kate, and Maureen—with love

ACKNOWLEDGMENTS

My special thanks to my daughter, Maureen, for her wonderful artwork. You have a talent!

As always, my love and appreciation go out to my family—Chris, Kate, and Maureen—and to our friends—Jamey and Tim—for their constant support and help with everything, including this resource.

And one more time, heartfelt thanks to Connie Kallback, my editor, for her skill, patience, and enthusiasm throughout this and other projects.

Still again, sincere thanks to Win Huppuch, whose wisdom and encouragement are always inspiring.

ABOUT THE AUTHOR

Jack Umstatter has taught English on both junior high school and senior high school levels since 1972, and has taught education and literature at Dowling College, Oakdale, NY for the past 11 years. He currently teaches English in the Cold Spring Harbor school district in New York.

Mr. Umstatter graduated from Manhattan College with a B.A. in English and completed his M.A. in English at S.U.N.Y.—Stony Brook. He earned his Educational Administration degree at Long Island University.

Mr. Umstatter has been selected Teacher of the Year several times and was elected to *Who's Who Among America's Teachers*. Most recently, he appeared in *Contemporary Authors*. Mr. Umstatter has taught all levels of secondary English classes, including honors and Advanced Placement classes. As coach of the high school's academic team, the Brainstormers, he led the team in capturing the Long Island and New York State championships in the American Scholastic Competition Network National Tournament of Champions in Lake Forest, IL. His teams have recently competed in the Questions Unlimited National Academic Championships in New Orleans and Los Angeles.

Mr. Umstatter's other publications include *Hooked on Literature!* (1994), *201 Ready-to-Use Word Games for the English Classroom* (1994), *Brain Games!* (1996), *Hooked on English!* (1997), and the six-unit *Writing Skills Curriculum Library* (1999), all published by The Center for Applied Research in Education.

ABOUT THIS RESOURCE

For some students, learning grammar is right up there with eating liver, receiving an immunization shot, or waking up before dawn on a chilly Saturday morning to help Mom or Dad clean the basement. "Who needs grammar?" and "When are we ever going to use this stuff?" are the refrains we often hear from our students. One of my favorites is, "In the real world, we will never use these things!" "Things," of course, means grammar.

Yet, we teachers realize that grammar serves many useful purposes. W. Somerset Maugham said, "It is well to remember that grammar is common speech formulated." Beside serving as the basic structure of our tongue, grammar is language and language, in turn, is the expression of life. And, yes, grammar is a part of the "real world." Every human utterance is somehow connected to grammar. More formally, standardized tests, such as the revised and, in many cases, more demanding state assessments, are in fashion today. So, too, are SATs, ACTs, ELAs, and other evaluations that test our students' knowledge of grammar. Obviously, grammar plays a part in the everyday lives of our students and all other human beings.

Even if we convince our students that grammar is a necessity, how then do we make the teaching of grammar exciting and fun for these children? To parse or not to parse? To diagram or not to diagram? These are the questions.

Grammar Grabbers! Ready-to-Use Games & Activities for Improving Basic Writing Skills is a collection of creative, fun-filled, and ready-to-use activities that make both teaching and learning grammar more enjoyable. These classroom-tested activities have been positively received by students who have become more interested in grammar, and, consequently, more skilled in their writing. The 203 activities can be used as individual, group, or whole-class activities. They can function as introductions, reviews, or homework assignments. Perhaps you will choose to use a specific activity as a quick time-filler, a competition, a makeup quiz, or an extra credit assignment. The possibilities are many! Formatted as crosswords, word finds, concealed quotations, cryptoquotes, scrambled and hidden words, riddles, magic squares, word-generating wheels, jumbles, and more, these activities will motivate and engage your students in exciting learning experiences. Grammar is now fun!

Section One, Parts of Speech—Working with Words!, features 26 activities that focus on the basic vocabulary of grammar—the parts of speech. Here the students will study the eight parts of speech, emphasizing their various forms and functions. Nine specific activities feature *all* the parts of speech, helping your students to know all eight of them well.

The 29 activities in the second section, Phrases and Clauses—Word Weavers!, continue the path toward the complete sentence. Here, students will start with two activities focusing on grammar terminology. They will then move on to identify and recognize the functions of prepositional, appositive, and verbal phrases, as well as main and subordinate clauses. Students will enjoy the activities that focus on how to intelligently include these phrases and clauses in daily writing assignments. They will gain a new appreciation for the *Gettysburg Address*, the Prologue to *Romeo and Juliet*, and even "Little Miss Muffet" while completing these interesting and fun activities.

The third section, Sentences—Grammar's Galaxy!, includes 26 creative sentence activities. Students will classify sentences according to structure and purpose while they learn to avoid fragments, run-ons, and comma splices. Utilizing the skills featured in the initial two sections, students will write powerful and convincing sentences in a variety of interesting formats.

Section Four, Usage—A Way with Words!, reviews those troublesome usage problems we see much too frequently as we review students' writings. In these 27 activities, students will become more skilled in language appropriateness, agreement, case, pronoun usage, verb situations, modifiers, avoiding double negatives, and other previously confusing areas.

Punctuation is dominant in the 20 activities that comprise Section Five, Mechanics—The Tools of the Trade! Some of the activities feature capitalization, spelling (spell checkers go only so far), and possessives. Those seemingly unconquerable comma problems are also featured here.

The sixth section, Grammar's Helpers—Taking Care of Business!, includes 24 activities highlighting words often confused, suffixes, plurals, idioms, expressions, and vocabulary to improve grammar and writing in general.

Section Seven, Grammar Games—And Away We Go!, features 29 grammar games that review the concepts found in the previous six sections. Your students will enjoy these activities that invite them to use their grammar, usage, and mechanics skills in a fun format. Whether individuals, small groups, or entire classes play these grammar games on parts of speech, vocabulary, sentences, word construction, or word recognition, the students will learn and have a good time.

The concluding section of *Grammar Grabbers!*, Final Tests—Knowledge Is Power!, is comprised of 22 Final Tests designed to test your students' knowledge and abilities in specific areas of grammar. Each Final Test is formatted as a genuine final or unit test and is worth 100 points. You will not have to compose tests on the parts of speech, clauses, grammar terms, types of sentences, agreement, complements, irregular verbs, clauses, phrases, commas, words often confused, punctuation, and more. They are right here, already prepared for you!

These ready-to-use activities provide students with the tools to use grammar more effectively in their writing. The writing process becomes less tedious and more enjoyable. The benefits are many, both for the students and for you! Students will become more proficient and comfortable with grammar, and they will become more eager to write. Teachers will have 203 ready-to-use activities at their fingertips—including 22 Final Tests!

Moliere once said, "Grammar . . . which can govern kings." Grammar's importance can never be underestimated. These activities emphasize the importance of grammar in an entertaining and productive way. So, allow your students to encounter grammar—that which governs kings—as presented in *Grammar Grabbers! Ready-to-Use Games & Activities for Improving Basic Writing Skills*. It will be a royal union!

Jack Umstatter

TABLE OF CONTENTS

Section One

PARTS OF SPEECH—WORKING WITH WORDS!

Section Two

PHRASES AND CLAUSES—WORD WEAVERS!

Section Three
SENTENCES—GRAMMAR'S GALAXY!

Section Four
USAGE—A WAY WITH WORDS!

Section Five

MECHANICS—THE TOOLS OF THE TRADE!

Section Six

GRAMMAR'S HELPERS—TAKING CARE OF BUSINESS!

Section Seven
GRAMMAR GAMES—AND AWAY WE GO!

Contents

Section Eight
FINAL TESTS—KNOWLEDGE IS POWER!

ANSWER KEYS (245-328)

PARTS OF SPEECH— WORKING WITH WORDS!

1. NOUNS AND NAMES

Circle the first letter of each noun in these sentences. Then write these letters in order on the line below number 10. If your answers are correct, you have spelled out seven first names.

1. The students found an umbrella near Evanston last night.

2. Some opinions will be discussed by reporters at their meeting.

3. The jury came to an understanding and an acceptance of the judge's notification.

4. We ladies thought the investigation was horrible.

5. After the scientist tested the acid, the microscope was sent to the academy.

6. When the research is published, interest in the artifacts will increase.

7. Stop it immediately!

8. Many inexpensive radios were purchased last October and November.

9. My dad has redone the entrance.

10. Please slice the bread.

The seven names are _____, _____, _____, _____,

_____, _____, and _____.

2. IS . . . IS NOT . . . IS . . . IS NOT . . . IS . . . IS NOT

Stop the arguing and decide for sure whether it *is* or *is not*! Circle the correct answer within the parentheses in each of these 20 sentences. Then, on the line next to the number, write the letter above the correct answer. Finally, write the letters, in order, of the "is" answers, and then do the same for the "is not" answers. If your answers are correct, the letters of the "is" and the "is not" answers will spell out two words associated with computers.

          p   l

1. _____ *Fido* (is, is not) a proper noun.

          r   o

2. _____ *Children* (is, is not) a plural noun.

         n   m

3. _____ *Bottle* (is, is not) a feminine noun.

         o   d

4. _____ *Monday's* (is, is not) an example of a possessive noun.

         g   e

5. _____ *Persistence* (is, is not) an abstract noun.

       e   u

6. _____ *Table* (is, is not) a plural noun.

       t   l

7. _____ *Love* (is, is not) a concrete noun.

       u   t

8. _____ *Himself* (is, is not) a predicate noun.

       r   s

9. _____ *Jury* (is, is not) a collective noun.

       y   i

10. _____ *Fragile* (is, is not) a compound noun.

© 2001 by The Center for Applied Research in Education

a   n

11. _____ *Mother-in-law* (is, is not) a compound noun.

m   e

12. _____ *Stardom* (is, is not) a singular noun.

m   r

13. _____ *Relaxation* (is, is not) an abstract noun.

a   m

14. _____ *Him* (is, is not) a subject noun.

e   b

15. _____ *Brother* (is, is not) a masculine noun.

w   e

16. _____ *Mine* (is, is not) a possessive noun.

m   d

17. _____ *Family* (is, is not) a plural noun.

v   i

18. _____ *Uganda* (is, is not) an abstract noun.

o   a

19. _____ *Playwright* (is, is not) a plural noun.

r   t

20. _____ *Candle* (is, is not) a concrete noun.

The "is" answers spell out _____. The "is not" answers spell out

_____.

3. FOUR-LETTER NOUNS AND VERBS

Twenty-five four-letter words that are both nouns and verbs are scrambled below. Unscramble these words and write them on the lines provided.

1. RDIA _____

2. NETO _____

3. FDNI _____

4. SWON _____

5. OJEK _____

6. YLLE _____

7. WLIA _____

8. DTNE _____

9. RTNE _____

10. HTSO _____

11. MTEE _____

12. RNIA _____

13. HDNA _____

14. IHCN _____

15. BTSE _____

16. CTAO _____

17. KCIK _____

18. SYAT _____

19. TTLI _____

20. DRAE _____

21. QIZU _____

22. PTRA _____

23. RLEE _____

24. ACRH _____

25. LNAO _____

4. PRONOUNS ARE IN!

Twenty-four pronouns are hidden in this word-find puzzle. They are listed beneath the puzzle, so you have some help. Circle the pronouns, arranged horizontally, backward, forward, diagonally, and vertically in the puzzle. Finally, next to each pronoun listed under the puzzle, write S if it is singular, P if it is plural, or S/P if it can be either singular or plural.

```
H  P  W  Y  M  G  W  E  Y  T  Q  S  C  P  R  Q  Z  X  W  F
W  T  D  X  X  C  N  B  O  Z  D  M  S  Y  S  C  W  X  J  L
C  Q  D  T  P  O  M  D  U  G  V  Q  Y  Z  X  J  Y  T  B  D
H  Z  W  T  Y  V  T  W  R  X  O  N  L  J  B  T  X  J  T  V
D  V  H  R  H  S  R  H  S  K  F  U  G  C  S  X  J  T  P  K
T  H  E  M  S  E  L  V  E  S  H  E  R  A  N  Y  B  O  D  Y
Z  V  C  K  H  V  I  X  L  M  P  D  X  S  Z  L  P  N  V  P
E  I  P  T  L  E  A  R  F  S  G  X  H  Y  T  K  H  H  X  X
T  H  I  S  V  R  L  W  E  S  A  N  O  T  H  E  R  K  S  H
W  E  Y  U  Q  A  L  M  I  C  O  H  B  L  M  N  N  Z  Y  F
N  Q  C  M  D  L  R  H  O  W  Y  M  R  X  H  O  F  G  Z  R
Y  O  U  R  S  E  L  V  E  S  M  X  E  W  B  M  I  N  E  S
F  X  M  G  T  R  K  W  W  P  T  Z  C  O  D  Z  R  P  F  C
R  Y  Z  W  B  W  F  Z  F  M  M  Z  D  M  N  V  D  D  F  C
J  N  G  H  V  L  S  P  V  D  P  Y  K  G  Q  E  V  L  V  K
```

ALL	OURS
ANOTHER	SEVERAL
ANYBODY	SOMEONE
EVERYONE	THEIR
HE	THEM
HER	THEMSELVES
HIS	THIS
IT	US
ME	WE
MINE	YOURSELF
MOST	YOURSELVES
NEITHER	
NOBODY	

5. THERE'S SOMETHING VERY DEFINITE ABOUT THESE INDEFINITES!

Indefinite pronouns can be tricky. Sometimes they sound like plural pronouns when they are really singular pronouns. You should memorize the pronouns to know which are singular, which are plural, and which can be either singular or plural.

Circle the correct indefinite pronoun in each sentence below. Then write the pronoun's corresponding two letters (above the pronoun) on the line next to the number. If your answers are correct, you will spell out the capitals of 5 countries. Write those five capitals on the line below the last sentence.

                        te   sa

1. _____ All of the books (was, were) brought to the storage room.

                        re   nt

2. _____ Each of the contestants (are, is) nervous about the show.

                        ia   nt

3. _____ Several of the contestants (are, is) receiving special awards.

                        le   go

4. _____ Everybody who saw the accident (are, is) asked to report to the precincts.

                        ne   so

5. _____ Anything in the athletic events (was, were) possible.

                        wd   ee

6. _____ Nobody from any of these towns (has, have) heard about the new regulations.

                        or   el

7. _____ Anyone from these areas (know, knows) how to prepare for these situations.

                                    hi   ru

8. _____ One of the brightest stars in the heavens (has, have) been visible for many years.

                                    he   io

9. _____ Something that you said during the festivities (was, were) bothering my sister.

                                      ls   po

10. _____ Some of the materials found in today's newspaper (contain, contains) funny material.

© 2001 by The Center for Applied Research in Education

                                                              co   in
11. _____ Neither of the choices for that political position (are, is) what we really
         expected.

                                                                            ki   ve
12. _____ Anyone who had ever been a member of any of Mrs. Muller's classes (had, have)
         been invited.

                                    da   af
13. _____ A few of these bracelets (happen, happens) to be on sale today!

                                    ma   pl
14. _____ Much of the current situation (won't, weren't) be resolved for a few months.

                                ko   sc
15. _____ Either of these desserts (sound, sounds) delicious.

                                                      su   us
16. _____ Each one of these twenty-two state officials (request, requests) more
         information from us immediately.

                            ca   tr
17. _____ Some of the cake (was, were) eaten by the older brothers.

                                          ut   nb
18. _____ Everything in these three bedrooms (need, needs) to be replaced.

                                sw   er
19. _____ Both of these beach chairs (was, were) lost last summer.

                                          nt   ra
20. _____ One of his most cherished possessions (are, is) his baseball cards.

The capitals of the five countries are _____

_____.

6. G(EE), THIS CAN BE FUN!

Twenty-five words are found in the boxes below. Draw an X through any box containing a word that is a verb (though it may be another part of speech as well). If your answers are correct, the shaded boxes will form a number. Write that number on the line below the grid. Finally, use any twelve of the words found on this grid in an original story. Entitle the story. Write that story on a separate sheet of paper.

go	graceful	grab	grounder	great
grow	graver	give	graduation	gross
growl	gyro	going	gaze	goose
grind	gondola	glide	geese	government
gust	gaggle	giggle	gumption	guppy

© 2001 by The Center for Applied Research in Education

7. FINDING THE VERBS ALPHABETICALLY

Twenty-six verbs are hidden in this puzzle. Each verb begins with a different letter, so there is a verb for each letter of the alphabet. These verbs are placed backward, forward, diagonally, horizontally, and vertically. Circle the verbs and write them in the space below the puzzle.

```
C  V  M  N  D  C  O  J  H  X  S  M  N  R  Q  A  K  G  J  F
R  S  F  B  P  P  H  X  J  Q  H  D  E  V  E  R  V  R  P  J
E  L  E  C  T  Z  O  O  M  Y  H  H  K  N  L  R  L  O  L  L
T  T  X  I  R  K  I  Y  O  S  E  K  F  W  D  I  E  W  I  N
T  V  O  R  E  N  M  R  I  S  S  A  O  B  N  V  A  L  F  D
U  N  P  H  A  J  D  N  Z  R  E  H  R  M  I  E  R  B  E  D
R  N  T  G  T  Y  I  I  R  S  Z  T  A  N  K  G  N  D  L  Z
G  U  P  Q  T  F  U  V  I  S  Y  S  R  Q  T  N  K  I  N  C
N  M  T  Q  L  Q  P  K  S  Y  R  Z  V  I  T  S  N  P  K  G
T  B  D  K  L  W  J  U  K  T  S  E  G  N  I  E  G  D  N  R
D  P  V  G  N  I  C  G  L  Z  N  E  X  D  D  P  R  C  G  L
G  M  X  Z  H  N  W  Z  T  L  B  X  C  X  W  P  R  P  J  G
J  M  L  T  G  T  W  D  P  C  V  S  K  J  K  F  D  P  J  P
Q  Y  Y  L  L  Z  L  Q  C  Q  Z  Q  B  J  F  D  V  S  L  H
P  K  R  H  Z  S  X  W  L  N  D  X  G  D  M  B  D  V  C  V
```

_____   _____   _____

_____   _____   _____

_____   _____   _____

_____   _____   _____

_____   _____   _____

_____   _____   _____

_____   _____

8. VERBS A-PLENTY

Twenty-nine four-letter verbs are this crossword's answers. Write your answers in the appropriate spaces within the crossword puzzle.

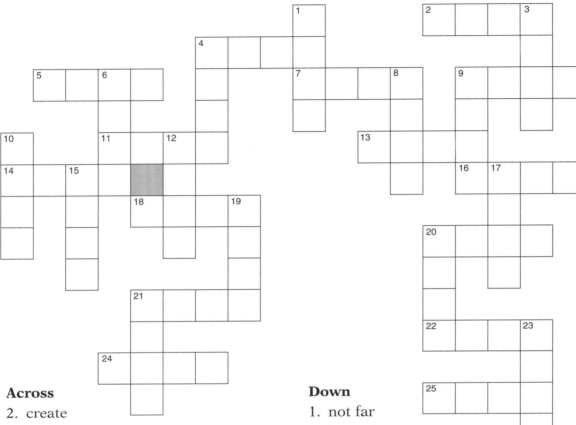

Across

2. create
4. to look intently
5. obscene
7. curve on bottom of foot
9. opposite of spend
11. get bigger
13. wreck
14. facilitate
16. to pull with force
18. to dress in
20. beat vigorously
21. final
22. stop
24. test
25. reveal

Down

1. not far
3. begrudge
4. shine brightly
6. convince
8. transport by wagon or truck
9. mail
10. carry
12. not closed
15. voice a melody
17. water from the sky
19. declaim violently
20. long for
21. praise
23. speak

Name_____ Date _____ Period_____

9. CALLING ALL VERBS! CALLING ALL VERBS!

Twenty-eight verbs are hidden within other words in these 15 sentences. The numbers in parentheses indicate the number of letters in these hidden verbs, in their order of appearance within the sentence. Circle the hidden verbs.

1. Have you done all of your research for the presentation? (6, 4)

2. We just loved the holiday display in the store window.   (4, 3)

3. Another informal meeting has to be scheduled for next month.   (4)

4. He is an interesting guy who believes completely in our cause.   (4, 8)

5. Marion, will you read the paragraph from the first chapter?   (5, 4)

6. At this stage of your life, you are looking for a more meaningful existence.   (4, 5)

7. Do you suppose they can seek independence by themselves?   (6, 3)

8. Plenty of residents came out to help their neighbors.   (4, 4)

9. The curious students looked for satellites and stars with their instruments.   (4, 5)

10. Those two passengers were discharged from the emergency room.   (4, 5)

11. Say "fervently flopping" five times fast.   (4, 4)

12. Some of the runners had been wrestling with the oppressive heat.   (5)

13. He will be remembered as a courageous and respectable human being.   (4, 7)

14. We ask that you please shut off all electronic devices while you are in the theater.   (5, 4)

15. It's hard to change the basic design of the forest.   (4, 4)

10. BE ALERT!

Twenty-nine verbs, all beginning with the letters *be*, are hidden in this puzzle. Circle each of these verbs. They are placed backward, forward, diagonally, horizontally, and vertically.

```
L E B G H B B N B B E F R I E N D L T D
F R E E E F E E Y E E X S H J N B S V B
H A G A G M E N S S D C H E N E L E B Y
B W R H J U T X I E B E A B Q B T V S N
B E M O A N I N G E F E T Z B E A M K B
T B E M X G I L S C G I G J Z H K L V Y
Z Q L P L G B E E H E T R E L E A F Z
X F G S E X E I B R V V D B U E E C Y Z
B G J B C C L C E R L L J V L D D E N R
E E Z K H E I B T F O M Q T S J G B W L
C N R V B S E H T H M W T P K V C E B Y
O Z H A K T V K E V Y I L Q D B N G J J
M J B S T B E B R Y L S Z K Q M K L J L
E V R P M E Z S W E S C L R N J L N W J
R K S S M F L X B T N B Q K N F W F X K
```

be	befriend	believe	besiege
beam	beg	belittle	best
bear	begin	bemoan	betake
beat	begrudge	bend	better
becalm	beguile	benefit	beware
become	behave	berate	
bedazzle	behold	beseech	
beep	belie	beset	

11. 26 MINUS X EQUALS 25

The English alphabet, of course, contains 26 letters. That will clue you in to the sense of this activity's puzzle, for each of the 25 adjectives that are the answers to these clues begins with a different letter of the alphabet. *X* has decided not to be included. Perhaps it is xenophobic! Anyway, write the correct answers for these 25 clues. The first letter of each answer is given to you. Have fun!

Across

1. not noisy
7. smart
10. violent
11. not new
17. easily broken
19. very old
20. slightly wet
21. not light
24. foolish or crazy
25. calm

Down

2. regular
3. fatigued
4. impassive
5. not muddy
6. charitable
8. irregular
9. not domesticated
12. severe

13. serious
14. not yet old or mature
15. not timid
16. unbiased
18. happy
22. unoccupied
23. suspicious

15

12. TAKE TWO MINUTES

Grammar certainly helps you to improve your writing. The same holds true for vocabulary and observation. Using appropriate vocabulary, the good writer observes well and notes well what is experienced. In this activity, you will combine grammar, vocabulary, and observation.

When you are outside the classroom, take two minutes per column and write down what you see and hear. Place your observations in the proper column. Thus, if you see a car, write *car* in the nouns column. If you see a person reading a newspaper, write *read* in the verbs column. If you see a tall man, write *tall* in the adjectives column. Try your best to fill in each column within two minutes. Good luck!

Nouns	Verbs	Adjectives
_____	_____	_____
_____	_____	_____
_____	_____	_____
_____	_____	_____
_____	_____	_____
_____	_____	_____
_____	_____	_____
_____	_____	_____
_____	_____	_____
_____	_____	_____
_____	_____	_____
_____	_____	_____
_____	_____	_____
_____	_____	_____
_____	_____	_____
_____	_____	_____
_____	_____	_____
_____	_____	_____
_____	_____	_____

13. THE LAST BECOMES THE FIRST

For each word in these columns, start the next word with the last letter of the preceding word. Thus, in the noun column, the word *sled* ends with the letter *d*. Thus, the next word in that column must be a noun that begins with the letter *d*. Do the same for the other two columns. Have fun!

Noun	Verb	Adjective
sled	switch	tall

Name_____   Date _____   Period _____

14. GALLERY OF ADVERBS

Twenty-five adverbs are hidden in this word-find puzzle. The words have been placed backward, forward, diagonally, horizontally, and vertically. The first letter of each adverb and the number of letters in each adverb are listed below the word-find. Circle the 25 adverbs.

```
N C O R R E C T L Y I F F Y Y X R E G W
I Q B E F W Q E S Q K N L A R Q R X K C
C M N D N M T K R Y Y M W K M Q L T N G
E R D N L T C H T T K A P K Q D K R X D
L L D U K D C H V J A V P W G X Q E Y G
Y S N H F A N T A S T I C A L L Y M Z R
S C O N F I D E N T L Y N Z T A Z E X G
U K K G C M N M H Z D L T L W D H L P M
D V T V R O N F Y Y B D K F Y V M Y W T
D S N Y I F G W Q B H E O Y Y E Q Q G V
E F Z S Q N W R U T K R T T L R E J N P
N M I K R G E R I G E U B H L S E M E F
L L F E C X L V T V N S J E A E L R H M
Y R V R M O D G E Y S U R E Y L Y L T T
S O S S X G G R Y R R A X E R Y L R T C
```

A _____(4)   I ___ (2)   S _____ (6)

A _____ (9)   M _____ (6)   S _____ (6)

A _____ (9)   N _____ (5)   S _____ (8)

C _____ (9)   N _____ (6)   T _____ (4)

C _____ (9)   N _____ (7)   T _____ (5)

C _____ (11)   O _____ (4)   U _____ (5)

E _____ (9)   Q _____ (5)   V _____ (4)

F _____ (7)   R _____ (6)

F _____ (13)   S ___ (2)

18

Name_____ Date _____ Period_____

15. HEY, CONJUNCTION, WE KNOW YOUR FUNCTION!

The three types of conjunctions and their examples are listed below. For each type of conjunction, write three sentences in which you include a different conjunction for each sentence. Thus, for the coordinate conjunction, you will write a sentence for each of three (of the six) conjunctions.

Coordinate conjunctions: *for, and, nor, but, or, yet* (Remember FANBOY—a mnemonic for the first letters of the six coordinate conjunctions.)

sentence 1:

_____

_____

sentence 2:

_____

_____

sentence 3:

_____

_____

Coordinate conjunctions: *whether . . . or; neither . . . nor; both . . . and; either . . . or; not only . . . but also* (Remember W.N. BEN, the first letters of the five coordinate conjunctions.)

sentence 1:

_____

_____

sentence 2:

_____

_____

sentence 3:

_____

_____

19

Subordinate conjunctions: *after, although, as, as if, as long as, as though, because, before, if, in order that, provided that, since, so, so that, though, unless, until, when, where, whereas, while*

sentence 1:

_____

_____

sentence 2:

_____

_____

sentence 3:

_____

_____

16. BREAKING NORTHWESTERN APART

Use the letters in the twelve-letter word *NORTHWESTERN* to form as many words as you can that have four or more letters. Place your words in the appropriate spaces according to the word's part of speech. Score 1 point for every four-letter word; 2 points for every five-letter word; 3 points for every word having six or more letters. Write your score under each column, and then total the scores for your final score.

Nouns	Verbs	Adjectives	Conjunctions
_____	_____	_____	_____
_____	_____	_____	_____
_____	_____	_____	_____
_____	_____	_____	_____
_____	_____	_____	_____
_____	_____	_____	_____
_____	_____	_____	_____
_____	_____	_____	_____
_____	_____	_____	_____
_____	_____	_____	_____
_____	_____	_____	_____
_____	_____	_____	_____
_____	_____	_____	_____
_____	_____	_____	_____
_____	_____	_____	_____
_____	_____	_____	_____
_____	_____	_____	_____

Scores:

_____ _____ _____ _____

TOTAL SCORE IS _____ points.

17. END IT CORRECTLY!

Twenty prepositions composed of two or more words are waiting for a word to end them correctly. Select a word from the list below to complete the preposition. *In addition to* that, write that word on the appropriate line to complete the preposition. *Apart from* that, just have a good time!

1. according _____

2. across _____

3. alongside _____

4. along _____

5. apart _____

6. aside _____

7. because _____

8. by means _____

9. except _____

10. in addition _____

11. from _____

12. in place _____

13. inside _____

14. on account _____

15. round _____

16. subsequent _____

17. together _____

18. down _____

19. instead _____

20. on top _____

about	of	of
among	of	to
from	of	to
from	of	to
from	of	with
from	of	with
from	of	

Name _____ Date _____ Period _____

18. TOP TWENTY-FIVE

Fill in the missing letters of the word in Column B to match the part of speech in Column A. The first one, *bake* (or bike), is done for you.

1.	verb	bake
2.	noun	in _ _ _ ration
3.	pronoun	h _ r _ e l _
4.	preposition	a _ _ ut
5.	preposition	b _ _ w _ _ n
6.	adverb	_ _ ortly
7.	adverb	a _ _ ea _ y
8.	pronoun	s _ v _ r _ l
9.	adjective	ea _ e _
10.	conjunction	f _ r
11.	noun and verb	i _ t _ rest
12.	interjection	_ _ llo
13.	pronoun	i _ s _ lf
14.	adjective	sp _ _ _ _ id
15.	noun	_ ea _ en
16.	verb	im _ _ _ te
17.	noun	c _ _ nt _ _
18.	verb and noun	m _ _ ti _ n
19.	verb	gr _ _ _ _ y
20.	adjective	hef _ _
21.	adjective	g _ _ at
22.	preposition	d _ _ in _
23.	preposition	w _ t _ _ n
24.	noun	l _ w _
25.	helping verb	s _ o _ l _

19. PARTS OF SPEECH MAGIC SQUARE

Match each word with its description. Write your answers in the correct spaces. When your answers are correct, all columns and rows and both diagonals will add up to the same number.

A=	B=	C=	D=
E=	F=	G=	H=
I=	J=	K=	L=
M=	N=	O=	P=

A. NIGHT
B. THAT
C. INTELLIGENT
D. THEIR
E. FREQUENTLY
F. HIM
G. FAMILY
H. OUCH
I. EVERYBODY
J. WHOM
K. MYSELF
L. DURING
M. AND
N. INTENSIFY
O. HAS
P. CHICAGO

1. helping verb
2. possessive pronoun
3. interrogative pronoun
4. adverb
5. indefinite pronoun
6. personal pronoun
7. proper noun
8. adjective
9. interjection
10. reflexive pronoun
11. common noun
12. main verb
13. relative pronoun
14. conjunction
15. collective noun
16. preposition

20. NURSERY RHYME TIME

Here are two nursery rhymes. First, indicate each word's part of speech above the word. Then, on a separate sheet of paper, write your own nursery rhyme using the same pattern (exact number of lines, number of words, and ordered parts of speech) as the nursery rhyme. Use the following abbreviations for the parts of speech: noun = n; pronoun = pn; verb = v; adjective = adj; adverb = advb; conjunction = c; preposition = prep; interjection = i. Share your original nursery rhymes with your classmates.

Jack and Jill

Jack and Jill went up the hill

    To fetch a pail of water.

Jack fell down and broke his crown

    And Jill came tumbling after.

Up Jack got and home did trot

    As fast as he could caper.

He went to bed to mend his head

    With vinegar and brown paper.

There Was an Old Woman

There was an old woman who lived in a shoe,

She had so many children she didn't know what to do.

She gave them some broth without any bread,

She whipped them all soundly and put them to bed.

21. YOU DO PARTS OF SPEECH RIGHT!

Below are 15 advertisements. Some are pretty clever. Now you can be clever by correctly identifying each word's part of speech. Place the correct abbreviation above each word in the advertisement. Use the following code: noun (n); pronoun (pro); verb (v); adjective (adj); adverb (advb); preposition (prep); conjunction (c); interjection (i); and article (art).

1. We do driving right!

_____

2. Our tires tread on!

_____

3. The best breakfast in town!

_____

4. Milk—the muscle builder!

_____

5. The news that's fit to print!

_____

6. We do it with you in mind!

_____

7. Built to last forever!

_____

8. We are a leg up on our competition!

_____

9. Fishing for fun!

_____

10. Better driving through us!

_____

11. Quality craftsmanship!

_____

12. Shoes for those on the go!

_____

13. The city that never sleeps!

_____

14. Growing along with your family!

_____

15. We will surround you in a sea of comfort!

_____

22. BULL'S-EYE

Fifteen words are found in the three circles below. Match the word with its correct description in the clues listed below the circles. Write the number next to the word within the circle. Use your dictionary to help you along.

Canada
ion
herself
hah
queue

down
wrought
occasional
forward
litigate

but
heave
Khan
into
rush

1. an adjective, adverb, verb, and noun

2. a verb and a noun

3. a noun only

4. a preposition, conjunction, adverb, and pronoun

5. an adjective only

6. a noun and a suffix often denoting a noun

7. a verb only

8. a preposition only

9. a pronoun only

10. an adverb, adjective, preposition, and noun

11. an interjection only

12. a verb, adjective, and noun

13. a noun and a verb whose last four letters are silent

14. a verb that is a past participle of the verb "to work"

15. a noun denoting a person's title

23. TWICE EACH

Fill in each of the 16 blank spaces with an appropriate word. Then, on the line next to that sentence, fill in the new word's part of speech. Each part of speech should be used twice.

1. _____ Most _____ opportunities do not present themselves very often.

2. _____ Last _____ seagulls surrounded the blanket.

3. _____ Can you read this _____ ?

4. _____ She left her sunglasses _____ her purse in the car.

5. _____ _____ of the packages can be brought out to the car now.

6. _____ Ken Logan runs quite _____.

7. _____ I have witnessed several accidents happen _____ that corner.

8. _____ The _____ basket held all the items.

9. _____ Either Channel 7 _____ Channel 9 will run the program.

10. _____ _____! Can't we go along with you?

11. _____ _____ of your photographs can be submitted in this contest.

12. _____ All the cartons were carried _____ the room.

13. _____ Jacques is one of the _____ capable students.

14. _____ The model _____ throughout the shoot.

15. _____ _____ ! That bee's sting really hurts.

16. _____ _____ if you need to be there by noon.

24. TEN AND TEN AND TEN AND TEN AND TEN
(AND THEN FIVE)

This activity will test your knowledge of vocabulary and parts of speech. In the spaces provided, write your responses following the directions given to you. Share those answers with your classmates.

A.   List 10 adjectives that deal with physical appearance and have positive connotations.

_____ _____ _____ _____ _____

_____ _____ _____ _____ _____

B.   List 10 nouns that are names of living quarters, such as *house*.

_____ _____ _____ _____ _____

_____ _____ _____ _____ _____

C.   List 10 verbs, such as *examine*, that deal with the learning process.

_____ _____ _____ _____ _____

_____ _____ _____ _____ _____

D.   List 10 adverbs, such as *carefully*, that have at least 8 letters and start with consecutive letters of the alphabet.

_____ _____ _____ _____ _____

_____ _____ _____ _____ _____

E.   List 10 nouns found at the beach.

_____ _____ _____ _____ _____

_____ _____ _____ _____ _____

F.   List 5 interjections that show happiness!!!

_____ _____ _____ _____ _____

25. FOLLOWING DIRECTIONS

Ten sets of directions to compose various sentences are found below. On the line below each directive, write your sentence. Then compare your sentences with those of your classmates.

1. Noun — linking verb — article — noun.

   _____

2. Noun — verb — noun.

   _____

3. Noun — linking verb — adjective.

   _____

4. Article — adjective — noun — verb — preposition — adjective — noun.

   _____

5. Helping verb — pronoun — verb — preposition — verb — article — noun?

   _____

6. Verb — article — noun — adverb.

   _____

7. Proper noun — conjunction — pronoun — helping verb — verb — adverb.

   _____

8. Pronoun — helping verb — adverb — verb — pronoun.

   _____

9. Preposition — pronoun—adjective — noun — pronoun — helping verb — verb — pronoun.

   _____

10. Verb — adverb.

   _____

Name_____ Date _____ Period_____

26. MORE THAN ONE

Each of the 20 words found in this word-find puzzle can function as more than one part of speech. Circle the 20 words that are placed horizontally backward and forward, diagonally and vertically. Then, on a separate sheet of paper, list the two (or more) parts of speech for each word. Write a sentence illustrating each word as each part of speech. As an example, the b ____ (2) word, *by*, can be used as a preposition and an adverb. Thus you should write a sentence illustrating *by* as a preposition and then another sentence using *by* as an adverb. The first letter and the number of letters in each hidden word are listed below the word-find.

```
R P P M G J S Q D M F K W K T R W C J P
V G T N I A P W R O L I G H T R O H S N
K C V V M R M T R E W J B R O L L S F P
L J Y L M F R E N N S N A F P M G I X V
R S N O W O C O F S Z P I H S W T D M K
J E R W K L H Q R T N T E R X Z L R P G
S Y C K T L D Y D M K Q V C S T A X C B
F W G O V O F J X K K J F R T H T N G W
K Q U K R W W R L F Z Y G N X C R P M J
Q X A H S D Y M O Y B D Y Q I J J D N M
G B R N L J L S Y S R M L Q T D G J K
Z F D D F Z B V R C T H F Z L C R N N X
W Y N M J X P M B Z R N B M M Y L S R Y
D Q L F J G S F Y H O L G Z V H Y X Q K
H G B Y C G Y L P C F W Y Q V W N J F Q
```

B___ (2)   L_____(5)

C_____ (8)   M_____(6)

D_____(4)   P_____(5)

D_____(4)   P_____(4)

F_____(6)   R_____(6)

F_____(5)   R_____(7)

G_____(4)   S_____(4)

G_____(4)   S_____(5)

G_____(5)   S_____(4)

H_____(4)   T_____(3)

© 2001 by The Center for Applied Research in Education

31

Section Two

PHRASES AND CLAUSES— WORD WEAVERS!

27. GETTING THE GIST OF GRAMMAR

Match the 16 grammar terms from Column A with their underlined examples from Column B. Write the two-letter answer in the space provided next to the appropriate number. If your answers are correct, the letters will spell out (in order) a sentence about this activity. Write that sentence on the line below the last question. Good luck!

Column A

1. _____ adverb clause
2. _____ adjective clause
3. _____ direct object
4. _____ fragment
5. _____ gerund phrase
6. _____ infinitive phrase
7. _____ main clause
8. _____ object of the preposition
9. _____ participial phrase
10. _____ predicate adjective
11. _____ predicate nominative
12. _____ run-on
13. _____ sentence
14. _____ subject
15. _____ verb
16. _____ verb phrase

Column B

AM. The car <u>that he bought</u> is sleek.

CA. <u>Running around the track</u>, Jack was winning the race.

EC. He is the <u>president</u>.

EN. These <u>scallops</u> are delicious.

ES. She was waiting for the <u>taxi</u>.

GI. This <u>is</u> the most convenient route.

GR. <u>After the store closed</u>, the employees went to the restaurant.

HA. <u>Skiing is fun I like going to the mountains</u>.

IS. <u>Yvonne exercises</u> whenever she can.

LL. <u>I am going to the store after lunch today</u>.

MA. We gave <u>presents</u> to the bus drivers.

NB. This tree is very <u>tall</u>.

NG. The weather <u>has been changing</u> rapidly.

RC. The principal wanted us <u>to go to the meeting</u>.

RE. <u>After the gymnasium emptied out</u>.

XE. <u>Treating us to dinner</u> was enjoyable for Jim.

The sentence reads _____.

© 2001 by The Center for Applied Research in Education

28. NO FRAGMENTED THOUGHTS HERE!

These 16 terms are commonly used in grammar. Be complete and not fragmented as you match the words (A to P) with their definitions (1 to 16). Write the correct number in the appropriate box within the Magic Square. When your answers are correct, all columns and rows and the two diagonals will add up to the same number.

A=	B=	C=	D=
E=	F=	G=	H=
I=	J=	K=	L=
M=	N=	O=	P=

A.   Gerund
B.   Nominative Case Words
C.   Tense
D.   Reflexive Pronouns
E.   Fragment
F.   Participle
G.   Predicate
H.   Modify
I.   Interjection
J.   Clause
K.   Possessive Case Words
L.   Run-On
M.   Article
N.   Objective Case Words
O.   Infinitive
P.   Indefinite Pronouns

1. verb form (to + verb) used as a noun, adjective, or adverb
2. group of words that has a complete subject and a verb but lacks a complete thought
3. describes or limits (changes) the meaning of another word
4. verb form used as a noun
5. the -*self* and -*selves* forms of the personal pronouns
6. group of words that is missing a subject, verb, or complete thought
7. nouns and pronouns that show ownership
8. nouns and pronouns used as direct objects, indirect objects, and objects of the preposition
9. verb form used as an adjective
10. time as expressed by the verb
11. most frequently used adjectives, such as *a*, *an*, and *the*
12. two or more sentences incorrectly joined together either by a comma or with no mark of punctuation
13. word expressing strong emotion
14. pronouns that do not refer to a specific person or thing
15. nouns and pronouns used as subjects and predicate nominatives
16. another name for a verb

29. U CAN DO IT!

Each of your answers will begin with the letter U. Simply write your answer on the appropriate line and make sure it begins with the letter U. Now show how *you* and *U* can do it!

1. Name a noun with more than 5 letters. _____

2. Name a verb with more than 5 letters. _____

3. Name any pronoun. _____

4. Name an adjective with more than 5 letters. _____

5. Name an adverb with more than 5 letters. _____

6. Name any conjunction. _____

7. Name any interjection. _____

8. Name any preposition. _____

9. Write a subordinate clause. _____

10. Write a gerund phrase. _____

11. Write a participle phrase. _____

12. Write a simple sentence. _____

13. Write an adverb phrase within a sentence.

_____

14. Write an adjective phrase within a sentence.

_____

15. Write a complex sentence.

_____

30. THE *GETTYSBURG ADDRESS*

The following is an excerpt from Abraham Lincoln's *Gettysburg Address*. Read the excerpt and then answer the questions on the lines provided for you. The text's lines have been numbered for your convenience.

(1) Four score and seven years ago our fathers brought forth upon this continent, a new
(2) nation, conceived in Liberty, and dedicated to the proposition that all men are
(3) created equal.

(4) Now we are engaged in a great civil war, testing whether that nation, or any nation
(5) so conceived and so dedicated can long endure. We are met on a great battlefield
(6) of that war.

(7) We have come to dedicate a portion of that field, as a final resting place for those
(8) who here gave their lives that that nation might live. It is altogether fitting and proper
(9) that we should do this.

(10) But, in a larger sense, we cannot dedicate—we cannot consecrate—we cannot
(11) hallow—this ground. The brave men, living and dead, who struggled here, have
(12) consecrated it far above our poor power to add or detract. The world will little note
(13) nor long remember what we say here, but it can never forget what they did here.

1. What is the prepositional phrase on line 1? _____

2. On lines 2 and 3, the words *that all men are created equal* appear.
   What type of subordinate clause is this? _____

3. What word is an adverb in line 3? _____

4. What part of speech is *endure* in line 5? _____

5. What is the infinitive in line 7? _____

6. What type of prepositional phrase is *of that field* in line 7? _____

7. Name the two adverbs in line 8. _____ and _____

8. Name the two pronoun/adjectives in line 8. _____ and _____

9. What are the two adjectives in line 8? _____ and _____

10. What part of speech is the word *But* in line 10? _____

11. What is the adjective clause in line 11? _____

12. The words *far* and *above* in line 12 are both what part of speech? _____

13. What word is an article in line 12? _____

14. What part of speech is the word *remember* in line 13? _____

15. What is the last pronoun in this excerpt? _____

© 2001 by The Center for Applied Research in Education

31. DISSECTING THE SENTENCE

Read the sentence displayed here and then answer the following 15 questions.

AFTER THE LONG MATCH THE PLAYERS RESTED MOMENTARILY BEFORE THEY BEGAN TO SIGN AUTOGRAPHS.

In this sentence . . .

1. What is the first common noun? _____

2. What is the adverb? _____

3. What is the prepositional phrase? _____

4. What is the verb of the main clause? _____

5. What is the subordinating conjunction? _____

6. What is the infinitive phrase? _____

7. What is the pronoun? _____

8. What is the subject of the main clause? _____

9. What is the dependent clause? _____

10. What is the direct object? _____

11. What part of speech is the word *long*? _____

12. What is the antecedent of the word *they*? _____

13. What is the second verb? _____

14. Is the word *they* a singular or plural pronoun? _____

15. Is the sentence a compound or complex sentence? _____

32. SEEING *ROMEO AND JULIET* GRAMMATICALLY

The Prologue to William Shakespeare's *Romeo and Juliet* summarizes the play's major events. Today, you will examine these lines of poetry grammatically. Read the Prologue and then answer the 15 questions on the lines provided.

> Two households, both alike in dignity, 1
>> In fair Verona, where we lay our scene, 2
> From ancient grudge break to new mutiny, 3
>> Where civil blood makes civil hands unclean. 4
> From forth the fatal loins of these two foes 5
>> A pair of star-crossed lovers take their life; 6
> Whose misadventur'd piteous overthrows 7
>> Doth with their death bury their parents' strife. 8
> The fearful passage of their death-mark'd love, 9
>> And the continuance of their parents' rage, 10
> Which, but their children's end, nought could remove, 11
>> Is now the two hours' traffic of our stage; 12
> The which if you with patient ears attend, 13
>> What here shall miss, our toil shall strive to mend. 14

1. What is the prologue's first prepositional phrase? _____

2. Is *In fair Verona* an adjective or adverb phrase? _____

3. What is the first noun in line 3? _____

4. What part of speech is *civil* in line 4? _____

5. What is the adjective phrase in line 5? _____

6. What noun does the adjective *misadventur'd* modify? _____

7. What part of speech is *doth* in line 8? _____

8. What part of speech is *strife* in line 8? _____

9. What word in line 9 can be used as a noun and a verb? _____

10. What part of speech is *continuance* in line 10? _____

11. What word in the eleventh line means *nothing*? _____

12. Name the adverb in the twelfth line. _____

13. What is the subordinating conjunction in line 13? _____

14. What part of speech is *attend* in the thirteenth line? _____

15. What is the infinitive phrase in the Prologue's concluding line? _____

33. WHAT EXACTLY IS A TUFFET?

You can still write the following ten sentences, though you might not know that a tuffet is a low stool or a tuft of grass. Do we assume that Little Miss Muffet sat on a low stool or a tuft of grass? Anyway, read the "Little Miss Muffet" nursery rhyme and then complete the ten tasks on the appropriate lines.

Little Miss Muffet

Little Miss Muffet sat on a tuffet,
Eating her curds and whey.
Along came a spider and sat down beside her
And frightened Miss Muffet away.

Write a sentence in which you . . .

1. use *Miss Muffet* as a direct object.

   _____

2. use *curds and whey* as direct objects.

   _____

3. use *on a tuffet* as an adverb phrase.

   _____

4. use *Little Miss Muffet* as part of an adverb clause.

   _____

5. use *spider* as a subject.

   _____

6. use *spider* as the subject and include a compound verb in the sentence.

   _____

7. use *eating* as a participle.

   _____

8. use *sat down beside her* as part of an adjective clause.

   _____

9. use *by the spider* as an adverb phrase.

   _____

10. use *on a tuffet* as part of a gerund phrase.

    _____

34. WALKING WEARILY

What an unusual title for an activity—Walking Wearily! Well, there is a reason for this specific title, since "walking wearily" suffices the activity's requirements. Fill in each blank with two words: The first is a verb ending with *-ing* and the second is an *-ly* adverb describing the verb. Both words should begin with the letter to the left of the blank. If you would like to reverse the order of the verb and the adverb to make the combination sound more pleasing to the ear, please do so. Try to make each combination sensible. It is challenging!

A. _____   M. _____

B. _____   N. _____

C. _____   O. _____

D. _____   P. _____

E. _____   Q. _____

F. _____   R. _____

G. _____   S. _____

H. _____   T. _____

I. _____   U. _____

J. _____   V. _____

K. _____   W. _____

L. _____   Z. _____

Name_____ Date _____ Period _____

35. PARTICIPLES AND VERBS

Today you are asked to offer regular and irregular verbs in their participle forms. As an example, the regular verb *annoy*, *annoyed* in its participle form, is a participle in the sentence, "*Annoyed* by the loud music, the neighbors complained to each other." The irregular verb *drive*, *driven* in its participle form, is a participle in the sentence, "*Driven* by the crowd, the wrestler went on to pin his opponent."

For each letter below, offer a word that begins with that particular letter and is a participle (like *annoyed* and *driven*). For any five words in each column, use the back of this page to write a sentence beginning with one of the words in its participle form.

Regular Verbs

a. _____

b. _____

c. _____

d. _____

e. _____

f. _____

g. _____

h. _____

i. _____

j. _____

k. _____

l. _____

m. _____

n. _____

o. _____

p. _____

q. _____

r. _____

s. _____

t. _____

u. _____

v. _____

w. _____

x. _____

y. _____

z. _____

Irregular Verbs

b. _____

c. _____

d. _____

e. _____

f. _____

g. _____

h. _____

k. _____

l. _____

r. _____

s. _____

t. _____

w. _____

36. DO YOU NOTICE THIS?

You will *notice* that all the directives in this activity ask you to use the word *notice* in one form or another. Compose 12 sentences including the various sentence components. Do not add endings to the word *notice*; leave the word in its present form for all 12 sentences. Write your responses on the appropriate lines.

1. Use *notice* as a subject.

_____

2. Use *notice* as a verb.

_____

3. Use *notice* as a predicate nominative.

_____

4. Use *notice* as a direct object.

_____

5. Use *notice* as the object of the preposition.

_____

6. Use *notice* as the last word of an adverb clause.

_____

7. Use *notice* as the last word of an adjective clause.

_____

8. Use *notice* as the last word of an infinitive phrase.

_____

9. Use *notice* as the last word of a participial phrase.

_____

10. Use *notice* as the last word of a gerund phrase.

_____

11. Use *notice* as the last word of an adjective phrase.

_____

12. Use *notice* as the last word of an adverb phrase.

_____

37. THERE ARE NO OPPOSING APPOSITIVES HERE

An appositive is a noun or pronoun that follows another noun or pronoun to explain it more thoroughly. Thus, in the sentence, "Wall Street, the world's financial business center, is located in New York City," *the world's financial business center* is the appositive phrase that further explains *Wall Street*.

Group One features 15 sentences, each missing an appositive. Match the 15 sentences with their appropriate appositives in Group Two. Write each appositive's two-letter answer on the line within the sentence. Then, write all the two-letter answers, in order, on the line below the last question. If your answers are correct, you will spell out a name and its appositive. One answer has already been given for you.

GROUP ONE

1. Magic Johnson, _____, played on many championship teams during his illustrious career.

2. P.T. Barnum, _____, had some very memorable quotes.

3. John Fitzgerald Kennedy, _____, was tragically murdered in 1963.

4. Ultramarathoning, _____, can humble even the most determined athletes.

5. Iced tea, _____, was served at the clergy's luncheon this past July.

6. Connecticut, _____, is the southernmost New England State.

7. Julia Childs, _____, has created many delicious dishes.

8. Mia Hamm, _____, is a positive role model for all.

9. Sharon Stone, _____, is a member of MENSA, a group of very intelligent people.

10. Agatha Christie, _____, wrote the novel *And Then There Were None*.

11. Adjectives, _____, are used quite well by most established writers.

12. Key West, _____, is a popular tourist location.

13. Chicago, _____, is on Lake Michigan.

14. Ontario, _____, is home to the Toronto Blue Jays.

15. Tom Joad, _____nd_____, was created by John Steinbeck.

GROUP TWO

ar.　a television gourmet chef

el.　a former NBA great

ey.　the Nutmeg State

ge.　a Canadian province

ka.　a talented actress

le.　the Windy City

ll.　a part of Florida

nd.　the First Lady of mystery novels

nd.　a character in *The Grapes of Wrath*

oc.　an outstanding soccer player

re.　a grueling test of endurance

ro.　those words that modify nouns and pronouns

sl.　a cool, refreshing drink

sp.　the 35th United States president

vi.　the great American circus showman

The two-letter answers spell out _____

© 2001 by The Center for Applied Research in Education

38. FINDING THOSE SIXTEEN PREPOSITIONAL PHRASES

The 16 prepositional phrases below are hidden in the word-find puzzle. They are placed backward, forward, diagonally, and vertically. Circle each phrase and then use any eight of them, each in its own sentence. Write these sentences on the reverse side of this paper.

```
P U B E S I D E S T H A T R S H F W S Y
B A N B E Y O N D T H E L A S T H I L L
Y P S D A B O U T S I X Y E A R S T F V
H Q T T E D R Y V Q D N F N B Q U H B V
I T X L H R X X C R E H T M N N K O B D
M F N I V E N J N Q K Z M H T T W U Y X
S F O K T F R E V F A X G I E G N T G V
E T O E C Y R E A Z L B L R Z P D H J R
L C N Y K N M L R T E T D X G S A E G Y
F V T O W A R D M Y H O U S E N J R N T
F L A U R W C V F E T M F Y M B B X K P
Z P R D D Z Y K N P Y D Y C L G T M F M
O N T H E A I R D D B Q B B T R S C T L
F Z F H X K Y T N E A R T H E R O A D K
W I T H I N T H E C A V I T Y D W X W V
```

about six years   near the road

at noon   on the air

besides that   past here

beyond the last hill   toward my house

by himself   underneath my bed

by the lake   until then

in the park   within the cavity

like you   without her

39. DON'T LET THESE PHRASES FAZE YOU!

These 20 phrases should not present a problem for you. Simply place the corresponding letter of the correct phrase (noun, verb, adjective, adverb, or preposition) on the line after the phrase's number. If your answers are correct, you will spell out five four-letter words associated with weather. So, even though the weather sometimes fazes you, don't let these phrases faze you!

1. _____ total chaos   (s) noun   (t) verb   (u) adverb

2. _____ took the photograph   (m) preposition   (n) verb   (o) adjective

3. _____ quite eerie   (n) adverb   (o) adjective   (p) noun

4. _____ far more relaxing   (w) adjective   (x) adverb   (y) preposition

5. _____ his own machine shop   (p) preposition   (q) verb   (r) noun

6. _____ during the matinee performance   (a) preposition   (b) verb   (c) noun

7. _____ like a bird   (h) verb   (i) preposition   (j) noun

8. _____ very swiftly   (n) adverb   (o) adjective   (p) verb

9. _____ by the fence   (f) adjective   (g) adverb   (h) preposition

10. _____ a loose cannon   (a) noun   (b) verb   (c) adjective

11. _____ since last Wednesday   (h) verb   (i) preposition   (j) adverb

12. _____ somewhat attractive   (j) noun   (k) adverb   (l) adjective

13. _____ too quickly   (m) adverb   (n) noun   (o) verb

14. _____ rather selfishly   (g) adjective   (h) noun   (i) adverb

15. _____ might have won   (r) preposition   (s) verb   (t) adverb

16. _____ little women   (r) adverb   (s) adjective   (t) noun

17. _____ did attend   (h) verb   (i) adjective   (j) noun

18. _____ has been searching   (a) verb   (b) adverb   (c) noun

19. _____ more respectable   (x) adverb   (y) preposition   (z) adjective

20. _____ pretty casually   (d) noun   (e) adverb   (f) verb

The five four-letter words associated with weather are _____, _____,

_____, _____, and _____.

40. PHRASES AND SCIENTISTS

Match the prepositional phrases from Group B with their appropriate sentence beginnings from Group A. Write the two-letter answer on the line next to each number. Then write each prepositional phrase on the line to complete the sentence. If your answers are correct, you will spell out the names of four famous scientists. Write those four names on the line at the bottom of the following page.

GROUP A

1. _____ Tim drew the white line _____.

2. _____ The farmer placed the grain bags _____.

3. _____ Our boat glided _____.

4. _____ An artist carried her easel _____.

5. _____ If you want to get there by one o'clock, you had better listen _____.

6. _____ Sheila has a copy _____.

7. _____ The professor was happy that there was not a sound _____.

8. _____ The bicycle shop is _____ of the dock.

9. _____ Our town was founded _____.

10. _____ These guest houses sit _____.

11. _____ Accommodation packages for this vacation plan start _____.

12. _____ Meals are served _____.

13. _____ The children received their birthday gifts _____.

14. _____ Who will be invited _____?

15. _____ While Joanne was watching the football game, she dropped her

     pocketbook _____.

GROUP B

AL. through the mail

AR. of the agreement

DE. into the atelier

EI. at $250 a week

EO. beneath the bleachers

IL. besides these people

IN. in 1683

NE. along the tennis baseline

NG. between five and eight o'clock

ON. with the current

SC. to his directions

SE. within walking distance

ST. by the wharf

TE. during the lecture

WT. near the barn

The four scientists are _____.

© 2001 by The Center for Applied Research in Education

© 2001 by The Center for Applied Research in Education

Name _____ Date _____ Period _____

41. GERUNDS

Four functions of the gerund are highlighted in this activity. First, underline the gerund phrase. Then, on the line next to the number, indicate whether the gerund phrase acts as a subject (s), direct object (do), predicate nominative (pn), or object of the preposition (op). Each function is used five times.

1. ____ After the incidents the chefs resumed cooking for the event.

2. ____ Blaine's decorating added much to the new apartment.

3. ____ The cat irritated the homeowner by scratching on the screen door.

4. ____ Diving to such depths was John's goal.

5. ____ Francine's new occupation is accounting.

6. ____ Researching her family's history took up much of Maureen's time.

7. ____ Nancy's running the New York City Marathon last November was a thrill.

8. ____ We realized the terrible mistake without their telling us.

9. ____ Turning on the lights too early ruined the surprise.

10. ____ The columnists' major goal was alerting her readers to the potential problem.

11. ____ Many people in that region enjoy skiing the slopes.

12. ____ Are you happy about seeing your relatives so often?

13. ____ The crew rehearsed rowing against a mild wind.

14. ____ We have enjoyed fishing with Uncle Ted.

15. ____ These students have helped their community by collecting canned goods.

16. ____ The problem is finding enough interested donors.

17. ____ Her favorite activity is photographing sunsets.

18. ____ Martin took great interest in bowling and fishing.

19. ____ Did he enjoy reading *A Tale of Two Cities*?

20. ____ Her most enjoyable experience was feeding the newborn.

42. TO BE OR NOT TO BE

Hamlet gave the infinitive (*to* + a verb) a whole new life when he said, *"To be* or not *to be."* Hamlet truly weighed some difficult issues with his famous infinitive. Today, you are asked to weigh some very important matters as well. On the appropriate lines, write five goals—either short-term or long-term goals—and two ways you will go about trying to reach each goal. Begin each of the goals and each of the ways with an infinitive.

   Example: One of my goals is *to make* the school orchestra. Two ways I will try to reach this goal are *to practice* more frequently and *to study* music more carefully.

One of my goals is . . . _____

Two ways I will try to reach this goal are

_____

_____

Another of my goals is . . . _____

Two ways I will try to reach this goal are

_____

_____

Another of my goals is . . . _____

Two ways I will try to reach this goal are

_____

_____

Another of my goals is . . . _____

Two ways I will try to reach this goal are

_____

_____

Another of my goals is . . . _____

Two ways I will try to reach this goal are

_____

_____

43. LUCKY SEVEN

Twenty-one infinitive phrases have been underlined. For each phrase, identify its function by writing the correct abbreviation on the appropriate line. The three functions and their abbreviations are subject (s), object (o), and predicate nominative (pn).

1. _____ <u>To win an Olympic medal</u> is her goal.

2. _____ Bethany decided <u>to attend Wheaton College in Massachusetts</u>.

3. _____ Jill wanted <u>to go back to school in September</u>.

4. _____ <u>To have failed that test was</u> devastating for the brilliant student.

5. _____ The Okies hoped <u>to build a new life in California</u>.

6. _____ The most difficult way is <u>to run there</u>.

7. _____ <u>To recite the names of the 50 states</u> was easy for Zack.

8. _____ <u>To roam around with his buddies</u> was fun for Fred.

9. _____ Claudine's goal was <u>to solve the crossword in half an hour</u>.

10. _____ Yesterday the snow seemed <u>to be thicker</u>.

11. _____ They were determined <u>to reach Colorado before sunset</u>.

12. _____ Marcia said <u>to remove the furniture from the other apartment</u>.

13. _____ Magellan's desire was <u>to circumnavigate the globe</u>.

14. _____ Her goal was <u>to know every aspect of Shakespeare's life</u>.

15. _____ <u>To close the gap between the two candidates</u> proved quite difficult for Seth.

16. _____ Mr. Monson's wish was <u>to see his grandchildren before that</u>.

17. _____ Her punishment was <u>to clean all the desks in the room</u>.

18. _____ <u>To err</u> is human.

19. _____ <u>To forgive</u> is divine.

20. _____ None of the workers promised <u>to be there after ten o' clock</u>.

21. _____ The prisoners asked <u>to be released by the first day of the next month</u>.

44. COMPLETING THE IDEA

Each of these 15 subordinate (adverbial) clauses needs a main clause in order to make the sentence complete. Write the main clause on the appropriate line. Notice the comma that separates the introductory subordinate clause from the main clause. If the subordinate clause does not begin the sentence, you do not need to insert the comma.

1. If you see my lost dog, _____.

2. _____ after you catch the ball.

3. _____ since there is no milk left.

4. While the waves crashed on the shore, _____.

5. Unless you think you can do it yourself, _____.

6. _____ whenever you can.

7. Before you turn eighteen years old, _____.

8. _____ where the jobs are.

9. _____ though she felt she should have been selected.

10. As if that was not trouble enough, _____.

11. Even if all his plans do work out, _____.

12. _____ while the family was at the picnic.

13. That is exactly what I told you _____.

14. Until all the soldiers have returned home from the war, _____.

15. None of the soldiers knew about the deal _____.

© 2001 by The Center for Applied Research in Education

45. BECAUSE OF THE CLAUSE

The clause is an important component of sentence construction. Here the clause is also important, for it will complete an idea. On the line next to the clause in Group A, write the letter of the sentence part in Group B that completes the idea. Each number and letter is used only once.

GROUP A

1. ____ Hearing a knock at the door,

2. ____ After the doctor examined the patient,

3. ____ Because it was very windy,

4. ____ Whether you go to the movies or not,

5. ____ If this is the best way to do it,

6. ____ If there is no planned party,

7. ____ Whenever you are grouchy,

8. ____ If you do not hurry,

9. ____ Since the swimmers went out too far,

10. ____ Because the lessons were about to begin,

GROUP B

A. let's have our own.

B. you don't stay that way for very long.

C. the teacher called for the students' attention.

D. we will go to the theater anyway.

E. Jill went to see who was there.

F. we will be late for the concert.

G. the ball carried a long distance.

H. then do it this way!

I. they were scolded by the angry lifeguard.

J. she asked to see the patient's chart again.

46. PHRASE AND CLAUSE INDICATORS

We can often tell what type of a phrase or clause a group of words is by its first word. Even without the rest of the words in the phrase or the clause, you will able to tell whether each of these words can start a prepositional phrase, verb phrase, verbal phrase, or subordinate clause. Some words may start more than one of these. Write your answers on the appropriate lines. The first one is done for you.

1. since: _____prepositional phrase and subordinate clause_____

2. about: _____

3. singing: _____

4. to: _____

5. within: _____

6. after: _____

7. is: _____

8. grounded: _____

9. as: _____

10. did: _____

11. although: _____

12. between: _____

13. unless: _____

14. until: _____

15. beside: _____

16. residing: _____

17. surrounded: _____

18. are: _____

19. overwhelming: _____

20. have: _____

47. STARTING AND ENDING

A subordinating conjunction begins a subordinate or dependent clause. Such a clause must include a subject and a verb. Fifteen subordinating conjunctions are featured below. Some of these conjunctions begin clauses that start the sentence, while others start a clause that ends the sentence. Complete each sentence in the space provided. Insert a comma after an introductory subordinate or dependent clause. Remember that, unless the sentence needs a comma for clarification, a comma is not necessary when the subordinating conjunction does not introduce the sentence.

1. Because _____.

2. Whenever _____.

3. Unless _____.

4. While _____.

5. As long as _____.

6. Before _____.

7. So that _____.

8. Although _____.

9. Wherever _____.

10. Until _____.

11. If _____.

12. When _____.

13. _____ where _____.

14. _____ as soon as _____.

15. _____ than _____.

48. PHRASES AND CLAUSES AND MORE

Let's take the confusion out of groups of words. For each underlined portion of the word groups below, write the appropriate letter on the line provided. There should be three of each letter if your answers are correct.

- A. Sentence
- B. Gerund Phrase
- C. Infinitive Phrase
- D. Participial Phrase
- E. Subordinate or Dependent Clause
- F. Run-On

1. ___ Are you going <u>to submit your manuscript</u>?

2. ___ <u>This is the finest moment of your life</u>.

3. ___ The road <u>leading out of town</u> was very congested yesterday.

4. ___ <u>Going to the store</u> was always exciting for the children.

5. ___ <u>Taking his normal lead off base</u>, the runner had a good jump.

6. ___ <u>While he took attendance</u>, the teacher used his black pen.

7. ___ The woman <u>whom you needed</u> is not here today.

8. ___ <u>Seeking a new way to the New World</u> was his mission.

9. ___ Signs <u>painted in only a single color</u> were noticed more readily.

10. ___ <u>To be one with nature</u> was her quest.

11. ___ <u>Can you feel the tension in this room</u>?

12. ___ <u>These keys were picked up here a minute ago are they yours</u>?

13. ___ The crowd left <u>as soon as the game ended</u>.

14. ___ <u>Writing her autobiography</u> brought back many happy memories.

15. ___ This is the score <u>to beat here</u>.

16. ___ <u>Tend to your own matters, Kyle</u>.

17. ___ <u>Are you going to the movie tonight I am</u>!

18. ___ <u>See who is on the phone it might be important</u>.

49. WIN'S NINE LIVES

In this activity, you can certainly win if you know how to use the word *win* in winning fashion. Construct the nine sentences as directed. Since they all ask you to use the word *win*, you cannot afford to lose. Write your sentences on the lines provided.

1. Use a form of the word *win* within a verb phrase.

   _____

2. Use a form of the word *win* within a gerund phrase.

   _____

3. Use a form of the word *win* within a participial phrase.

   _____

4. Use a form of the word *win* within an infinitive phrase.

   _____

5. Use a form of the word *win* within an adverb phrase.

   _____

6. Use a form of the word *win* within an adjective phrase.

   _____

7. Use a form of the word *win* within an adverb clause.

   _____

8. Use a form of the word *win* within an adjective clause.

   _____

9. Use a form of the word *win* within a noun clause.

   _____

50. WEATHERING THESE PHRASES, CLAUSES, AND SENTENCES

Below are five phrases, five clauses, and five sentences. On the lines provided, write the letter P next to the each phrase, the letter C next to each clause, and the letter S next to each sentence. Next, list each group of phrases in alphabetical order according to its first word. Do the same for the clauses and then for the sentences. A letter follows each group of words. If you have correctly identified each group of words, its letters will spell three words related to weather. Write those three words at the bottom of the page. Note that the initial word in each group is intentionally printed in lowercase.

_____ you should read more magazines (T)

_____ after the hurricane (S)

_____ as soon as the moon wanes (N)

_____ since the morning show (M)

_____ unless you find a better way to do it (D)

_____ let us mend the fences (E)

_____ when these cars make the turn (Y)

_____ before the flood (T)

_____ during the summer months (O)

_____ in the beginning (R)

_____ it is raining now (L)

_____ after all the papers are delivered (W)

_____ after the storm subsided (I)

_____ if you fix the cabinet, I can help you reinstall it (S)

_____ when you see her, tell her I miss her (E)

The three words related to weather are _____, _____, and _____.

51. FILLING IN THE BLANKS

Compose original sentences by filling in the blanks with the correct part of speech. Share your answers with your classmates.

1. _____ _____ _____.
       pronoun   verb   adverb

2. _____ _____ _____ _____.
       proper noun verb   article   noun

3. _____ _____ _____ _____?
       helping verb pronoun   pron/adj   noun

4. _____ _____ _____.
       verb   pronoun adverb

5. _____ _____ _____ _____ _____ _____ _____.
       pronoun   conj   pronoun   help. verb verb   prep   pronoun

6. _____ _____ _____ _____.
       adverb   verb   pronoun   adverb

7. _____ _____ _____ _____ _____.
       proper noun verb   adverb   preposition pronoun

8. _____, _____ _____.
       adverbial clause   pronoun verb

9. _____ _____ _____ _____ _____.
       article   adjective   noun   verb   prepositional phrase

10. _____ _____ _____ _____.
       pronoun   helping verb verb   infinitive phrase

11. _____, _____ _____ _____.
       adverbial clause   pronoun verb   adverb

12. _____ _____ _____ _____ _____.
       article   noun   adjective clause   verb   prepositional phrase

13. _____ _____ _____ _____.
       pronoun   adverb   verb   noun

14. _____ _____ _____ _____ _____ _____.
       pronoun verb   article   adjective   noun   prepositional phrase

15. _____ _____ _____ _____.
       prepositional phrase pronoun verb   infinitive phrase

52. COMBATING THIRTEEN

Match the 13 items in Group One with the 13 underlined items in Group Two by writing the two-letter answer next to the Group Two item on the line adjacent to its corresponding Group One item. If your answers are correct, the answers will help you to combat 13, a number that some people think is unlucky. Write your answers on the line below the last Group Two member.

GROUP ONE

1. ____ adjective clause
2. ____ adverb clause
3. ____ comma splice
4. ____ declarative sentence
5. ____ fragment
6. ____ gerund phrase
7. ____ imperative sentence
8. ____ infinitive phrase
9. ____ interrogative sentence
10. ____ participle phrase
11. ____ prepositional phrase
12. ____ run-on
13. ____ verb phrase

GROUP TWO

(ab) <u>Since they were already selected</u>, nothing can be done.
(an) <u>Do this immediately, Richard</u>.
(ar) The woman <u>who helped you</u> is Mrs. Ficken.
(bi) <u>These charts are very telling, they will certainly aid our search</u>.
(ck) <u>Trying her best</u>, the skater received fine scores at the competition.
(da) Roy wanted <u>to take the water to the team members</u>.
(en) <u>Please turn off the light it is too bright in this room</u>.
(fo) <u>Ruining all of our plans that night</u>.
(lu) <u>Is this all</u>?
(ny) Ursula <u>is studying</u> the maps carefully.
(ot) <u>Telling those kinds of stories</u> is not wise.
(ts) <u>We can surely accomplish these tasks now</u>.
(yp) <u>For this class</u>, we must arrive on time.

What helps to combat 13, a number some people think is unlucky? _____

_____

© 2001 by The Center for Applied Research in Education

53. WHY?

Answer each question with two reasons. Write your responses on the lines provided.

1. Why is "in the morning" a prepositional phrase?

_____

_____

2. In the sentence, "The desk near the water fountain is mine," why is "near the water fountain" an adjective phrase?

_____

_____

3. In the sentence, "He walked near the water fountain," why is "near the water fountain" an adverb phrase?

_____

_____

4. Why is "because Tameka smiles so beautifully" a clause?

_____

_____

5. Why is "when Jed spent his money so intelligently" a subordinate or dependent clause in the sentence, "His parents were happy when Jed spent his money so intelligently"?

_____

_____

6. Why is "Reading the signs along the road" a fragment?

_____

_____

7. Why is "A clown scared my little sister, she cried" a comma splice?

_____

_____

8. Why is "Turn at the next corner" an imperative sentence?

_____

_____

9. Why is "that he recovered" an adjective clause in the sentence, "The fumble that he recovered made the difference"?

_____

_____

10. Why is "Squirrels love to scamper across our yard they are fun to watch" a run-on?

_____

_____

54. SINGING ALONG

Here are 20 song titles. On the line next to each, tell whether the title is a sentence (S), clause (C), or phrase (P) by writing the appropriate abbreviation. There are 10 sentences, 5 clauses, and 5 phrases. Each word of the song's title is purposely capitalized. Finally, on the reverse side of this paper, write 3 song titles that are sentences, 3 that are clauses, and 3 that are phrases. Do not use any titles from this page.

1. _____ Rock Me Gently

2. _____ On The Wings Of Love

3. _____ Since I Don't Have You

4. _____ The Thrill Is Gone

5. _____ Check It Out

6. _____ Crying In The Chapel

7. _____ Rhythm Is A Dancer

8. _____ Dancing In The Street

9. _____ For Your Love

10. _____ If You Remember Me

11. _____ When You Dance

12. _____ Take A Bow

13. _____ This Is How We Do It

14. _____ Because They're Young

15. _____ Everybody Wants To Rule The World

16. _____ Big Girls Don't Cry

17. _____ Round And Round

18. _____ Before You Walk Out Of My Life

19. _____ My Boyfriend's Back

20. _____ Papa Was A Rollin' Stone

Name_____ Date _____ Period_____

55. TWO SENTENCES TELL IT ALL!

Read the two sentences below, and then answer the questions regarding the sentences. Write your answers on the appropriate lines.

    (A) I have not seen her since the Smiths went skiing in Colorado.

    (B) The annoying cat that constantly comes into our yard has been missing.

1. What is the article in sentence A? _____

2. What is the first noun in sentence B? _____

3. What is the pronoun adjective in sentence B? _____

4. What is the adverb in sentence B? _____

5. What is the prepositional phrase in sentence B? _____

6. Is *annoying* in sentence B used as an adjective or an adverb? _____

7. What is the subordinate clause in sentence B? _____

8. What is the adverbial clause in sentence A? _____

9. What is sentence A's gerund? _____

10. What is the only plural noun in either sentence? _____

11. What tense is the verb *went* in sentence A? _____

12. What type of phrase is *has been missing*? in sentence B? _____

13. What is the adverb in sentence A? _____

14. Is sentence A's phrase *in Colorado* a prepositional or participial phrase? _____

15. Is sentence B's prepositional phrase *in our yard* an adjectival or an adverbial phrase? _____

Section Three

SENTENCES— GRAMMAR'S GALAXY!

Activity	Focus	Page

Name _____ Date _____ Period _____

56. THE COMMON WORD

For each group, write three sentences that include the common word used as part of a phrase, a clause, and a sentence. Keep the word in its present form. Tell what type of phrase (verb, gerund, or participial), clause (main, adjective, or adverbial), or sentence (simple, compound, complex, or compound-complex) you have written. An example is given to you. Write your answers on the appropriate lines.

Example Group:

common word *placing*

(participial phrase) Placing an ad in the paper, the man hoped to sell his car soon.

(adverb clause) While he was placing the ad, he heard the good news.

(complex sentence) The man was placing an ad on the wall, and he hoped to have a buyer within a few days.

Group One: common word *sold*

(_____ phrase) _____

(_____ clause) _____

(_____ sentence) _____

Group Two: common word *seeking*

(_____ phrase) _____

(_____ clause) _____

(_____ sentence) _____

Group Three: common word *found*

(_____ phrase) _____

(_____ clause) _____

(_____ sentence) _____

Group Four: common word *researching*

(_____ phrase) _____

(_____ clause) _____

(_____ sentence) _____

Group Five: common word *lost*

(_____ phrase) _____

(_____ clause) _____

(_____ sentence) _____

57. ODD ONE OUT

One member in each group does not belong. Circle that member's letter, and be prepared to tell why it does not fit in with the others. If your answers are correct, the twelve letters will spell out two words associated with the word *odd*. Write the twelve letters on the line below the last question. What are the two words?

1. Which is not a prepositional phrase?
   (o) which is the way
   (p) near the street
   (q) by the road

2. Which is not a sentence?
   (e) This is the way we do this dance.
   (f) By the time I get to Phoenix.
   (g) Are you going to finish the ice cream soon?

3. Which is not a fragment?
   (f) We scored in the middle of the third quarter last night.
   (g) Reading the sentence.
   (h) Jose, at the proper time.

4. Which is not a run-on?
   (a) This is the first run tomorrow will be the second run.
   (b) You should remember exactly what you were told here tonight.
   (c) Can you help us with the project we could really use another hand.

5. Which underlined portion is not an infinitive phrase?
   (c) Hillary wanted <u>to see the giraffe</u>.
   (d) This is the woman <u>to ask now</u>.
   (e) All the musicians went <u>to the rehearsal</u>.

6. Which underlined portion is not a participle phrase?
   (a) <u>Walking for thirty minutes</u> is good exercise.
   (b) <u>Walking for thirty minutes</u>, the researcher checked his blood pressure.
   (c) Those three women, <u>walking for thirty minutes</u>, talked about their families.

7. Which underlined portion is not a verb phrase?
   (t) Usually we need to get <u>to the job by eight o'clock</u>.
   (u) Madeline <u>is challenging</u> the other group.
   (v) Perhaps you <u>could meet</u> the principal now.

© 2001 by The Center for Applied Research in Education

8. Which underlined portion is not an adverb phrase?

(u) <u>In the morning</u> we go to the bagel store.

(v) Will you see him <u>in the morning</u>?

(w) The fog <u>in the morning</u> made driving quite difficult.

9. Which underlined portion is not an adjective clause?

(d) The woman, <u>who is your new director</u>, has many talents.

(e) <u>Because the octopus is so interesting</u>, we studied the creature for a long time.

(i) The car <u>that your family rented</u> is very stylish.

10. Which underlined portion is not a gerund phrase?

(d) <u>Skiing in the Alps</u> is very exhilarating.

(e) <u>Swimming with his brothers</u> was John's idea of a good time.

(i) Yogi was <u>catching with the pitcher</u>.

11. Which is not a declarative sentence?

(r) Take it to them.

(s) This is the finest linen we carry in this exclusive store.

(t) We are the champions of the world.

12. Which underlined portion is not a dependent clause?

(d) These cartoon monsters <u>are very frightening to the younger children</u>.

(e) <u>Because they were terrific musicians</u>, they were booked often.

(f) You can change rooms <u>if you need to do so</u>.

The two words associated with odd are _____ and _____.

Name_____ Date _____ Period_____

58. UNSCRAMBLING THE SENTENCES

The words in each group below can be rearranged to form a complete sentence. On a separate sheet of paper, rearrange the words to form a sentence. The capitalized word is the sentence's first word. Add the necessary end punctuation. Good luck!

1. rest a Take

2. finish Can the you test

3. beautiful is a This day

4. there be Some will them of

5. awarded scholarship been Tom a has

6. do you so can please him, If help

7. that you pretty The is found bracelet

8. note wrote She an dad her interesting

9. Paula our he and group will represent

10. My has car two past been for the days in the repair shop

11. When to the you to go to go decide with you want meeting, I

12. sentence, you break complete a take this After

© 2001 by The Center for Applied Research in Education

59. MAKING SENSE

The words in each of the twelve groups below are out of order. On the line below each group, write the words in the correct order so that the revised sentence makes sense. The capitalized word is the first word of the revised sentence.

1. it Bring here.

_____

2. you Do it see?

_____

3. enjoys ravioli eating He.

_____

4. batteries their They recharge will.

_____

5. researched situation the Scientists already have.

_____

6. succeed under to is pressure NASA.

_____

7. anything Did it they hear about?

_____

8. It is about the talk to weather time.

_____

9. slowly increasing The humidity is.

_____

10. have stories Malamud's We Bernard of read most.

_____

11. understand all of it You will not.

_____

12. when me announcement radio hear the you Call.

_____

Name_____ Date_____ Period_____

60. SOME GOOD ADVICE

Unscramble the words in these quotes by Aesop, a famous ancient Greek author. Write the unscrambled versions on the appropriate lines. Then, above each word in the unscrambled version, write each word's part of speech, using the these abbreviations: noun (n), pronoun (p), verb (v), adjective (adj), adverb (advb), preposition (prep), conjunction (c), interjection (i) and pronoun adjective (p/a).

1. "eDtysro het dese fo eilv ro ti wlli gorw ot eb uryo runi."

The unscrambled version is: _____

2. "Cusyml sngtije si on kejo."

The unscrambled version is: _____

3. "eW tnofe ssedpie hwat si stom fueslu ot su."

The unscrambled version is: _____

4. "vreEy rrelu si hshra howes reul si nwe."

The unscrambled version is: _____

5. "evreN sturt het iacevd fo a mna ni ffcidutiseli."

The unscrambled version is _____

61. LET'S GET SOME ORDER HERE!

Fifteen sentences have been scrambled. On the line below each group of words, place each sentence's words in their proper order. The capitalized word is the sentence's first word. The word with the punctuation mark after it is the sentence's last word. There might be more than one way to reconstruct a sentence. Have fun!

1. We yesterday. to store the went

_____

2. This reason! best the is

_____

3. Can games they now? video these play

_____

4. Since she tall will is play she so center.

_____

5. Keep another. touch one with in

_____

6. The yard. continued around the wind leaves to the blow

_____

7. Jim's door. near left was front the valise

_____

8. Yesterday sun the picnickers. was the roasting

_____

9. Will the to book return you library? my

_____

10. Please and forgive forget.

_____

11. You you you me know that. when say make laugh

_____

12. This typical very is a family.

_____

13. Push change drop down .will and your button the

_____

14. They mashed us extra for the charged potatoes.

_____

15. Can you when occurred? that event remember

_____

62. CONSECUTIVE LETTERS

Today you will write sentences, clauses, and phrases in a rather different way. Alphabetically! That's right. Each group of words has a specific direction. As an example, if the first one is a sentence that has the letters A, b, c, d, and e, you could write, "All boys can dance expertly." Observe when you must use capital letters. On the lines provided, write the ten groups of words as directed.

1. B c D e.   (sentence)

_____

2. L m n o p q.   (sentence)

_____

3. K L m n o.   (sentence)

_____

4. S T u v w,   (clause)

_____

5. B c d e f,   (clause)

_____

6. A b c d e,   (clause)

_____

7. I J k L,   (clause)

_____

8. i t t t   (verb phrase)

_____

9. h i k   (verb phrase)

_____

10. S t u   (participial phrase)

_____

63. FIRST AND FOREMOST

The idea here is simple: Construct sentences using only words that begin with the letter in the parentheses. The minimum number of words per sentence is five, and the maximum number of words is up to you. Yet, the sentence must make sense. Write the sentences on the lines provided.

1. (w) _____

2. (f) _____

3. (t) _____

4. (o) _____

5. (c) _____

6. (s) _____

7. (b) _____

8. (g) _____

9. (h) _____

10. (p) _____

64. STEP BY STEP

You will be building sentences "step by step" as you follow the directions on what to add and, perhaps, where to add it. Write the additions on the appropriate lines given to you. Write intelligently and creatively.

1. Rob ran.

Add an adverb. _____

Start the sentence with a prepositional phrase. _____

Add another subject. _____

Add another prepositional phrase. _____

2. You sing.

Change sing to a past tense verb. _____

Add another subject. _____

Add an adverb indicating *how often*. _____

Add a prepositional phrase. _____

_____

3. They gave.

Add a direct and an indirect object. _____

Add an adverb phrase showing *how*. _____

Start the sentence with a prepositional phrase. _____

_____

Make the declarative sentence a question. _____

4. Liz fell.

Add an adverb. _____

Add a prepositional phrase. _____

Add a subordinate clause. _____

_____

© 2001 by The Center for Applied Research in Education

65. THE STUFF OF SENTENCES

Start with the verb *drive*. The add the required sentence parts as directed. When you finish the tenth direction, you will have made a terrific sentence!

1. (Add a subject.)

_____

2. (Add a helping verb.)

_____

3. (Add an adverb.)

_____

4. (Add a conjunction.)

_____

5. (Place the comma before the conjunction.)

_____

6. (Add a pronoun subject following the conjunction.)

_____

7. (Add a helping verb and a main verb for that new subject.)

_____

8. (Add an adverb for that new verb.)

_____

9. (Add a prepositional phrase to the part of the sentence preceding the comma.)

_____

10. (Add a prepositional phrase to the part of the sentence following the comma.)

_____

66. DOING WHAT'S REQUIRED

Today you will construct ten sentences. Each sentence has either three or four requirements. Write the sentence on the line below the sentence's requirements. Label each requirement.

1. This sentence needs eight words and a prepositional phrase, and the last word must be an adjective.

   _____

2. The interrogative sentence must include nine words and a second-person plural pronoun.

   _____

3. This four-word sentence must have a first person singular pronoun and a predicate nominative in it.

   _____

4. This compound sentence includes twelve words, a day of the week, and a prepositional phrase.

   _____

5. This eight-word sentence has a subordinate clause, a prepositional phrase, and a plural pronoun in it.

   _____

6. This sentence of five words must include a relative pronoun.

   _____

7. Having seven words, this sentence includes an adjective clause and a predicate adjective.

   _____

8. An interrogative sentence, this six-word group also includes a proper noun.

   _____

9. This three-word imperative sentence must have a pronoun and an adverb in it.

   _____

10. With eight words, this sentence includes a compound verb, a prepositional phrase, and a feminine pronoun.

   _____

67. TIME AND TIDE WAIT FOR NO MAN! (SO MANY A PHILOSOPHER HAS SAID)

Get psyched! It is time to think and write quickly—and intelligently! Picking up on the activity's title, "Time and tide wait for no man," we will get started as soon as your teacher gives the okay. Simply follow the directions listed below. Write all sentences on a separate sheet of paper.

You have ten minutes to write seven sentences following these directions.

1. Write a sentence that starts with *Time* and ends with *you*.

2. Write a sentence including the word *and* and two adjectives.

3. Write a sentence that starts with *The tide* and includes the word *sailboat*.

4. Write a sentence that starts with *Wait* and includes the words *handsome* and *interesting*.

5. Write a sentence that starts with *For* and ends with *police*.

6. Write a sentence that starts with *No* and includes two adverbs.

7. Write a sentence that starts with *A man* and ends with *woman*.

You have ten minutes to write six sentences following these directions.

A. Write a sentence with *so* as the first word of a subordinate clause.

B. Write a seven-word sentence that begins with *many*.

C. Write an eight-word sentence that starts with *A* and includes an animal.

D. Write a sentence that includes *philosopher* and two days of the week.

E. Write an interrogative sentence beginning with *Has*.

F. Write a sentence that includes a direct quote and the word *said*.

68. IN THE BEGINNING AND AT THE END

The directives for the first and last words of a possible sentence are given to you. It is your job to fill in the rest of the words to make a complete sentence. Write your sentences on the lines provided.

1. prepositional phrase . . . adverb

   _____

2. subordinate clause . . . *-ing* word

   _____

3. participial phrase . . . prepositional phrase

   _____

4. pronoun . . . predicate noun

   _____

5. plural noun . . . predicate adjective

   _____

6. girl's name . . . adverb

   _____

7. boy's name . . . subordinate clause

   _____

8. subordinate clause . . . prepositional phrase

   _____

9. compound subject . . . compound verb

   _____

10. name of a city . . . subordinate clause

    _____

11. gerund . . . prepositional phrase

_____

12. infinitive phrase . . . noun

_____

13. prepositional phrase . . . prepositional phrase

_____

14. *-ion* word . . . *-ing* word

_____

15. *-ly* word . . . prepositional phrase

_____

69. SOPHISTICATION IS IN

The following groups of sentences need your immediate help. Each group should be combined into a single sentence. Compose ten sophisticated sentences using combining tools including conjunctions, phrases, clauses, and more. Write the new, more sophisticated and mature sentences on the lines below each group. Compare your answers with those of your classmates.

1. The girl is tall. The girl is smart. The girl has two sisters.

   _____

   _____

2. We saw the movie star. The movie star was in his sports car. The movie star waved to us.

   _____

   _____

3. My mother bought a new rug. The rug is oval and red. The rug was purchased for $300.

   _____

   _____

4. Our English class homework is to read three chapters from our novel, *The Adventures of Tom Sawyer*. It should take me about 45 minutes to read those pages. I will read those pages in my bedroom tonight.

   _____

   _____

5. It is sunny today. We plan to go to the beach this afternoon. We will take our supper with us when we go to the beach this afternoon.

   _____

   _____

6. My brother went shopping for my birthday present today. I hope he buys me a new CD player. My other CD player broke last month.

   _____

   _____

7. The police searched for the missing car. The car was a new Chrysler. It belongs to the Kenson family.

_____

_____

8. Our family physician told my dad to get more exercise. He told my dad to reduce his cholesterol. He told my dad he needed to improve his eating habits.

_____

_____

9. Yesterday oil was spilled on the road near our house. We called the hazardous materials bureau workers to report the situation. The problem was taken care of immediately.

_____

_____

10. My cousin recently married her boyfriend. They spent their honeymoon in South America for a week. They had been dating for three years.

_____

_____

70. SHOWING YOUR BUILDING SKILLS

Seven columns of words are listed below. Construct ten sentences, using as many words as possible from these columns. Score 1 point for a sentence that has 5 words; 2 for sentences that have from 6 to 8 words; 3 for sentences having 9 or more words. Insert the proper punctuation. Write your sentences on a separate sheet of paper.

Pronouns	Helping Verbs	Adverbs	Verbs
he	had	foolishly	ate
I	has	intelligently	eaten
me	have	intensely	read
others		keenly	runs
she		often	spoken
them		seldom	talks
they		usually	walked
us			
we			
you			

Prepositions	Articles	Nouns
in	a	flowers
near	an	forest
on	the	music
to		room
with		store
		street
		subway
		umbrella

71. TWO (OR MORE) INTO ONE

Combine each group of sentences (two at the least and four at the most) into one by using your combining skills, including conjunctions, phrases, clauses, and such. Write the new sentences on the appropriate lines.

1. I am eighteen. I can now drive.

_____

_____

2. Geraldo is a talented magician. He can perform many interesting tricks. Geraldo is a professional magician.

_____

_____

3. Marina heard a knock at the hotel door. Marina went to open the door.

_____

_____

4. The sun was shining. The wind was blowing. The children were playing in the fields.

_____

_____

5. She drove her car. The car was new. The car was a convertible.

_____

_____

6. Our garden contains many beautiful plants and flowers. My father spends much time working in our garden.

_____

_____

© 2001 by The Center for Applied Research in Education

7. Their bedroom has been redecorated. New photographs have been hung up on the bedroom walls.

   _____

   _____

8. Our English assignment focuses on Mark Twain. I will have to go to the library to get more information. The paper has to be at least seven pages long.

   _____

   _____

9. The Taggert family had to put their cat to sleep. The cat was old. Nancy was especially saddened by this event.

   _____

   _____

10. Her computer needed repairs. The repairs were costly. She brought her computer to the local computer store.

   _____

   _____

72. PUTTING THE WORDS IN THEIR PLACES

Forty-one words that were parts of six original sentences are listed below in their proper parts of speech column. Construct your own sentences using as many of these words as possible. Can you use them all in six sentences? Fewer? More? Write your sentences on a separate sheet of paper. Do your best and show your creativity. For the curious among you, your teacher has the original six sentences.

NOUNS	VERBS	ADJECTIVES
day	be	heavy
light	been	her
newspapers	caused	living
plan	did	many
problems	has	new
residents	fix	the
room	needed	the
snow	opposed	the
watch	read	the
	repaired	the
	raining	town's
		traffic
		two

PRONOUNS	PREPOSITIONS	ADVERBS
it	of	carefully
some	throughout	
we	to	
you		

73. I LOVE TO COMB YOUR HAIR, JOE!

Yes, it is a rather different activity title, but it does make sense, considering what you are asked to do. You see, those seven words are taken from this box of 25 words. Using any of these 25 words, construct at least 10 sentences of 5 or more words.

No word can be repeated in the same sentence. Leave the words in their original form. Show variety in your sentence construction! Write your answers on a separate sheet of paper.

a	cut	Joe	remember	usual
be	hair	lose	see	way
can	he	love	the	will
car	I	never	then	you
comb	in	on	to	your

74. WRITING A SHORT, SHORT STORY

Today you are asked to write a short, short story that includes each of the words listed below. The subject of the story is your choice. Make the story as interesting as you can, and use effective grammar and usage. Then proofread your story to check your work. Underline all the words you were asked to include. You might want to share your story with others. Write your story on a separate sheet of paper.

Nouns: car, fence, shack, sun, and two proper nouns of your choice

Verbs: (You may change the tense if needed.) ride, skid, talk, walk

Pronouns: he, it, she, them

Adjectives: drastic, fast, handsome, sturdy, tall

Adverbs: carefully, carelessly, quickly, slowly

Conjunctions: and, but, or

Prepositions: in, to, under, with

75. ARE YOU UP TO THE CHALLENGE?

Fifteen questions challenge your knowledge of sentences as classified by structure and purpose. Read the sentence for each number, and then circle the correct three-letter answer. Write those three letters on the line preceding each sentence. Finally, write each three-letter answer, in order, on the line below sentence number 15. If your answers are correct, you will spell out an important observation on life.

1. ____ Do you think this is possible?   com. interrogative   per. exclamatory
lon. compound

2. ____ Our house, which has 14 windows, is 25 years old; our neighbor's house is
even older.   son. simple   eso. compound   pet. complex

3. ____ This is the new mall that the Smith Brothers built.   edo. simple
iti. complex   oug. imperative

4. ____ I can't even imagine you could do that to me!   onb. exclamatory
pol. interrogative   fed. declarative

5. ____ Since you cannot address the graduates, Bert will gladly do it.
wil. declarative   you. simple   rin. complex

6. ____ After they volunteer to collect the food, you can organize them.
oon. compound-complex   gso. complex   dol. imperative

7. ____ My glove is missing; my bat is too.   tre. complex   sto. compound-complex
utt. compound

8. ____ This is the best route.   heb. simple   len. imperative   yke. exclamatory

9. ____ They will wait at the station until you arrive.   est. complex
jac. compound   ood. interrogative

10. ____ Your ideas are great, and we will certainly consider them at the next meeting.
an. compound   ion. imperative   pog. compound-complex

11. ____ Throw the ball.   ort. declarative   dwo. imperative   ify. interrogative

12. ____ Look.   rst. imperative   iss. complex   nni. declarative

13. ____ Although he is a bit clumsy, he caught the ball, and then he sprinted down
the field for a touchdown.   in. compound-complex   ent. compound
oss. complex

14. ____ She sings beautifully.   int. interrogative   don. imperative   peo. declarative

15. ____ I like popcorn.   ple. simple   pin. compound   dow. complex

76. WHAT TYPE OF SENTENCE IS THIS?

On the line next to each sentence, indicate the sentence's type, according to structure, by writing out *simple*, *compound*, *complex*, or *compound-complex*. There are four simple, three complex, five compound, and three compound-complex sentences. Do your best!

1. _____ I have never eaten and rested so well.

2. _____ Marbury is the player who received the most applause.

3. _____ You can take the present to them, and they should readily accept it.

4. _____ Since the orchestra is now ready, the concert will start immediately.

5. _____ Your antique books are quite rare, and you could easily sell them for a lot of money.

6. _____ Since Long Island is so populated, its residents who commute demand much from the LIRR, and the railroad officials have listened to the commuters' requests.

7. _____ These are the easiest ways to do it, Rachel.

8. _____ Can spring be far behind?

9. _____ The soldier whom you met is a brave man and he is going to receive a medal for his bravery.

10. _____ Find your keys, and then these people can drive you home.

11. _____ Yesterday I studied hard for today's test, but I did not score very well on it.

12. _____ I enjoyed the show that you directed, and I hope to see it again soon.

13. _____ You had better believe in miracles, Jose.

14. _____ My grandmother will be there, although she will probably be a little late.

15. _____ Ian and Bill were the commentators, and they called an excellent game.

© 2001 by The Center for Applied Research in Education

77. DOING THE DIAGRAMMING

Here are five sentences to diagram. On this and the reverse side of the paper, diagram the sentences. Label each word's part of speech. Discuss your answers with your classmates.

1. Hector handed his mother the package.
2. This magazine contains good photographs and articles.
3. These elite athletes modeled for our magazine.
4. Take this to the director.
5. Mr. Williams is our neighbor to the right.

78. DECIPHERING THE DIAGRAMMING

Diagramming sentences can be troublesome at times. Why are the words placed where they are? Why do some words go on the lines that are below the original line? For each word in these four diagrams, write its part of speech next to it. Use these abbreviations: noun (n), pronoun (p), verb (v), adjective (adj), adverb (advb), preposition (prep), conjunction (c), and interjection (i). Then, on another sheet of paper, set up a diagram for your original sentence using the same formats as seen here.

1. The fancy clothes were not purchased.

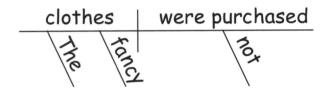

2. A very intelligent student usually excels.

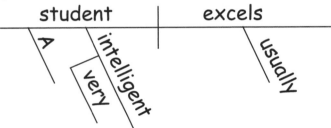

3. Both recordings sold well.

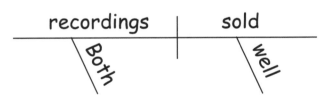

4. The tall and handsome models spoke and walked gracefully.

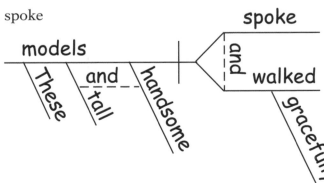

79. MATCHING THE DIAGRAMS

Match the five sentence diagrams and the five sentences by placing each sentence's words in their correct spaces within the diagram. Write the sentence's number in the parentheses before the corresponding diagram.

1. The annoying fly had bitten Rudy.
2. Kerry washed the cars and bicycles.
3. You and I were not selected.
4. My father is smart and humorous.
5. She seldom told him a secret.

A. (　)

B. (　)

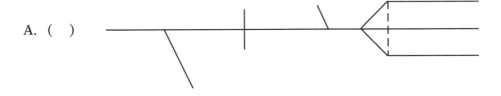

C. (　)

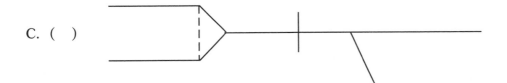

D. (　)

E. (　)

80. TO SPLICE IS NOT SO NICE!

Rather than using a period, semicolon, colon, or a conjunction and a comma, writers sometimes incorrectly join statements with a comma, essentially creating a run-on sentence. "The woman in the blue dress is my neighbor, she is rather tall." These two sentences serve as an example of a comma splice. Here is a correct method: "The woman in the blue dress is my neighbor. She is rather tall."

Nine of the following examples are comma splices. Place a check next to those numbers. If your answers are correct, they will total an even 100. Then, on another sheet of paper, correct the comma splices.

1. ___ After Kenny played the drums, he sang several songs with his band.

2. ___ Francine likes to swim and sail, she hopes to make her college team.

3. ___ Without missing a day of work, the nurse quickly recovered from her fall.

4. ___ My brother, a chiropractor, usually works six days a week.

5. ___ These are the days to remember, they will never come again.

6. ___ Running from the authorities, the bank robber was finally caught in the next state.

7. ___ Grab these shirts, James, they need to be washed immediately!

8. ___ These benches will be painted next weekend, then they will be more presentable.

9. ___ New York, the Empire State, is the home of several sports teams.

10. ___ Both Ursula and Michelle, the Watson twins, will leave for Europe next month.

11. ___ No, these are not the correct pants, Lyle.

12. ___ These new automobiles, in my opinion, are terrible overpriced.

13. ___ My dearest friend, Isaac Smith, will graduate this week, he will then attend college in Maryland.

14. ___ Helen of Troy will be remembered as the face that launched a thousand ships, can you name any of those ships?

15. ___ "Frankly, my dear, I don't give a damn" is a line from a famous movie, do you remember the movie's title?

16. ___ Because it has rained nearly every day this week, the grass has really grown.

17. ___ Edison lived in Menlo Park, that is why he is called The Wizard of Menlo Park.

18. ___ It is obvious that she is bright, charming, and friendly.

19. ___ Can this be the correct road, it seems too far away from the stadium.

20. ___ The group learned that Charles Dickens, a famous British author, wrote many interesting novels.

© 2001 by The Center for Applied Research in Education

81. THE SENTENCE POEM

This is different from most poems you have read. It is called a Sentence Poem because it is all sentences arranged in a specific format. An example Sentence Poem entitled "Reading" is given to you. There are seven distinct lines. On a separate sheet of paper, write your own Sentence Poem, choosing any topic you want. You might read your poem aloud in class. Enjoy!

The format of the Sentence Poem is as follows:

line 1: simple sentence

line 2: compound sentence

line 3: complex sentence

line 4: interrogative sentence

line 5: complex sentence

line 6: compound sentence

line 7: simple sentence

The following is a Sentence Poem about Reading:

"Reading"

Reading is a worthwhile activity.

It teaches you new facts, and it can take you away from your problems for a while.

A book that is interesting will open new interests for you.

What else can reading do?

As Emily Dickinson said, "There is no frigate like a book to take us lands away . . ."

Many people like to read, and you will too.

Reading is good for you.

Section Four

USAGE—A WAY WITH WORDS!

82. GRAMMAR VOCABULARY

Match the word (A to P) with its description (1 to 16). Place all your answers in the magic squares below. If your answers are correct, all columns and rows and the two diagonals will add to the same number.

A=	B=	C=	D=
E=	F=	G=	H=
I=	J=	K=	L=
M=	N=	O=	P=

A.	would've	1.	reflexive pronoun
B.	others	2.	main verb
C.	motor	3.	plural pronoun
D.	jury	4.	adverb
E.	should	5.	interjection
F.	is	6.	singular noun
G.	me	7.	past tense verb
H.	herself	8.	helping verb
I.	had read	9.	adjective
J.	hurrah	10.	linking verb
K.	seldom	11.	past tense verb phrase
L.	for	12.	collective noun
M.	mesmerize	13.	contraction
N.	can't hardly	14.	conjunction and preposition
O.	pretty	15.	singular pronoun
P.	began	16.	double negative

83. GRAMMAR SPANNING

Match the number of the underlined portion of the sentence with its corresponding letter. Place your answers in the magic square below. Thus, *captain*, the underlined word in number 7, matches up with A (predicate nominative). Place 7 in the letter A box. If your answers are correct, all columns and rows and the two diagonals will add up to the same number.

A=	B=	C=	D=
E=	F=	G=	H=
I=	J=	K=	L=
M=	N=	O=	P=

A. predicate nominative
B. helping verb
C. preposition
D. gerund as subject
E. pronoun
F. adjective
G. adverb
H. direct object
I. verb
J. interjection
K. indirect object
L. conjunction
M. participle
N. noun as subject
O. infinitive
P. object of the preposition

© 2001 by The Center for Applied Research in Education

1. <u>Flaunting</u> his muscles, the lifeguard walked along the shore.

2. The <u>magical</u> elves enchanted the children.

3. Thomas scored the winning <u>basket</u> that night.

4. I have always wanted <u>to go</u> to Brazil.

5. George <u>and</u> Marcie were leading the field of runners.

6. <u>After</u> the dance, we went to the diner with our friends.

7. She is the team's <u>captain</u>.

8. <u>Ha</u>! I caught you at your own game.

9. Receiving the flowers gave <u>her</u> a warm feeling.

10. <u>Playing</u> in the snow is always enjoyable for the kids.

11. Visibility <u>might</u> be a problem on the roads.

12. They seldom <u>require</u> this much postage.

13. A few <u>kites</u> were flying above the sand dunes.

14. Are <u>several</u> of the contestants coming back next week?

15. These jars will be <u>completely</u> filled.

16. He always pays attention in <u>class</u>.

84. JUGGLING THE IRREGULARS

The order of the letters in each of these 20 irregular verbs has been changed. Each irregular verb appears in its present tense form. After you have spelled these 20 verbs correctly, write each verb's past and past participle forms in the appropriate columns.

	PRESENT	PAST	PAST PARTICIPLE
1. OG	_____	_____	_____
2. ETA	_____	_____	_____
3. OKWN	_____	_____	_____
4. ISMW	_____	_____	_____
5. GIBNE	_____	_____	_____
6. EFZREE	_____	_____	_____
7. INBGR	_____	_____	_____
8. EABRK	_____	_____	_____
9. RSBTU	_____	_____	_____
10. VGEI	_____	_____	_____
11. EASKP	_____	_____	_____
12. OSCEOH	_____	_____	_____
13. ITWER	_____	_____	_____
14. NRGI	_____	_____	_____
15. OD	_____	_____	_____
16. UTP	_____	_____	_____
17. INSKRH	_____	_____	_____
18. KTEA	_____	_____	_____
19. TOWHR	_____	_____	_____
20. EASLT	_____	_____	_____

85. A PRO WITH PRONOUNS

Circle the correct pronoun in each sentence and then write that pronoun on the line provided. Add up the letters in those correct pronouns. The total for Group 1's pronouns is 21. The total for Group 2's pronouns is 29. Have fun!

GROUP 1

1. _____ Kameesha and (I, me) went to the mall yesterday.

2. _____ The cake was eaten mostly be Hugo and (her, herself).

3. _____ The newly elected secretary is (he, him).

4. _____ (We, Them) soldiers will surely attend the ceremony next Sunday.

5. _____ Either the minister or (he, him) will do the reading.

6. _____ Please take Frankie and (I, me) with you.

7. _____ The task will be completed by her and (I, me).

8. _____ The woman, (who, whom) is your coach, is talented and patient.

9. _____ (Who, Whom) related that to you?

10. _____ Paula and (I, myself) live on the same street now.

Total: _____

GROUP 2

11. _____ The letters were addressed to both Sue and (I, me).

12. _____ Cory told us that the winners were Sarah and (she, herself).

13. _____ (Who, Whom) is you choice for president this year?

14. _____ To (who, whom) are you sending that package?

15. _____ These students (who, whom) you know are seldom absent.

16. _____ (He, Him) is knocking on the door.

17. _____ They will interrogate both the group of spectators and (he, him).

18. _____ She is one of the scholars who (is, are) receiving a commendation.

19. _____ Did someone see (who, whom) dropped this wallet?

20. _____ Neither of the pilots saw (it, itself).

Total: _____

86. HOW IRREGULAR!

In the space provided within each sentence, write the correct form of the present tense verb listed before the sentence. On another sheet of paper, write a paragraph using at least five of the present tense verbs (or their past or past participle forms) displayed here.

1. choose   He had _____ the correct box.

2. grow   How he had _____ so tall is beyond me.

3. lead   She had _____ throughout the game against North.

4. see   Have you _____ the new television program yet?

5. ride   They _____ on horseback during that hot day.

6. know   Do you _____ the way to get to the park, Maury?

7. drive   We could have _____ there much faster.

8. begin   It has _____ to rain, I'm afraid.

9. burst   The pipe in the basement _____ because of the cold.

10. bear   She had _____ all her difficulties courageously.

11. say   Did you _____ that they were beginning the race here?

12. eat   I could have _____ much more, but I did not.

13. creep   He stealthily _____ into the closet near the door.

14. come   The settlers had _____ twenty years before that.

15. break   In only two years she _____ all the swimming records.

16. speak   He has _____ with such eloquence at other ceremonies.

17. swim   All of the swimmers have already _____ their laps.

18. sing   Could they have _____ any better?

19. write   It was _____ clearly above the door.

20. swear   They _____ that they would do their best work for you.

87. THE SUBJECTS OF SCIENCE

Circle the subject in each sentence. Then write each subject's first letter on the line below the last sentence. If your subjects are correct, the letters will spell (in order) four words you would hear in science class. Write those four words on the second line following the last sentence.

1. These past three days have been quiet and enjoyable.
2. Interest in the MTV schedule of shows has risen since last year.
3. All the cars purchased during these three years must be reexamined.
4. Has Georgia seen you since Tuesday night?
5. Suddenly, some realization hit him.
6. Annapolis is the home of the United States Naval Academy.
7. Near the car is the machine.
8. The student's graduation was a cause for celebration.
9. At the same time, the regiment successfully moved forward.
10. During the main portion of the trial, the attorney seemed confused.
11. Part of the solution involves this piece of evidence.
12. This year, Halloween will be a very special time for the twins.
13. Children are special people.
14. Only after three warnings did the hound obey.
15. His favorite album is missing.
16. Can the regulars attend all of these sessions?
17. The peevish toddler is usually the center of attention in his family.
18. Many of these tools were gifts to the carpenter.
19. The chemical's activity is the big concern here now.
20. Protocol must be followed at all times.

Write the 20 letters here. _____

The four words you hear in science class are _____, _____,

_____, and _____.

88. BROADWAY BOUND

Underline the first letter of both the subject and the main verb in each sentence. Then write these 26 letters (in order) on the line below the last sentence. If you have done this correctly, you have spelled out the names of two well-known Broadway plays. Write the names of the plays on the indicated line.

1. We must enter our names in the contest.

2. Several of the dogs tried to outrun the car.

3. Suicide is a very sad topic to discuss during the holiday season.

4. Such delicacies must be enjoyed.

5. Some of the waves tossed the swimmers.

6. The others will probably restore the supply soon.

7. You must never lose this precious ruby.

8. Everything in this store sold for well below its original price.

9. Much of the news today includes your favorite summer events.

10. The search entered its fourth day today.

11. Recently, Raymond acted in the musical.

12. The bundle was left in the meadow.

13. Each will certainly serve you well.

The letters of the 26 words are _____.

The two Broadway plays are _____ and _____.

89. THINKING ABOUT THE PAST

Twenty present tense verbs are listed in Column A. Their 20 supposed past tense verbs are listed in Column B. If the verb in Column B is correct, write C (for correct) on the line next to the number. If the verb is incorrect, write I (for incorrect). If your answers are correct, their will be 10 C's and 10 I's, and their corresponding numbers (the number next to each C or I) will total 105. For the 10 incorrect verbs, write the correct past tense forms next to the incorrect form in Column B.

COLUMN A

1. ___ break
2. ___ burst
3. ___ choose
4. ___ come
5. ___ draw
6. ___ drink
7. ___ drown
8. ___ flow
9. ___ give
10. ___ lead
11. ___ raise
12. ___ ring
13. ___ run
14. ___ shake
15. ___ show
16. ___ shrink
17. ___ strive
18. ___ tear
19. ___ wear
20. ___ write

COLUMN B

broke
bursted
choosed
came
drawn
drunk
drowned
flowed
gived
led
raised
rang
runned
shaked
showed
shrunk
strove
torn
weared
wrote

The correct past tense verbs are in numbers _____.

The incorrect past tense verbs are in numbers _____.

90. FIVE ADJECTIVES

Circle the word indicated by the italicized word or words preceding each sentence. Then write the first letter of each answer (in order) on the line below the last sentence. If you do all this correctly, you will spell out five adjectives. Write those five adjectives on the indicated line.

1. *Subject*   The sophisticated scientist delivered an informed presentation.

2. *Verb*   Most people like themselves.

3. *Predicate adjective*   The outlaw was quite ornery.

4. *Indirect object*   Kyle gave Wendy his car for the weekend.

5. *Direct object*   The women gave radios to one another.

6. *Predicate nominative*   His most prominent trait is his intelligence.

7. *Predicate adjective*   The cat is quite cautious.

8. *Subject*   The athlete's heart was studied by the team of cardiologists.

9. *Verb*   The audience members groaned because of the comedian's silly joke.

10. *Direct object*   Reggie was returning the letter to the post office.

11. *Indirect object*   He would give anybody anything.

12. *Subject*   In the middle of the field stood a deer.

13. *Verb*   None of the fifteen gymnasts noticed the change in his floor program.

14. *Direct object*   Pauline left her father's umbrella on the train last night.

15. *Predicate nominative*   George is the most talented member of the rock group.

16. *Predicate adjective*   Her face was especially beautiful.

17. *Indirect object*   We gave the beautician a holiday gift.

18. *Verb*   The sergeant ordered her company to move more swiftly.

19. *Subject*   The lease on the apartment expires next June.

20. *Direct object*   The skilled driver fortunately avoided the ditch.

Write the 20 letters here. _____

The five adjectives are _____, _____, _____, _____,

and _____.

© 2001 by The Center for Applied Research in Education

91. MUSICALLY INCLINED

Twenty of the thirty words listed below can be used as complements. These complements include direct objects, indirect objects, objective complements, predicate nominatives, and predicate adjectives. The other ten words cannot function as complements. Circle these ten words. List the first letter of these ten words on the line below the thirty words. Then unscramble these letters to spell out a style of music. Write the style's name on the indicated line. Have fun!

actually	intelligent
aimlessly	loosely
automobile	mother
business	my
clear	myself
computer	painful
effigy	panel
entirely	pleasure
eventually	relic
famous	researchers
gracious	spectacular
gravity	suitcase
hazard	tremendously
her	very
hoisted	youthfully

The first letters of the ten words that cannot function as complements are

_____.

These letters spell the style of music known as _____.

© 2001 by The Center for Applied Research in Education

Name_____ Date _____ Period_____

92. YOU RAISE A SON, BUT A SUN RISES

Some verbs that are particularly tricky are found in this activity. Here, the verb's present infinitive is found within parentheses after the question's number. Read the sentence and fill in the correct form of the verb. Then, look at the number following the sentence. On the line below the last sentence, write the letter of the word you filled in that matches that number. Thus, for the first fill-in, the letter is S because it is the fifth letter of the correct answer choose. Fill in the remaining 14, in order; if your answers are correct, you will spell out four words. Rise to the occasion!

1. (choose) Did you <u>choose</u> a dress, Mary? (5)

2. (begin) They had _____. (4)

3. (rise) Yesterday the sun _____ at 6:30. (1)

4. (set) Where had you _____ that down, Derek? (2)

5. (sit) Those cats have been _____ on the wall for the past five minutes. (4)

6. (burst) The leaky pipes finally _____ open yesterday. (2)

7. (tear) All of the campers had _____ up the papers. (3)

8. (raise) Gasoline prices have _____ these last few months. (5)

9. (lie) Is the coat _____ on the floor again? (2)

10. (lay) Last night I _____ the package on the shelf in our den. (2)

11. (take) Some of these seats are _____ already. (3)

12. (fly) Because he had _____ so many miles, he was given a free trip to Europe. (4)

13. (use) Had they _____ their radar detector at that juncture? (3)

14. (ask) Never have I _____ you for anything as important as this. (4)

15. (make) The director has not _____ the schedule yet. (3)

The letters are _____.

The four words are _____, _____, _____, and _____.

113

93. GETTING PERSONAL

Sixteen personal pronouns are described in the clues below. Match each pronoun with its correct description by placing the number within the appropriate box in the magic square. The number after the description indicates the number of letters in the pronoun. If your answers are correct, all the rows and columns and both diagonals will add up to the same number. You may want to consult your grammar book or notes.

A=	B=	C=	D=
E=	F=	G=	H=
I=	J=	K=	L=
M=	N=	O=	P=

A. WE
B. YOURS
C. OUR
D. ME
E. OURS
F. YOU
G. THEIR
H. YOUR
I. HIS
J. HERS
K. MY
L. THEY
M. ITS
N. SHE
O. HIM
P. HER

1. singular — possessive — neuter (3)
2. singular or plural — nominative or objective (3)
3. singular or plural — possessive — masculine or feminine (4)
4. singular — objective — masculine (3)
5. plural — nominative (4)
6. plural — possessive — masculine or feminine (3)
7. plural — nominative (2)
8. singular — possessive — feminine (4)
9. singular — possessive — masculine or feminine (2)
10. singular — objective — masculine or feminine (2)
11. singular or plural — possessive — masculine or feminine (5)
12. singular — possessive — masculine (3)
13. singular — nominative — feminine (3)
14. plural — possessive — masculine or feminine (4)
15. plural — possessive — masculine or feminine (5)
16. singular — objective — feminine (3)

94. SOMETHING'S WRONG HERE—HALF THE TIME

Ten of these sentences contain an incorrectly used word. Do nothing to those sentences containing only correctly used words. However, for the other ten, cross out the wrong word and write the correct word in the space after the sentence. Then write the two letters next to these ten sentences (in consecutive order) on the line below the last sentence. If your answers are correct, you will spell out a famous saying.

1. (er) The car's brakes were repaired yesterday by Hank. _____

2. (ra) My aunt sat beside me at my sister's musical concert. _____

3. (ro) Did you really want to by that parasol today? _____

4. (do) May we have ice cream for dessert? _____

5. (n't) Unfortunately, my message was not heard over the crowd's noise. _____

6. (me) I did not feel that I truly new the correct address. _____

7. (wa) The string on the package was to loose. _____

8. (se) Eric was quite happy to be asked to the prom. _____

9. (sn) Cindy, the lacrosse team's most gifted player, hurt her heal. _____

10. ('tb) How will this test score effect my grade? _____

11. (ol) Jim bought these papers at the stationery store. _____

12. (op) My grandparents love to talk about the past. _____

13. (ui) They did not have to make such a seen at the movies last night. _____

14. (lt) Mike did not know weather to go or to stay. _____

15. (en) It does not seem right that Yvonne has to do most of the group's work. _____

16. (in) Your not the only one who owes me money, Kendra! _____

17. (ad) I will leave you and than I will go with the other mountain climbers. _____

18. (pe) Nobody can possibly learn that much in this short span of time. _____

19. (ay) We found a large amount of coins in the basement. _____

20. (rt) Can I right the wrongs of this family? _____

The saying is _____.

© 2001 by The Center for Applied Research in Education

95. JUST IN CASE

Either a noun or a pronoun is underlined in each sentence. Determine which case of the underlined word is used—nominative, objective, or possessive. A three-letter combination is found next to each sentence. Write these letter combinations, in order, on the appropriate line below the last sentence. If your answers are correct, you will spell out the names of three famous Americans.

1. (JUD) They found <u>her</u> sitting in the room by herself.

2. (MAR) I could not believe that you were the only <u>one</u> who attended the meeting.

3. (THO) My sister could not find <u>her</u> jewelry box after she returned from camp.

4. (MAS) These playing cards are <u>theirs</u>.

5. (KTW) <u>Ben</u> will be attending this Colorado college in the fall.

6. (AIN) Is your <u>computer</u> working properly now, Phil?

7. (EDI) They could very easily find <u>his</u> address in this book.

8. (YBL) Hand me the planks so I can fit <u>them</u> in here now.

9. (UME) Have you memorized these <u>dates</u> for today's quiz, Charlene?

10. (SON) This car has been <u>my</u> headache for too long.

Nominative case: _____

Objective case: _____

Possessive case: _____

On the reverse side, write three sentences illustrating the nominative case, three illustrating the objective case, and three illustrating the possessive case.

96. LET'S EXAMINE THOSE CASES!

Knowing the case for a specific pronoun helps in cases of usage and for your writing in general. This activity will challenge your knowledge of cases. On the line next to the number, write the letter N for a pronoun that is nominative, O for one that is objective, P for one that is possessive, and NO for one that is both nominative and objective. Here is a big hint for you: There are four Ns, nine Ps, five Os, and two NOs. The total of the sentence numbers for the Ns and Os is 105—the same as the total of the Ps and NOs! Best of luck!

1. _____ hers

2. _____ you

3. _____ mine

4. _____ me

5. _____ we

6. _____ it

7. _____ their

8. _____ he

9. _____ him

10. _____ his

11. _____ your

12. _____ she

13. _____ theirs

14. _____ our

15. _____ they

16. _____ himself

17. _____ us

18. _____ yours

19. _____ them

20. _____ my

97. CASING OUT THE PUZZLE

These 18 words are hidden in this word-find puzzle. Circle the words and then write whether each is an example of the nominative (N), objective (O), or possessive (P) case. Some can be used as examples of two cases. After you have located the 18 words, write a sentence for each word illustrating the case. If a word can be used in more than one way, show both examples. Write these sentences on a separate sheet of paper.

```
L H D H I X Y P P H T H H E R S P X B V
J S X B Z T D Q C X P H S X T C B P J H
P P S N S S K C X C P N E R R V P V S B
M X G Q M T K H R G W P T I R Z F B W Z
D D K R R F D F L V M H H Z R K Q L N Q
M W F T X S X F C X H F P W G S F N K G
L B M K W R L V Y Z Z R F R J D W L Z C
Z Y M M C J J R W O G F O C K V K S J E
Z W H L B N B R T N U W U N Y S H L N K
Q Q P I S V W M H J R R R D O H Y I W G
Z W D U S X S Q E R B S S X U E M E M T
V Q M C D K S H Y H T Z D Z P E W V H H
Z M S H M V S J M I J P L Z H N M C Q N
K Q C N S G F L K R Y B X T Y M V B X F
X B T D X N C Q C W D F J H X L K K K V
```

he	ours
her	she
him	theirs
his	them
it	they
its	us
me	we
mine	you
my	yours

98. DON'T OBJECT TO THESE THIRTY OBJECTS!

Thirty objects are found in these sentences—thirteen direct objects (DO), twelve objects of the preposition (OP), and five indirect objects (IO). Underline each object and then write the two-letter abbreviation above the appropriate objects.

1. Many prizes were given to the children.

2. My sister and he gave them another present.

3. When will the director post the list of characters?

4. John delivered his speeches to small crowds.

5. His psychiatrist wrote him a prescription for a new medication.

6. This Chicago highway always offers an interesting view of the city's skyline.

7. Give Serena the list of books to borrow from the library.

8. Some of these grapes were bought at this store.

9. Mike lent Sam twenty dollars for the tickets.

10. Have these activities inspired Brett?

11. You have yet to submit a poor excuse to the teacher.

12. The DVD player gave the family another electronic device.

13. See no evil.

14. Dad has cooked salmon for you.

15. An apple a day keeps the doctor away.

99. IS THAT OBJECT A SIGN?

If the word can be used as a direct object, indirect object, or an object of the preposition, circle the word *yes* and the letter next to it. If it cannot, circle the word *no* and the letter next to it. In consecutive order, write all the Yes letters on the Yes line and all the No letters on the No line. If your answers are correct, you will see some signs.

1. him	yes A	no L
2. water	yes R	no E
3. she	yes B	no L
4. us	yes I	no T
5. our	yes A	no E
6. we	yes D	no O
7. you	yes E	no B
8. it	yes S	no C
9. her	yes V	no E
10. they	yes H	no S
11. their	yes I	no C
12. Lawrence	yes I	no F
13. them	yes R	no G
14. my	yes L	no O
15. I	yes M	no R
16. me	yes G	no J
17. mine	yes O	no P
18. Francine	yes O	no K
19. he	yes P	no I
20. your	yes N	no O

Yes: _____

No: _____

100. THE FARMER GREW MY YOUNGER BROTHER?

If you read the first sentence of this activity, the title does make sense. But the sentence does *not* make sense! What is wrong is that the writer has misplaced the modifier, *Grown by the farmer*. *The pieces of fruit*, and not *my younger brother*, were grown by the farmer. So, a better sentence is, "My younger brother ate the pieces of fruit grown by the farmer" or "Grown by the farmer, the pieces of fruit were eaten by my younger brother."

    Six of the following sentences use modifiers correctly. Circle those six numbers. Then, on a separate sheet of paper, correct the other eleven sentences by fixing the misplaced modifier problem and writing the sentence in a clear, logical form. Assume that sentence 1 has been corrected through the above examples.

1. Grown by the farmer, my younger brother ate the pieces of fruit.

2. Sitting on the dock, the view was enjoyed by my sister.

3. Frolicking on the den's rug, the puppy played with the ball of yarn

4. Reasoning with the class, the teacher said homework would be canceled.

5. Nearing the end of the marathon, the finish line was spotted by my gym teacher.

6. Listening to my telephone conversation, the man in the next phone booth was interested in what I was saying.

7. Dunking the basketball, the seven-footer looked quite at ease.

8. Looking out the window, the accident was seen by the young girl.

9. Having finished her term paper, the dog was walked by Darlene.

10. Visiting New York City for the first time, the Statue of Liberty was a popular attraction my family visited.

11. Looking for Commerce Street, the map was perused by his wife.

12. Relaxing on the beach chair, the sun was too bright for me.

13. Snow, glistening beautifully in the moonlight, caught our eye.

14. Revving her engine, the Indy 500 driver prepared for the race's start.

15. Angered by the passenger, the train conductor cooled off very well.

16. Burnt in the oven, the chef took out the charred bread.

17. The spectator cheered the home run hitter rounding the bases.

18. Yawning from the long day, the moon was spotted by Jasmine.

© 2001 by The Center for Applied Research in Education

101. WHEN TOO MUCH IS TOO MUCH!

Each sentence contains an example of superfluous words. You would not have to say that someone is "light in weight" when "light" by itself will suffice. Cross out the superfluous words in each sentence. When necessary, replace them with more exact and less wordy substitutes. Write the new sentences on a separate sheet of paper.

1. Her beautiful hair was brown in color.

2. At the present time there are no plans to construct another bridge to the island.

3. The bank robber was later fatally murdered by the guard.

4. If you open an account in our bank, you will receive a free gift.

5. What will be the end result of all these arguments about the budget?

6. The characters made me laugh throughout the whole novel.

7. Let's study all the past history about that war now.

8. In view of the fact that our treasury is almost depleted, we need to think of ways to raise money.

9. Those basketball players are tall in height.

10. Most of these models are quite handsome in appearance.

11. Here is a check in the amount of $350.

12. I would like to reflect back on the old days.

13. I do not think we had received any prior notice.

14. Do you want me to repeat the directions again?

15. This gift is on the occasion of my parents' thirty-fifth anniversary.

16. Kenny really has no use for those foreign imports.

17. The police seem to think that it was an unintentional accident.

18. How many new innovations made that big a difference this decade?

19. This day marks the final end of our time together.

20. This is the start of the beginning of the novel.

© 2001 by The Center for Applied Research in Education

102. IT'S ALL HAPPENING AT THE ZOO

Here are 15 sentences all dealing with the zoo. There are underlined portions of each sentence. Circle the underlined word or mark of punctuation if it is correct. If it is grammatically wrong or spelled incorrectly, draw a box around it. Then write your circled answers, in order, on the line entitled Correct. Write your boxed answers, in order, on the line entitled Incorrect. If all your answers are correct, the two lines, Correct and Incorrect, should spell out a line of a show tune from a popular movie that was also a Broadway show. (Assume all the material is factual.)

                         th   es

1. These puppies have <u>grown</u> so much in such a short <u>time</u>.

                    ea   cl

2. Each of these cats <u>has</u> found <u>their</u> own mouse.

                  re   af

3. Neither the <u>giraffe</u> nor the elephant enjoyed <u>his</u> time at the zoo.

                  ew

4. That is a tiny <u>,</u> cute monkey in the other cage.

            of   my   fa

5. On Thursday <u>,</u> June 29, 2000 <u>,</u> my family went to the zoo for the second time that <u>week</u>.

              vo   ri

6. Is Edward <u>Albee's</u> play, *The Zoo Story*, really about a zoo?

                          te   th

7. We saw many <u>monkeys</u>, pandas <u>,</u> and bears the last time we went.

              im

8. Both <u>tiger's</u> behavior was certainly worth noting.

                        be

9. Three other families had <u>ate</u> with us in the cafeteria.

           in

10. There <u>wasn't</u> enough time for us to visit all the animals.

ve

11. <u>Less</u> animals were sleeping during our last trip.

ry

12. <u>Everywheres</u> we looked we saw happy children.

mo   gs

13. The <u>guides'</u> enjoy teaching others about the various <u>animals'</u> habits.

un   ta

14. We <u>was</u> taught that the cheetah is faster <u>then</u> any other land animal.

in

15. The llama's cage was located <u>besides</u> the chimpanzee's cage.

Correct _____

Incorrect _____

103. MAKING CHANGES

Follow the directions given after each sentence and make any other necessary changes to the sentence. Write your responses on the appropriate lines.

1. Several toys were found under the shelf. (Change *toys* to *toy*.)

   _____

2. Either of the choices is a good one. (Change *is* to *are*.)

   _____

3. A person is not expected to tolerate such rude behavior from his or her friends. (Change *person* to *persons*.)

   _____

4. I am quite happy to see you. (Change *I* to *Hank*.)

   _____

5. Some of the animals built their homes across the river. (Change *Some* to *One*.)

   _____

6. Here is a note for you. (Change *note* to *notes*.)

   _____

7. One dollar is not a high asking price for that. (Change *One* to *Five*.)

   _____

8. Jane is the best of those three dancers. (Change *three* to *two*.)

   _____

9. There was much philosophical disagreement between the two states. (Change *two* to *four*.)

   _____

10. Why don't these drivers change their schedules? (Change *don't* to *doesn't*.)

_____

11. Every one of the tires in this store is on sale today. (Change *Every one* to *All*.)

_____

12. I know that Jamey is at the store. (Add *and Kate* to the sentence.)

_____

13. The gift is these cards. (Change *gift* to *gifts*.)

_____

14. Both Edie and Tommy devised their own skits. (Drop *and Tommy* from the sentence.)

_____

15. Was any of the bread eaten? (Change *bread* to *breads*.)

_____

104. HOW AGREEABLE!

Nine of the fifteen sentences below show correct agreement between the subject and the verb. On the line next to each sentence, write the letters CA for correct agreement and the letters IA for incorrect agreement. If you have done this correctly, the CA total is 66.

1. _____ The lights on top of the building were beautiful.

2. _____ Some of the papers was ripped from the rain.

3. _____ Each of the students has the correct answer.

4. _____ Several members of the team were absent for the picture.

5. _____ Seventy-five cents are not enough.

6. _____ Ham and eggs is his breakfast selection.

7. _____ Mumps are a common childhood illness.

8. _____ Here are your sister and brother.

9. _____ The decisions of the umpires have not frustrated the team.

10. _____ All of my friends were happy to go to the assembly.

11. _____ Both of the musicians have been selected for the next musical.

12. _____ Most of the magazines is ready for delivery.

13. _____ Many of the breads is prepared on the premises.

14. _____ Have all the pictures been developed yet?

15. _____ Neither the boy nor his sisters is happy about the plan.

105. DON'T GET NONE OF THESE QUESTIONS WRONG!

Please do not be upset with the usage mistake in this activity's title. The problem, of course, is the double negative. Instead, it should read, "Do not get any of these questions wrong!" or "Get none of these questions wrong!" Below you will find 15 sentences, each having a double negative problem. On a separate sheet of paper, rewrite each sentence, correcting the double negative problem.

1. We don't need no education.

2. I can't get no satisfaction.

3. They can't hardly run the required distance.

4. Harry doesn't have no reason to complain.

5. The seagulls do not ever resist the waste receptacles at the beach.

6. Our choir members can't scarcely hear the director's cue.

7. It really does not make no difference to them.

8. When we looked for disposable razors on the shelf in the drugstore, we found that there wasn't none.

9. Unfortunately, the search party hasn't found none of the missing airplane parts.

10. My mother couldn't locate none of the other Web sites.

11. After doing so many pushups, Benny couldn't hardly lift his arms.

12. Our treasurer reported that we haven't but fifty dollars left in our account.

13. You don't need no fancy tools to do that job, Martin.

14. Some of the bird watchers haven't spotted none of the orioles.

15. There isn't no way that I am going to fall for his silly tricks!

© 2001 by The Center for Applied Research in Education

106. EXPLAIN WHY!

Explain what the specific grammatical or usage problem is in each of these 15 sentences. Write your responses on the appropriate lines.

1. Each of the cats were found near the parking lot.

_____

2. There is no weigh that we can complete that on time.

_____

3. Please keep this very important secret between you and I.

_____

4. Why ain't there a better route to the main road?

_____

5. All the team members were real tired after the overtime period.

_____

6. Jacques is the better of these four hockey players.

_____

7. After their weekend engagement was completed, they travel to Canada.

_____

8. They formerly had been members of that voting block.

_____

9. They enjoy biking, bowling, and visits to the Caribbean.

_____

10. You are not that different than your brother.

_____

11. In most of Shakespeare's plays, he includes an interesting morale.

_____

12. Him and I can carry the charcoal from the car to the picnic area.

_____

13. The grapes who are on the counter need to be washed.

_____

14. Burning in the oven, the man took out the chicken.

_____

15. Neither the mayor or his campaign manager needs our advice.

_____

107. THE OLD "WHO VERSUS WHOM" PROBLEM

When do you use *who* and when do you use *whom*?" For years, people have been troubled by this question. Since most sentences that use *who* or *whom* in a subordinate clause are really two former sentences combined into one, see whether you can replace *who* for *he* or *she* and *whom* for *him* or *her*. In the sentence, "John, *who* is fourteen, is tall," the two former sentences are "John is tall" and "John (He) is fourteen." If the interrogative sentence reads, "To *whom* should I give the present?" answer it, "I should give the present to *him*.

Circle the correct word in each sentence. Eight answers will be *who* and seven answers will be *whom*.

1. (Who, Whom) is your favorite singer?

2. She is the woman (who, whom) ran so well in the Penn Relays.

3. I think I will remember (who, whom) she is.

4. Lester Kingsfield, (who, whom) you highly recommended, is a great person.

5. Teresa Bowman, (who, whom) I can recall quite easily, has brown hair and blue eyes.

6. Do you often wonder (who, whom) wrote that note to you last week?

7. I now remember (who, whom) I told yesterday.

8. Do you know of anyone (who, whom) plans to attend the Art Council's Holiday Gala?

9. She, (who, whom) is one of the world's best tennis players, gave me her autograph.

10. Is Tony the musician (who, whom) you were raving about last week?

11. Will you please tell me (who, whom) that dancer is, Murray?

12. To (who, whom) should I give this receipt?

13. There is somebody (who, whom) really knows me well.

14. The professor (who, whom) I talked with at lunch is Mr. Hollman.

15. Marshall Timmons is a vocalist (who, whom) I can listen to at any time.

108. WHAT ON EARTH?

Circle the correct choice in each sentence. Then, on the line below the last sentence, write each choice's corresponding letter. If your answers are correct, you will spell out three five-letter words that share something in common. Do your best!

                        e   t

1. Each of (us, we) batters took practice swings.

                                          r   a

2. Mr. Simmons taught Helene and (I, me) how to crochet.

                      s   r

3. Molly, (who, whom) you have met, will be my prom date.

          o   t

4. (Us, We) clarinet players have practiced many hours for the concert.

                    h   i

5. Tiko and (she, her) have been friends for nearly eight years.

                                  h   e

6. Give the cards to Betty and (her, she).

                    c   a

7. Who is dating (who, whom)?

                                        u   t

8. Do you firmly believe that the instigator is (her, she)?

                                      e   t

9. My recollection is that Ricardo is taller than (he, him).

                            r   o

10. Our new officers, Carol and (he, him), will be sworn in next Wednesday evening.

                                r   h

11. The latest raffle winners are Sylvester and (her, she).

© 2001 by The Center for Applied Research in Education

                                  e   m

12. Mrs. Bauer and (I, me) were decorating the hall for the holiday dance.

                                          n   a

13. Was the phone call for Peter or for (I, me)?

                                 e   r

14. This is strictly between you and (I, me).

                            s   t

15. Are you as fast a runner as (her, she)?

The three words are _____, _____, and _____.

What do these three words have in common? _____

Section Five

MECHANICS—THE TOOLS OF THE TRADE!

109. IS THAT WHAT IT IS?

Match these 16 names of punctuation marks with the marks themselves. If your answers are correct, all rows and columns and the two diagonals will add up to the same number. Good luck!

A=	B=	C=	D=
E=	F=	G=	H=
I=	J=	K=	L=
M=	N=	O=	P=

A.	SEMICOLON		1.	;
B.	PERIOD		2.	?
C.	DASH		3.	`
D.	BRACKETS		4.	,
E.	COMMA		5.	' '
F.	EXCLAMATION MARK		6.	" "
G.	SINGLE QUOTATION MARKS		7.	:
H.	PARENTHESES		8.	—
I.	HYPHEN		9.	. . .
J.	ACCENT		10.	[ ]
K.	APOSTROPHE		11.	( )
L.	QUOTATION MARKS		12.	'
M.	ASTERISK		13.	-
N.	QUESTION MARK		14.	!
O.	ELLIPSIS		15.	.
P.	COLON		16.	*

110. TELEPHONE SPELLING

Using the letters associated with each number on this diagram, spell as many words as you can following the general directions below. For each word, you can: (A) Use the same number no more than two times. Thus, you can go back to the number again, but only one time. (B) Use the same number on two consecutive turns (It may be the same letter, or it may be two different letters on the same number.) Place the digit's number above each letter to ensure that you have stayed within the rules.

Each word must be a minimum of four letters. Here is how you will accumulate points: Each four-letter word is worth 1 point; a five-letter word is worth 2 points; a six-letter word is worth 3 points; any word of seven or more letters is worth 4 points. Write all your spellings on a separate sheet of paper. Total all your points and see how well you did!

1	2	3
	ABC	DEF
4	5	6
GHI	JKL	MNO
7	8	9
PQRS	TUV	WXYZ

A. Spell four words that fill the blank in the sentence, "The plane flew _____ the clouds."

B. Spell four names of people, places, or things. (No word can start with a capital letter.)

C. Spell four words that describe people, places, or things.

D. Spell four words that are action words.

E. Spell four words that end in -*ly*. (These words must include four letters in addition to the -*ly* combination.)

© 2001 by The Center for Applied Research in Education

111. A CAPITAL OFFENSE . . . NOT GETTING 37!

Do you want to avoid committing a crime that is a capital offense? If so, do well on this capital letter activity, and you can go straight. Just circle the letters that should be capitalized. If your count is 37, you are as free as a bird! If not, you have committed the ultimate capital offense! Good luck.

1. i am going to go to shea stadium with my family this saturday night.

2. do you think that geometry is harder than english?

3. her favorite musical group is playing at radio city music hall in february.

4. the people who come over the canadian border are stopped by the police officials there.

5. clinton county in new york is a beautiful upstate area.

6. did you study the debates between kennedy and nixon?

7. maurice richard was an outstanding hockey player years ago.

8. *the last of the mohicans* was written by cooper.

9. we visited several japanese and chinese restaurants on our vacation.

10. we love to celebrate mother's day in may and father's day in june each year.

112. SPELLING MNEMONICS (PART ONE)

Below are 15 spelling demons, words that are easy to misspell. For each word, invent a mnemonic, a way to remember how the word is spelled. Write your "memory jogger" on the line next to each word. An example is provided for you.

1. all right: ____all right is better than all wrong_____

2. amiable: _____

3. beginning: _____

4. buoyant: _____

5. cadence: _____

6. charlatan: _____

7. clientele: _____

8. collaborate: _____

9. competent: _____

10. controversy: _____

11. denounce: _____

12. dissect: _____

13. gallery: _____

14. indomitable: _____

15. navigator: _____

113. SPELLING MNEMONICS (PART TWO)

Below are 15 spelling demons, words that are easy to misspell. For each word, invent a mnemonic, a way to remember how the word is spelled. Write your "memory jogger" on the line next to each word. An example is provided for you.

1. optimistic: _____TIM is always opTIMistic!_____

2. paramount: _____

3. pessimistic: _____

4. promenade: _____

5. protagonist: _____

6. reprimand: _____

7. sedentary: _____

8. separate: _____

9. session: _____

10. tantalizing: _____

11. tutor: _____

12. veneer: _____

13. villain: _____

14. volatile: _____

15. wrangle: _____

114. MUSICALLY SPEAKING

Circle the correct word in each sentence. Then write the letter found after the correct word on the line below sentence 15. Unscramble these 15 letters to form the names of three musical instruments. Write their names on the appropriate line. Bravo!

1. It is this lady's (O), ladies' (R) purse.

2. We are good friends of theirs (I), their's (T).

3. Who's (N), Whose (M) fish is that on the deck?

4. Everybody's (A), Everybodys' (H) ideas will be heard at the meeting.

5. She will finally meet her three boss's (Y), bosses' (I) husbands.

6. The game was her's (E), hers (U) to win or lose.

7. This is Tom and Lucy' s home (D), Tom's and Lucy's home (L).

8. Can anybody find Sherry's (R), Sherrys' (C) hat?

9. You can trust that it is nobody elses' (S), nobody else's (N) business.

10. This will be accomplished within two year's (R), years' (U) time.

11. These aren't (T), are'nt (O) the correct shoes for the dance.

12. There are three e's (P), es' (L) in the word *eerie*.

13. Someone's (A), Someones' (G) emotions are quite fragile.

14. Chris's (R), Chris' (E) relatives are very funny and friendly.

15. Sheeps' (M), Sheep's (G) wool is needed for this task.

Write the fifteen letters on this line. _____

The three musical instruments are _____, _____, and _____.

115. UNLUCKY SEVEN

Thirteen of these possessives are correct, and seven are wrong. For each incorrect possessive, write the correct version on the line provided. If the possessive is correct, the line should be left blank. Add up the numbers of the incorrect possessives; they should total 60.

1. the car of Mitch   Mitch's car   _____

2. the records of the students   student's records   _____

3. the lotion of the druggist   druggists' lotion   _____

4. the words of the senator   senator's words   _____

5. the sounds of the radios   radio's sounds   _____

6. the scarf of Mrs. Jones   Mrs. Jones's scarf   _____

7. the cars of the boys   boys' cars   _____

8. the bicycle you own   you're bicycle   _____

9. the room of the women   womens' room   _____

10. the food of the mouse   mouse's food   _____

11. the home of the mice   mice's home   _____

12. the recipes of the cooks   cooks' recipes   _____

13. the vote of the people   people's vote   _____

14. the house they own   their house   _____

15. the feet of the geese   geese's feet   _____

16. the side of the box   boxes' side   _____

17. the worth of four cents   four cent's worth   _____

18. the idea of someone   someone's idea   _____

19. the color of it   its color   _____

20. the size of the oxen   oxen's size   _____

116. GETTING TECHNICAL AND STAYING EVEN

The title, when you think about it, does makes sense. Grammar and usage require technical skills. Knowing when to use italics, bold letters, underlines, and quotation marks when writing the titles of novels, plays, and short stories is important. There's the technical! For each of the following titles, write the number 1 if the title can use italics, bold letters, or underlines (these are interchangeable), or 2 if the title requires quotation marks. Both 1 and 2 will appear the same number of times as answers—8. That's how they stay even! So get technical and stay even—and have fun!

1. _____ To Kill a Mockingbird (novel)

2. _____ Julius Caesar (book-length play)

3. _____ A Wonderful Summer (article)

4. _____ Titanic (ship)

5. _____ The Plot Thickens (book chapter)

6. _____ Evangeline (poem)

7. _____ David (statue)

8. _____ The Pit and the Pendulum (short story)

9. _____ Carmen (opera)

10. _____ You Are the Sunshine of My Life (song)

11. _____ Seventeen (magazine)

12. _____ The New York Times (newspaper)

13. _____ merci (foreign word)

14. _____ Why I Love to Yodel (essay)

15. _____ I love you madly (direct quotation)

16. _____ Law and Order (television program)

© 2001 by The Center for Applied Research in Education

117. THE COMMA COUNT IS THIRTY-TWO

Thirty-two commas are needed to correctly complete the punctuation. Insert the commas where needed, and then total them up. You should have 32 commas!

1. Murray will you please send this letter to Duluth Minnesota?

2. To tell you the truth you really should have made the team.

3. The couple married on Saturday August 25 1973 on Long Island New York.

4. Our chef considered roast beef veal chicken and steak as possible entrees.

5. When you reach the department store on the corner of Main Street and Hudson Avenue turn left.

6. Jesse is a warm playful puppy.

7. Irene left the game but we decided to stay until it was over.

8. I am sure that I can go to the movies but I question whether they will decide to go.

9. Marcia Smithers who is a television news personality has a great delivery.

10. *Oliver Twist* written by Charles Dickens is a popular read for English majors during their college years.

11. Selecting the smaller home the family members knew that they could be happy there.

12. By the stream behind our junior high school our science class conducted several experiments.

13. Yes the correct answer is letter A!

14. Until the rowdy neighbors choose to act differently others will be adversely affected.

15. Jeremiah of course was a bullfrog.

16. My dad however does not see it the same way as I do.

17. Mark I assume will go along with the new arrangements.

18. This political candidate is in one man's opinion the best qualified.

19. Please send the announcement to Seaford Delaware.

20. Her birth date was March 24 1980.

118. COMING ALONG WITH COMMAS

Six uses of the comma are listed below. Within the 18 sentences, insert the comma(s) where needed. Then write the reason's letter in the space next to the number. Each reason will be used three times.

A. Set off appositives and appositive phrases.

B. Set off interrupting or parenthetical expressions.

C. Set off direct address.

D. Separate items in dates and addresses.

E. After the salutation of a friendly letter and the closing of any letter.

F. Separate two or more adjectives preceding a noun.

1. ___ March 24 1980 was a very special day.

2. ___ Do you remember Artie Sherwood the former mayor?

3. ___ Roberto will you help with these packages?

4. ___ Most sincerely

5. ___ The relentless aggressive defense continued to hound the quarterback.

6. ___ Mickey Mantle I think was one of the most popular players of his day.

7. ___ Here are the priceless oft-talked about diamonds.

8. ___ Yours truly

9. ___ In truth the essential question was not asked.

10. ___ They did not however remember to close the door behind them.

11. ___ The subject of last night's program obesity has become a major concern.

12. ___ Do you remember how important July 31 1977 was for all of us?

13. ___ There are many reasons why you should be there Juan and Carlos.

14. ___ Jaspers the nickname of the Manhattan College teams was written on the poster.

15. ___ The reason my friends is easy for all of us to see.

16. ___ Dearest Grandmother ,

17. ___ This is certainly a beautiful engaging poem.

18. ___ The family has moved to 65443 Georgetown Boulevard Wesleyville Ohio.

Name _____   Date _____   Period _____

119. THE VERSATILE COMMA

Seven functions of the comma are used in this activity. Within each sentence, insert the comma(s) where needed. Then, on the line next to the number, write the corresponding letter for the comma's use. Each function is used three times.

A.   Separate independent clauses joined by *and, nor, for, but, or,* and *yet.*

B.   Separate an introductory adverbial clause.

C.   Separate items in a series.

D.   Set off nonessential clauses and nonessential participial phrases.

E.   Set off introductory elements such as words such as *well, yes, no,* and *why.*

F.   Set off introductory participial phrases.

G.   After a succession of introductory prepositional phrases.

1. ___ Well is this your final answer?

2. ___ In her depiction of young children the author displays great sensitivity.

3. ___ I would like to ask her to the prom and I hope she will accept.

4. ___ While the doctor reviewed the patient's records the nurse helped explain the options.

5. ___ Mitch Carter who won the tennis tournament last year has moved to Seattle.

6. ___ Reset by the doctor Karen's forearm mended well.

7. ___ Her birthday presents included a bracelet CD player and a trip to Holland.

8. ___ Over the river and through the woods the children ran to grandmother's house.

9. ___ Near the door to the smaller gym I left my equipment.

10. ___ The test was long boring and very difficult.

11. ___ Unless these dinners are reheated they will not be very tasty.

12. ___ As soon as the tree was cut down the workers began to chop it up.

13. ___ Why I did not know that!

14. ___ No this is not the best way to the highway.

15. ___ This is a beautiful painting but I think it is overpriced.

16. ___ Drafted by Vancouver the basketball player was later traded to Houston.

17. ___ Purchased last year Dad's car already has 20,400 miles on it.

18. ___ Either you can drive there yourself or we can arrange to have you driven.

19. ___ He called upon his friends his teachers and even his enemies for help in the trying situation.

20. ___ Edison who invented many useful products is known as The Wizard of Menlo Park.

21. ___ *An American Tragedy* written by Theodore Dreiser depicts the problems inherent in the American Dream.

120. IS A SEMICOLON HALF A COLON?

Anyone who knows punctuation can answer this question. The correct response is, "Of course not!" A semicolon and a colon are equally important punctuation marks, and each has its own function. Either a semicolon or a colon has been purposely left out of each sentence. For each sentence, insert the proper punctuation mark, and then write its corresponding four-letter answer, in order, on the Semicolons or Colons line below the last sentence. If your answers are correct, you will spell out two pieces of advice for life.

1. (YOUS) Initially, I was going to memorize my speech then I decided to read it.

2. (SEIZ) The first five answers are as follows A, B, B, D, and C.

3. (ETHE) Mr. Pryal, our English teacher, said that we must read the following books *Ethan Frome, Catcher in the Rye,* and *I Know Why the Caged Bird Sings.*

4. (HOUL) This is a great location moreover, the price is also quite agreeable.

5. (GREA) Please meet her by the ticket station no later than 630 A.M.

6. (DALW) These boxes should be enough for now however, we do need to order more of them immediately.

7. (AYSP) I chose not to apply for the summer camp position instead, I will work in the carpenter shop with my uncle.

8. (TTIM) We discussed Genesis 26 20-25 in class today.

9. (RACT) You have done extremely well on your state tests consequently, you have earned a noteworthy citation.

10. (ICEW) Our treasury needs replenishing furthermore, we must decide to do that immediately.

11. (HATY) Two of the vans need repair therefore, the principal has decided to rent a bus for the trip.

12. (ESIN) The mail arrived at exactly 9 30 A.M.

13. (OUPR) We will select a new representative accordingly, we will need to have names submitted by the people.

14. (EACH) Our plumbing problem has been repaired hence, we can start to fill the swimming pool.

15. (LIFE) Our teacher described the various parts of the plot background, initial incident, rising action, climax, falling action, and denouement.

Semicolons: _____.

Colons: _____.

121. HALF A HUNDRED AND YOU'RE HOME!

Fifty words need immediate CPR (Capitals Problem Relief)! Circle any letter that should be a capital letter. If you total 50—half a hundred—you're home and your CPR work has saved 50 more lives. Go to it!

1. have you ever heard mariah carey sing "love takes time" or spin doctors sing "two princes?"

2. what do the members of the veterans of foreign war group intend to do for the fourth of july?

3. when fordham university plays manhattan college, there is much excitement.

4. time and fortune are two magazines that mr. jackson reads each weekend.

5. the new york times is an outstanding daily newspaper.

6. edgar allan poe's short story, "the fall of the house of usher," is more than interesting.

7. at the conference we met people of many different religions.

8. los angeles and vancouver are two beautiful cities near the pacific ocean.

9. how far south of new jersey is georgia?

10. officer thompson and officer goodren responded immediately to the call.

© 2001 by The Center for Applied Research in Education

122. PUNCTUATING DIALOGUE

All punctuation marks that should be in this dialogue have been purposely omitted. Insert them where needed. The indentation is correct. Then complete the dialogue. Use the back of this sheet if more room is needed. When you are finished, compare your answers with those of your classmates.

I havent had time to call you Steve said to Maria What has been happening with you Nothing much Same old same old

What are your plans for this summer Will you be going away to Nova Scotia again Jane asked as she opened her pocketbook

My entire family will be going to Vermont this July Steve said I think we will be there for the whole month We will probably be staying with my fathers sisters family the Robertsons

With a questioning look Jane asked Do you think you will be home in time to try out for the schools soccer team If you are not there for the weeks tryout you cannot be on the team Do you think you should speak to Coach Butler before you go away

That's not a bad idea Jane I hadnt even thought about that This could really be a problem I guess Theres no way my parents will let me stay home by myself though

With a helpful gesture Jane asked Steve why dont you have your parents talk to the coach That might solve the problem

Steve quickly replied

123. PUNCTUATING PROPERLY AND PURPOSEFULLY (PART ONE)

Today you will be working with six marks of punctuation—the apostrophe, the colon, the comma, the dash, the exclamation mark, and the period. Place these punctuation marks, and only these punctuation marks, where they belong within these sentences. Each is used at least once. Some may be used several times.

1. After she finished reading the newspaper Marlene washed the breakfast dishes.

2. These are the US states we will study this month Nebraska Kansas Missouri and Wisconsin

3. Its about 1230 so we should be heading for the fire departments picnic

4. The best years of Mitchs life were from 1980 1995

5. Softball tryouts will be held from 10 230

6. We told them that they could stay for one week and one week only

7. The house on Webster Street the one owned by the Murphy family is quite beautiful

8. Our family firmly believes in this commandment Do unto others as you would have them do unto you

9. Heads up everybody

10. But can we believe him

11. Serenas serve is equal to her sisters serve

12. The magician worked with the following props rabbits handkerchiefs wands and hats

13. Since we were sitting in traffic for over two hours we arrived home at 1130

14. Barbara the following are the cars that my dad has owned a 1992 Toyota a 1995 Cadillac and a1998 Dodge

15. Jill will be moving to Milwaukee Wisconsin at the end of August

124. PUNCTUATING PROPERLY AND PURPOSEFULLY (PART TWO)

Today you will be working with brackets, the comma, parentheses, the period, the question mark, quotation marks, single quotation marks, and the semicolon. You will insert these, and only these, punctuation marks within these sentences. Each one is used once, and some are used much more than that. Good luck!

1. Billy Joel loves to sing his hit song Piano Man

2. When Sylvia asked are they going on vacation

3. Molly Mrs. Glynn our English teacher asked did Robert Frost write And that has made all the difference

4. We shipped out two hundred 200 packages of books Joe

5. The evenings main speaker Donald Trump was quite informative [Do not use a comma for this answer.]

6. How do the British pronounce the word schedule Tim asked

7. When will they resume the tennis match Dottie

8. Please shut the window Tawana it is getting cold in here

9. I like her plan better furthermore it will be the more efficient as well

10. Franco are you and Pedro the other assigned officer patrolling both parades next weekend

11. The tilde ~ is found on the left side of the keyboard

12. Unfortunately this medication did not work nevertheless we will continue to pursue other more effective medications

13. My mom often tells me These are the best times of your life Christine

14. James was born on August 27 1977 in Topeka Kansas

15. Our invitees include Dr. William Brennan chiropractor Professor Martha Gavigan literature enthusiast and Dr. David Gilliam our keynote speaker

125. FITTING THEM IN PROPERLY

Punctuation is the word of the day in this activity. Fill in the missing 16 commas, 5 apostrophes, 11 periods, 4 question marks, 4 pairs of quotation marks, and 2 hyphens.

1. Herman Hesse wrote those two novels *Siddhartha* and *Steppenwolf*

2. Are you James asked Emma going to the playground later

3. Is this the movie guide you misplaced Sharon

4. Was it Shakespeare who wrote . . . a pair of star crossed lovers take their lives

5. Almost all the water has evaporated but I still feel the area is quite slippery

6. Wishing and hoping the cheerleaders did their best to remain calm as the judges tallied their votes

7. The day trader purchased stocks mostly in technology health care and farm products

8. Ryan Smythe is a cordial warm hearted employer

9. Our humble home located on the corner of Clendon Street and Stuart Road is 20 years old

10. These problems that challenged most of my classmates were designed by the college professor

11. The beach with its 500 acres and beautiful shoreline is a valuable tourist attraction for our county

12. Herman Melvilles most successful novel *Moby Dick* was published in 1851

13. Our familys Thanksgiving plans were changed due to the days inclement weather

14. Both ambassadors papers had been reviewed by the mediator

15. Have you listened to everybodys suggestions

© 2001 by The Center for Applied Research in Education

126. HOW BAD CAN IT GET?

The incompetent electric printer has played some games on us here. So much for machines! Many punctuation marks are either in the wrong places or omitted. Help out by placing the punctuation marks in their proper spots.

1. Robertos' wallet was found near the sofa.

2. Bettys' and Lucy's new bedroom set was delivered yesterday.

3. Stu's and Brad's wardrobes show their exquisite taste's in clothing.

4. Has anybody seen the towns financial records' lately?

5. Because the concert has been rescheduled: the promoted groups will have to reset the date.

6. Art Carney, the actor who starred in the movie *Harry and Tonto* is a versatile performer.

7. Our dog did not hear the whistle; moreover . . . she did not even hear our calls.

8. Basketball as most fans recall was invented by Dr. James Naismith.

9. Remember, folks, to take off your shoes — upon entering the house.

10. Although he seldom speaks out of turn Gerald let us all know what he felt.

11. Well discuss the careers of the following celebrities, Jay Leno Marlon Brando, and Chevy Chase.

12. Also, the studios are set up in those, three locations.

13. He doesnt realize that everybodys' opinion is important Robbie.

14. Obviously it was a careless immature thing to do.

15. Behind the barn, near the stream, the artist often achieved his greatest work.

16. "Why cant they pick us up here," Susan asked, "It won't be a major problem."

17. Please adjust the mirror — the sun's' glare is too much for me.

18. A great deal of effort went into decorating the gymnasium for the dance, the band, however, did not meet our expectations.

19. The seven packages have arrived and, you can now distribute them.

20. Don't leave the car unlocked—this is a tough neighborhood.

127. PITY THIS POOR PRINTER!

To put it mildly, there are many apostrophes that have been left out by the inexperienced printer. Help save the printer's job by correctly filling in all the missing apostrophes. If you do well, the printer will be forever beholden to you. Thanks for your knowledge and help!

1. Tina doesnt know where shed be without her parents help in this matter.

2. Its beginning to look as if theyll be moving within two months time.

3. How many 8s and how many 12s should I add to this total?

4. He's a fixin to carry out his daddys plans to expand the farm.

5. There are many childrens books that Mikes great-grandmother has passed down to the family.

6. Mr. Williams will deliver the two families gifts to you.

7. The mens department, and not the womens department, has the sale now.

8. My bosss car was purchased at Ben Londons All- Star Automotive.

9. We love to listen to Crosby, Stills, and Nashs old hit songs.

10. Because Janes so understanding, shell listen to almost anyones sad story.

11. Larrys sister-in-laws job is both interesting and stressful.

12. Do you think you had taken somebody elses jacket by mistake?

13. Our class studied Theodore Roosevelts, Franklin Roosevelts, and Dwight Eisenhowers speeches.

14. You have earned how many As and how many Bs this semester?

15. Wasnt it Pink Floyds lyric that stated, "We dont need no education"?

© 2001 by The Center for Applied Research in Education

128. PRETTY BAD PUNCTUATION

These groups of sentences certainly have one thing in common. Each group needs to have its punctuation improved. There are no spelling errors, but there are enough punctuation errors to keep you busy! Insert the necessary marks of punctuation, and then compare your answers with those of your classmates. Rewrite the corrected paragraphs on the appropriate lines.

A.   This is, probably the last time our entire class, will be together; In a few months we will be moving on to different colleges and jobs— ; lets make the most of our last week's together.

_____

_____

_____

B.   My next-door neighbors own a dog, that barks throughout the day. Since the neighbors; Alice and Tom—work long hours; the dog receives little attention. Wow? This noise has really become a major annoyance to my family, and other families in the neighborhood.

_____

_____

_____

C.   After we have, our holiday dinners together—either I will drive my grandparents home or my parents will. When Mom and Dad are too tired to do it I will still volunteer my services, because I love to listen to my grandparent's stories of the past?

_____

_____

_____

© 2001 by The Center for Applied Research in Education

Section Six

GRAMMAR'S HELPERS—
TAKING CARE OF
BUSINESS!

129. THEY SOUND THE SAME BUT . . .

Each of the 24 words that are your clues has an answer that sounds much like the word itself. Of course, the answer is spelled differently! Write the letters in their appropriate spaces and fill in the puzzle. On a separate sheet of paper, define each of these words and their partners, starting with the Across clues and answers and then working through the Down clues and answers.

Across
1. prophet
3. wade
6. quay
7. sun
8. haul
9. pale
10. teem
12. groan
14. aide
15. knight
17. pane
18. creek
20. hire

Down
1. pier
2. flee
3. whine
4. grate
5. duel
7. slight
9. peel
11. chord
13. navel
16. guest
19. hymn

© 2001 by The Center for Applied Research in Education

161

130. THE PRINCIPAL GAVE ME DESSERT AND QUITE A COMPLIMENT!

Four answers to this crossword are found in this activity's title. Twenty-two other answers, all words often confused, are to be placed in their appropriate boxes.

So, piece your answers all together, do what is moral, and don't be idle! Any more hints needed?

Across
1. not moving
2. group's spirit
6. to complete; make full
9. win's opposite
10. to perceive through the senses
12. not here but _____
13. state house
15. to shatter
16. adverb indicating degree
18. portion
20. war's opposite
21. stopping device
22. flattering remark
23. building leader; most important

Down
1. person or thing worshipped
2. virtuous
3. not tight
4. not there but _____
5. dry, sandy region
7. not fancy
8. owned by them
11. rough
14. completely
16. opposite of loud
17. flat surface; airplane; tool
19. path; academic class

131. ACCEPT A WEAK MINER

This crossword puzzle's title contains three answers to this puzzle. Twenty-six other words should be filled in as you examine words that are often confused. Read the clues, fill in the correct letters, and have a good time!

Across

1. revealed
3. to take or receive willingly
7. outdoors condition
11. word indicating a choice
12. more than enough
13. opening
14. entire
15. to purchase
17. garbage
20. musical or mathematical term
21. element such as gold or iron
22. setting or location
23. hurled
25. not legally an adult; small

Down

2. seven days
4. thick string or thin rope
5. one plus one
6. in one side and out the other
8. preposition and part of an infinitive
9. to leave or take out; exclude
10. past tense of shine
11. opposite of strong
16. an award
17. middle part of one's body
18. total
19. one who digs for valuable ore
21. quality of character
22. past participle of see
24. certain unknown number or part

132. HOMOPHONES CROSSWORD PUZZLE

Twenty-five homophones are the clues to this puzzle. Write the clue's homophone in the spaces within the puzzle. The first answer is given to you. After you have finished the puzzle, review each homophone's definition. Have fun!

© 2001 by The Center for Applied Research in Education

Across

2. cent	16. hire
3. wry	17. except
5. reed	19. slow
7. you	20. wood
8. time	21. roll
10. sea	22. cite
15. lose	

Down

1. brake	11. ate
2. sum	12. flow
3. road	13. hie
4. mien	14. course
6. all together	18. counsel
9. yule	20. whet

133. DEFINING THE CONFUSING

Match the 25 often confused words with their definitions. Write your answers in the magic square below. If your answers are correct, all columns and rows will add to the same number.

A=	B=	C=	D=	E=
F=	G=	H=	I=	J=
K=	L=	M=	N=	O=
P=	Q=	R=	S=	T=
U=	V=	W=	X=	Y=

A. they're
B. brake
C. effect
D. complement
E. sent
F. two
G. board

H. cent
I. further
J. there
K. scent
L. capitol
M. steel
N. capital

O. affect
P. heir
Q. their
R. steal
S. compliment
T. bored
U. heal

V. farther
W. air
X. break
Y. heel

1. coin
2. contraction for *they are*
3. refers to distance
4. praise or admiration
5. to influence
6. possession
7. money; city; most important
8. the past tense of *send*
9. what we breathe
10. the number
11. to destroy
12. place or location
13. metal

14. one who will inherit
15. stopping device
16. council or not excited
17. result or to produce
18. restore to health
19. building
20. refers to additional time, quantity, or degree
21. smell
22. piece of wood
23. that which completes
24. the back of the foot
25. taken without permission

134. HOMOPHONES WORD FIND

Twenty-five homophones of the words listed below the word-find are hidden in this puzzle. Circle the 25 words that are placed backward, forward, diagonally, and vertically.

```
H  C  I  H  W  V  Z  R  W  W  Z  T  B  B  G  W  H  T  M  J
X  D  G  H  E  Q  Z  S  P  P  G  W  E  T  S  R  C  A  R  J
M  Z  R  G  A  X  T  C  J  F  Y  Y  E  D  R  T  A  D  I  G
S  L  N  S  T  H  M  R  F  N  D  D  N  D  P  J  G  T  N  R
M  V  C  J  H  X  V  V  W  Y  J  T  V  J  L  R  J  R  E  C
B  T  L  Z  E  K  N  B  T  R  V  R  R  S  C  K  B  L  Q  C
X  L  K  Q  Z  Q  L  L  Q  R  S  J  Z  L  T  B  K  B  X  T
G  V  H  K  D  H  J  W  W  C  Q  C  W  D  K  W  D  K  H  Y
H  F  V  C  T  S  T  L  L  L  S  M  F  Y  N  S  T  C  N  Q  B
Z  H  G  P  B  R  H  B  O  L  H  T  I  J  E  X  C  R  R  D
K  N  F  C  T  E  M  E  M  A  O  V  N  N  E  V  I  '  E  B
K  N  W  D  N  F  I  V  A  I  N  F  N  D  P  '  B  R  T
L  K  V  O  G  D  T  W  I  R  E  H  A  T  A  W  L  T  G  E
T  O  N  I  A  P  E  P  D  S  U  N  M  R  Z  W  L  S  E  W
```

aisle	made	so
bee	mane	son
bin	might	vane
fined	mined	whether
great	need	witch
hare	nun	wrap
here	pane	wring
know	seen	
lone	shown	

Name_____ Date _____ Period_____

135. TOOOOOOOOO GENERAL

Each of these ten sentences lacks specificity. They are all too vague, too general. By adding more specific words, phrases, and clauses, you can make these dull sentences come to life. On the line below each sentence, write an improved sentence by adding or deleting words. Keep the original idea. When you have written these sentences, share them with your classmates. An example is provided for you.

Example: He walked here.

<u>The tall police officer sauntered along our town's two main streets.</u>

1. She sang it.

_____

2. They saw him.

_____

3. The noise was bad.

_____

4. Her remark was interesting.

_____

5. She talked to them.

_____

6. My sister listened and then spoke.

_____

7. It was there.

_____

8. We held a meeting.

_____

9. The cheerleaders yelled.

_____

10. It did not happen here.

_____

© 2001 by The Center for Applied Research in Education

136. IT'S THE END THAT COUNTS

The 15 suffixes found in this activity will help you to tell a word's part of speech. On the line next to each example, write the part of speech indicated by the suffix and its accompanying example. Then, on the line next to each suffix, write two more examples of that suffix. The first one is done for you.

1. <u>adjective</u>   "ful" as in sorrowful   <u>tearful, mouthful</u> _____

2. _____   "able" as in unbeatable   _____

3. _____   "ness" as in tenderness   _____

4. _____   "ion" as in protection   _____

5. _____   "ly" as in slowly   _____

6. _____   "ate" as in eliminate   _____

7. _____   "ible" as in invisible   _____

8. _____   "ity" as in femininity   _____

9. _____   "ation" as in hesitation   _____

10. _____   "ic" as in majestic   _____

11. _____   "ify" as in magnify   _____

12. _____   "ous" as in tremendous   _____

13. _____   "eive" as in receive   _____

14. _____   "ize" as in maximize   _____

15. _____   "less" as in painless   _____

137. SWEET SIXTEEN

Circle the correct answer to each of these 15 questions. Then total the corresponding numbers of the correct answers in each group. If each group's total is 16, all your answers are correct!

GROUP ONE

A. Which is **not** found in a dictionary entry? (3) meaning (4) spelling of verb forms (5) part of speech (6) guide word

B. Which is **not** a class in the Dewey Decimal System? (1) Language (0) Technology (1) The Arts (2) Sports

C. Which is **not** a part of speech? (2) adjective (3) clause (4) verb (5) interjection

D. Which is **not** a word? (3) alot (4) bored (5) chord (6) infinity

E. Which word is a homophone? (2) through (3) suggested (4) direction (5) freshly

TOTAL _____

GROUP TWO

F. Which word is spelled correctly? (2) stratagy (3) warant (4) symmetrical (5) vellocity

G. Which is a plural noun? (4) crisis (5) oxen (6) appendix (7) criterion

H. Which is an adverb phrase? (2) in the afternoon (3) hit hard (4) the dog's sharp teeth (5) a fair-weather friend

I. Which word is a modifier? (1) greatly (2) slid (3) among (4) write

J. Which word is an example of the superlative form? (3) better (4) worst (5) less realistically (6) speedily

TOTAL _____

GROUP THREE

K. Which is an example of the passive voice? (1) I have called upon them. (2) They will select the president's hotel. (3) We had been informed of the meeting. (4) The ball flew over the fence.

L. Which is an indefinite pronoun? (2) neither (3) they (4) I (5) she

M. Which is **not** a use of the comma? (7) to set off an appositive (8) to separate words in a series (9) to end a sentence that makes a statement (10) to separate two independent clauses joined by a coordinating conjunction

N. Which is **not** an acceptable form to indicate a novel's title? (1) brackets (2) italics (3) underlining (4) bold

O. What is the mark of punctuation used to form a fraction? (1) diagonal (2) circumflex (3) leader (4) underscore

TOTAL _____

138. THE PLURALS PUZZLE

Is the plural of ox *oxes* or *oxen*? Is the plural of data *datum* or *datums*? These and other tricky plurals are questions you will answer in this crossword puzzle. Fill in the correct letters to form the plural form of each singular noun clue. Have fun!

Across
1. brunch
4. datum
10. ox
11. mouse
12. calf
13. solo
14. goose
15. roof
17. aerial
18. sky
19. mouthful
21. crisis
22. wife

Down
1. baby
2. cupful
3. echo
4. donkey
5. try
6. monkey
7. potato
8. fence
9. child
16. fly
17. analysis
20. tooth

139. WHEN Y SOUNDS LIKE A AND I

The 25 words hidden in this word-find are verbs that end with the letter *y*. Some of them end with the "i" sound (as in *fly*), and some of them end with the "a" sound (as in *pray*). All the words are composed of three, four, or five letters. Circle the words that are arranged horizontally both backward and forward, diagonally, and vertically. On the reverse side of this paper, use ten of these words in a two-paragraph description of a literary character you have studied.

```
P  J  J  V  M  H  B  Y  N  R  X  Y  F  V  T  J  R  N  K  L
Z  H  V  M  C  V  C  F  H  M  B  Q  N  Q  F  Q  R  X  Q  S
T  S  Q  M  K  F  N  Q  M  F  R  L  L  S  X  R  Q  C  N  X
Y  F  J  D  D  T  Z  D  K  P  A  D  F  R  S  X  B  N  R  N
A  F  H  W  F  M  J  K  E  P  L  G  T  D  B  M  P  L  F  C
L  J  O  C  W  C  M  W  S  N  L  V  Y  R  U  R  Z  K  W  Y
F  L  Y  R  Z  Q  S  T  R  A  Y  A  S  K  Y  A  C  E  D  P
S  N  D  Z  A  Q  A  P  G  L  L  D  Y  L  A  V  Z  E  V  V
P  W  V  B  C  Y  P  N  E  S  C  W  P  T  S  T  L  S  P  J
R  Q  X  V  F  D  R  R  V  B  H  P  D  V  H  A  Q  G  A  N
A  E  S  P  Y  Y  A  W  S  B  A  F  R  Y  Y  C  W  F  Y  Q
Y  F  Z  K  J  H  Y  D  S  K  S  S  A  K  F  Q  S  L  R  Z
G  Z  P  B  D  K  Q  Z  H  W  L  R  W  L  P  J  J  X  N  W
J  Y  T  K  N  S  J  G  B  G  B  Y  Y  F  C  Y  G  N  K  H
Y  L  Z  G  N  Y  P  W  Z  K  X  G  C  R  F  P  Y  K  J  V
```

ally	delay	foray	pray	slay
apply	deny	fry	pry	spray
bray	espy	pay	rely	stay
buy	flay	play	say	stray
decay	fly	ply	sky	try

Name_____ Date _____ Period_____

140. LET'S GO TO THE MOVIES!

One word in each of these 20 pairs of words below is spelled correctly. Circle this word and then write its corresponding letter, in numerical order, on the line below the last pair of words. If your answers are correct, you will spell out a famous movie line. See if you can identify the movie as well!

1. tomorow (O)   tomorrow (T)

2. squirel (N)   squirrel (O)

3. allowed (M)   alowed (A)

4. interrupt (O)   interupt (K)

5. forfeit (R)   forfiet (P)

6. cashier (R)   casheir (E)

7. exercise (O)   exercize (U)

8. burglar (W)   burgular (M)

9. colossal (I)   collosal (A)

10. condem (O)   condemn (S)

11. labratory (L)   laboratory (A)

12. desirable (N)   desireable (S)

13. cemetary (I)   cemetery (O)

14. boundary (T)   boundery (W)

15. guardian (H)   guardien (R)

16. litenning (H)   lightning (E)

17. persuade (R)   pursuade (U)

18. perferred (E)   preferred (D)

19. impossable (L)   impossible (A)

20. professor (Y)   profesor (T)

The movie line is _____

173

141. DIVIDED DESCRIBERS

Each of the 15 describers (adjectives) below is broken up into three parts. Join a part from each of the three columns (in order) to form the describer. Thus, the first word becomes *blossoming*, since you took a part from each column. Write the other 14 words below the three columns.

COLUMN A	COLUMN B	COLUMN C
bloss	at	able
e	ate	ant
embell	bul	ed
gr	cept	ent
in	ect	ful
indom	ish	ible
intell	ist	ic
op	it	igent
per	mat	ing
pre	om	ive
pred	pend	ory
rel	port	ous
stu	tell	ual
styl	uct	une
tur	vas	ure

bloss_____   per_____

e_____   pre_____

embell_____   pred_____

gr_____   rel_____

in_____   stu_____

indom_____   sty_____

intell_____   tur_____

op_____

Name_____ Date _____ Period_____

142. DARING? TIMID? OPTIMISTIC? WHAT ARE YOU?

The three adjectives in the activity's title are strong vocabulary words to use in your writing. It is good to have a wide vocabulary because grammar and vocabulary are often dependent on each other. Below are 10 major words and 30 synonyms for those 10 major words. On the line next to each major word, write its three synonyms. Use your dictionary if necessary.

1. chamber (noun): _____

2. daring (noun): _____

3. grab (noun or verb): _____

4. improper (adjective): _____

5. lawless (adjective): _____

6. lenient (adjective): _____

7. optimistic (adjective): _____

8. promote (verb): _____

9. timid (adjective): _____

10. undecided (adjective): _____

afraid	debatable	grasp	rebellious
apartment	disobedient	hearten	room
assured	easygoing	hopeful	snatch
boldness	encourage	incorrect	stall
boost	erroneous	insurgent	unresolved
bravery	expectant	liberal	unsettled
clutch	fearful	mistaken	
courage	frightened	permissive	

143. "ROMAN" AROUND

Each of the 16 words in this magic square came into our English language from the Latin spoken by the Romans. Match the word with its origin. Use a dictionary to help you. When your 16 answers are correct, all columns and rows and the two diagonals will add up to the same number. When you have completed the magic square, write a story including eight of the words from this activity.

A=	B=	C=	D=
E=	F=	G=	H=
I=	J=	K=	L=
M=	N=	O=	P=

A. SPONSOR
B. SINUS
C. STADIUM
D. TETANUS
E. CAMPUS
F. PATELLA
G. TRIVIA
H. STATUS
I. RADIUS
J. DISH
K. IGNORAMUS
L. VIRUS
M. MAJOR
N. OPERA
O. HIATUS
P. TENOR

1. one who promises solemnly for another
2. works
3. to throw
4. plain or field
5. place where three roads meet
6. slimy liquid
7. hold
8. measure equaling 600 feet
9. to yawn
10. spasm of the muscles
11. to stand
12. former legal term
13. ray, rod, or spoke
14. small pan or dish
15. bent surface or curve
16. great

144. THE PREFIXES AND ROOTS MAGIC SQUARE

Match the 25 prefixes and roots with their meanings in this magic square. Place the meaning's number in its appropriate box within the square. When your answers are correct, all columns and rows and the two diagonals will add to the same number. Finally, on another sheet of paper, list two words for each prefix or root. For example, *equi* is the root for *equilateral* and *equilibrium*.

A=	B=	C=	D=	E=
F=	G=	H=	I=	J=
K=	L=	M=	N=	O=
P=	Q=	R=	S=	T=
U=	V=	W=	X=	Y=

A. equi	N. di	1. shut	14. eight
B. hetero	O. vert	2. equal	15. different
C. jur	P. oct	3. faith	16. good
D. hyper	Q. morph	4. one	17. law
E. cred	R. phil	5. turn	18. write
F. deca	S. mono	6. form	19. see
G. non	T. bene	7. two	20. all
H. clud	U. graph	8. belief	21. before
I. omni	V. fid	9. against	22. not
J. multi	W. anti	10. ten	23. above
K. pre	X. hypo	11. below	24. five
L. spec	Y. penta	12. many	25. love
M. biblio		13. book	

145. IT'S GREEK (AND ROMAN) TO ME!

Twenty-five Greek and Roman prefixes are in Column A below. Their meanings are found in Column B. On the line next to the number, write the corresponding two-letter answer as you match the word to its definition. Two answers are given to you. If your answers are correct, you will spell out an interesting idea that relates to this activity's title. Good luck!

COLUMN A

1. _____ abs-
2. _____ aster-
3. _ng_ auto-
4. _____ cid-
5. _____ cogn-
6. _____ dict-
7. _____ dox-
8. _____ eu-
9. _____ geo-
10. _____ graph-
11. _____ hom-
12. _____ hydr-
13. _____ log-
14. _____ manu-
15. _____ micro-
16. _____ ortho-
17. _____ prob-
18. _____ re-
19. _____ sed-
20. _____ sub-
21. _re_ sym-
22. _____ ten-
23. _____ tract-
24. _____ tri-
25. _____ vert-

COLUMN B

an. seat
at. prove
ch. speech
dg. under, below
ek. hold
es. same
ge. earth
in. back, again
it. small
la. say, speak
li. kill
mu. water
~~ng.~~ self
ng. belief
ot. three
ou. away from
ow. write
~~re.~~ star
re. together
ro. draw
sh. know
sl. straight
s! turn
to. hand
ua. good

The sentence is _____.

© 2001 by The Center for Applied Research in Education

146. SOME FOOD FOR THOUGHT

Using 15 words associated with foods, fill in the blanks in these idioms. Then, on a separate sheet of paper, define each idiom.

COLUMN A	COLUMN B
1. to put all your _____ in one basket	apple
2. to bring home the _____	bacon
3. to spill the _____	bananas
4. piece of _____	beans
5. happy as a _____	cake
6. upset the _____ cart	clam
7. holy _____	dough
8. cut the _____	eggs
9. rolling in the _____	fruitcake
10. no small _____	herring
11. red _____	mackerel
12. with a grain of _____	mustard
13. nutty as a _____	oats
14. to go _____	potatoes
15. to feel one's _____	salt

147. IGNORANCE IS NOT BLISS!!!

Match the 20 idioms in Column A with their meanings in Column B. Write the correct letter in the appropriate space. If your answers are correct, you will have spelled out 5 four-letter words. Write those five words in the spaces indicated. Good luck!

COLUMN A

1. _____ up the creek
2. _____ nitty-gritty
3. _____ ignorance is bliss
4. _____ burn the candle at both ends
5. _____ hit the spot
6. _____ face the music
7. _____ cat got your tongue
8. _____ shoot the breeze
9. _____ take down a peg
10. _____ get one's goat
11. _____ keep one in stitches
12. _____ foot the bill
13. _____ bring home the bacon
14. _____ paper tiger
15. _____ once in a blue moon
16. _____ up in the air
17. _____ ants in your pants
18. _____ off your rocker
19. _____ take a crack
20. _____ egg on one's face

COLUMN B

a. approach an unenviable situation
b. puncture one's self-importance
c. not talking much
d. stay up half the night at work or play
e. peace of mind from not knowing some information
e. embarrassment
f. undesirable situation
g. make an attempt
h. condition of being fidgety or restless
i. posturing aggressor without bite
k. talk informally
l. serious business
m. earn
n. make another laugh heartily
o. to tease or aggravate
p. satisfy
s. not often
t. undecided
u. not of sound mind
y. pay for

© 2001 by The Center for Applied Research in Education

The 5 four-letter words are _____ (1–4), _____ (5–8), _____ (9–12),

_____ (13–16), and _____ (17–20).

148. PULLING OUT THE STOPS

Pulling out the stops is an idiom that means "going all out" or really doing your best. That is what you are asked to do here. On a separate sheet of paper, compose a story using any 10 of these 15 idioms. "Put your nose to the grindstone" and make sure your story is "up to snuff." The idioms and their definitions are listed below. Good luck!

beat her to the punch: be quicker than another in doing something

bee in his bonnet: to be obsessed with one idea

catch some Z's: sleep

every Tom, Dick, and Harry: everybody

feeling blue: to be melancholic or depressed

get off one's back: leave one alone after a period in which you have given trouble

happy as a clam: very happy

hem and haw: to avoid making a point or commitment; falter

knock for a loop: to punch very hard; to defeat or overcome

lead by the nose: to dominate completely

make bricks without straw: to do something without the necessary material

make no bones about it: to state something without hesitation

on the button: exact or exactly

steal one's thunder: to use someone's ideas or methods without permission and without giving credit

up for grabs: available to the highest bidder or the most aggressive person

149. COMPLETING THE APHORISMS

Aphorisms are wise sayings. Each of the 15 aphorisms here (some more serious than others) has been broken up into two parts. Match the Column A and Column B parts by placing the correct letter on the space next to the number. If your answers are correct, they will spell out, in order of the answers from 1 to 15, another aphorism. Good luck!

COLUMN A

1. _____ If at first you don't succeed, _____.

2. _____ If the shoe fits, _____.

3. _____ These are the times _____.

4. _____ Be the best _____.

5. _____ If he hollers, _____.

6. _____ Eat, drink, and be merry _____.

7. _____ Great riches have sold more men _____.

8. _____ The artist doesn't see things as they are, _____.

9. _____ Grace is to the body _____.

10. _____ What does not destroy me, _____.

11. _____ Necessity poisons wounds _____.

12. _____ Whenever I feel afraid, _____.

13. _____ When gossip grows old, _____.

14. _____ Blessed are the meek _____.

15. _____ The worst cliques are those _____.

© 2001 by The Center for Applied Research in Education

COLUMN B

al.   try, try again

as.   but as he is

ay.   for tomorrow we may die

ct.   it becomes myth

ec.   makes me stronger

fe.   that try men's souls

lw.   let him go

me.   which consist of one man

oa.   wear it

or.   which it cannot heal

ra.   that you can be

re.   I whistle a happy tune

sh.   than they have bought

th.   what clear thinking is to the mind

ti.   for they shall inherit the earth

© 2001 by The Center for Applied Research in Education

150. DON'T BE DOWN IN THE DUMPS

An idiom is defined as an "untranslatable expression." Below are 20 words that complete 20 idioms. Write the correct word in each space and then, on a separate sheet of paper, write an illustrative sentence for each idiom. The first one is already done for you.

airs	cheek	heart	midstream
arms	down	hook	nose
break	envy	jump	raise
cast	fist	make	stern
champ	head	means	wrench

1. __down__ in the dumps: sad or depressed (After the rout by their biggest rivals, the losing players felt <u>down in the dumps</u>.)

2. _____ something from scratch: begin with the basic ingredients

3. _____ some eyebrows: to shock or surprise people mildly

4. _____ the first stone: to be the first to attack

5. _____ out in a cold sweat: to perspire from fever, fear, or anxiety

6. from stem to _____: from one end to another

7. live within one's _____: to spend no more than one has

8. throw a monkey _____ in the works: to cause problems for someone's plans

9. green with _____: jealous

10. in over one's _____: with more troubles than one can manage

11. hand over _____: rapidly

12. pay through the _____: spend too much for something

13. put on _____: to act in a superior fashion

14. get off the _____: to free from an obligation or an uncomfortable situation

15. _____ at the bit: to be prepared and eager to do something

16. change horses in _____: to make changes in an activity once it has already begun

17. _____ the gun: to start before the assigned time

18. have a _____ of gold: to be generous, kind, and sincere

19. turn the other _____: to ignore an abuse or an insult

20. up in _____: angry

Name_____ Date _____ Period _____

151. ST WI TH TW LE

Your eyes are still fine. It is just that the title gives you a big hint as to what you are asked to do in this activity. The full title is START WITH THESE TWO LETTERS. See, you are given five two-letter combinations for each part of speech. Using any of these two-letter combinations, expand the word, and join it with other two-letter combinations to form sentences. Allow *or* as a conjunction and *to* as a preposition to remain as words without adding any letters. The number of words in the sentence you compose gives you that many points, so a six-word sentence earns six points. Write your sentences on a separate sheet of paper. GO LU AN EN! (GOOD LUCK AND ENJOY!)

NOUNS	PRONOUNS	VERBS	ADJECTIVES
be	mi	ar	ac
ca	ou	be	la
le	sh	ha	pr
pr	th	wa	sm
to	yo	wi	st

ADVERBS	CONJUNCTIONS	PREPOSITIONS	INTERJECTIONS
ca	an	ab	go
gr	bu	in	hu
sl	fo	ne	su
to	or	on	wo
vi	ye	to	yi

152. THE TERMS OF GRAMMAR

Sixteen terms used in grammar are found within the magic square. Match the terms with the sentence featuring that term. If your answers are correct, all the rows and columns and the two diagonals will total the same number.

A=	B=	C=	D=
E=	F=	G=	H=
I=	J=	K=	L=
M=	N=	O=	P=

A. adjective clause
B. adverb clause
C. adverb phrase
D. gerund phrase
E. interrogative sentence
F. infinitive phrase
G. exclamatory sentence
H. run-on
I. imperative sentence
J. compound subject
K. participial phrase
L. fragment
M. past tense verb phrase
N. adjective phrase
O. comma splice
P. declarative sentence

1. You can do it, just try harder.
2. Bob and Monica will be the eventual winners.
3. This is the final leg of the race she can win it here.
4. The man who registered us showed us the game's format.
5. Winning the event was his goal.
6. Did you receive your package yet?
7. Winning the bet, Graham shared his prize.
8. The man in the picture is interesting.
9. To win the contest was her goal.
10. He belongs to three local clubs.
11. Hester Prynne was ignored by the man.
12. Under the provisions of the State Charter.
13. Wash the car, Charles.
14. I went to the store yesterday.
15. After the meal was eaten, the table was cleared.
16. I don't want to do it now!

© 2001 by The Center for Applied Research in Education

Section Seven

GRAMMAR GAMES—
AND AWAY WE GO!

153. ENGLO

ENGLO is much like BINGO—with a few exceptions. Your teacher will give you the directions on how to set up your card. Listen carefully to the directions and have some fun!

E   N   G   L   O

154. THE ALPHABET GAME

Here is a game you can play with your classmates or by yourself. The rules are simple. Rule number 1 is: "Have fun." Rule number 2 is to start each sentence with the next letter of the alphabet. Rule number 3 is to stick to the subject, say, Music or Teenage Life or Extracurricular activities and so forth.

So, as an example, if the subject were *cars*, the game could go something like this . . .

Automobiles are quite expensive these days.

But everyone loves to be seen in a cool-looking car.

Classic cars are out of my price range.

Driving around town can be fun and interesting.

(And so on down the alphabet . . .)

Your teacher, you, and your classmates will select the topics. You might also write what type of sentence each is (simple, compound, complex, compound-complex). Is the sentence declarative, interrogative, imperative, or exclamatory? Underline prepositional phrases. Point out a word's part of speech. Insert the necessary punctuation. These and other ideas will make the Alphabet Game fun and educational. Start on this side of the page and continue on the reverse side.

_____

_____

_____

_____

_____

_____

_____

_____

_____

_____

155. SCORING WITH SENTENCES

This activity combines math and parts of speech. A point value is assigned to each sentence. Using the values given to each part of speech, combine words to form a sentence that adds up to that point value. Label each word's part of speech above the word. There is no minimum or maximum number of words for each sentence. Just suffice the point value, form a sentence, and you are a winner! An example sentence is done for you.

noun = 4

pronoun = 4

verb = 3

adjective = 2

adverb = 3

preposition = 2

conjunction = 1

interjection = 1

Example: <u>(6) Go now!</u>

(above "Go now!": v   adv)

1. (7) _____

2. (10) _____

3. (12) _____

4. (13) _____

5. (14) _____

6. (16) _____

7. (18) _____

8. (19) _____

9. (21) _____

10. (24) _____

156. ROLL THE DICE!

Take out the dice, select a partner or two, and prepare to have some fun. Follow the rules below and fill in the spaces. When you have finished, please hand your sheet in to your teacher.

Rules: Roll the dice. If you roll a specific number, write the part of speech, phrase or clause in the space. If you roll the same number more than once, write another example of that same requirement. Thus, if you roll the number one three times, you should list three nouns. After you have rolled the dice, your partner(s) will do the same.

Enjoy!

If you roll a two, list a noun: _____

If you roll a three, list a pronoun:_____

If you roll a four, list a verb: _____

If you roll a five, list an adjective: _____

If you roll a six, list an adverb: _____

If you roll a seven, list a preposition:_____

If you roll an eight, list a conjunction: _____

If you roll a nine, list a prepositional phrase: _____

If you roll a ten, list an adjective clause: _____

If you roll an eleven, list an adverb clause: _____

If you roll a twelve, list a word that is both a noun and a verb: _____

Name_____ Date _____ Period _____

157. TIMING IS EVERYTHING!

Set your watch and get ready to go. Your teacher will tell you how much time you have for each column. Each word you write must be that column's part of speech, must have at least four letters, and must begin with the last letter of the word before it. Thus, in the noun column, you could start with *boat*, then *triple*, then *eagle*, and so forth. If you need more space, use the reverse side of this paper. Score one point for each word. Total all three columns up at the end of the competition. Write your three-column total here.

_____

NOUN	VERB	ADJECTIVE
_____	_____	_____
_____	_____	_____
_____	_____	_____
_____	_____	_____
_____	_____	_____
_____	_____	_____
_____	_____	_____
_____	_____	_____
_____	_____	_____
_____	_____	_____
_____	_____	_____
_____	_____	_____
_____	_____	_____
_____	_____	_____
_____	_____	_____
_____	_____	_____
_____	_____	_____
_____	_____	_____

Score: _____   Score: _____   Score: _____

158. THE GENERATING WHEEL

Using only the letters in this wheel that spell out GENERATE, form 25 words. You cannot use the letter G more than once in a word, since it appears only once in GENERATE. Yet, the E can be used three times in a word, since it appears three times in the word GENERATE. List the words below the wheel. Next to each word, write its part of speech. Some words can be more than one part of speech.

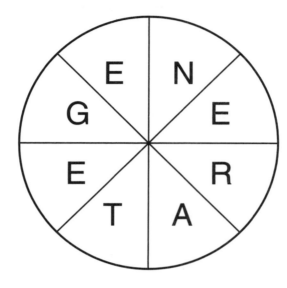

Name_____ Date _____ Period_____

159. THE LAST AND THE FIRST

This is truly a mind-expanding (and perhaps a bit aggravating) activity. The rules are quite simple. Start with the word *beach* in Column A (all nouns). Then take the last two letters of *beach*, *ch*, to start the next word. Then take the last two letters of that word to start the next word. Then repeat the process until you fill in the remaining 14 spaces in Column A. Then do the same for Column B. You can only use a specific two-letter combination once per column. The nouns can be singular or plural; the verbs can be present or past tense. All words must have four or more letters. Have fun!

COLUMN A (NOUNS)

beach

_____

_____

_____

_____

_____

_____

_____

_____

_____

_____

_____

_____

_____

_____

COLUMN B (VERBS)

wash

_____

_____

_____

_____

_____

_____

_____

_____

_____

_____

_____

_____

_____

_____

160. I'LL TAKE THE FIFTH

This activity can be played and replayed again and again. A word or phrase appears next to each line. For that specific answer, use the required word as the fifth word of a sentence. Your sentence can be about any topic so long as it has that specific requirement in the fifth slot.

1. noun: _____

2. pronoun: _____

3. verb: _____

4. adjective: _____

5. adverb: _____

6. conjunction: _____

7. preposition: _____

8. proper noun: _____

9. past tense verb: _____

10. adverb phrase _____

11. noun ending with -ion _____

12. first-person plural pronoun _____

13. adjective denoting size _____

14. subordinating conjunction _____

15. adverb denoting place _____

161. GRAMMAR POEMS

Writing poems can be enjoyable! Writing grammar poems can be a bit more challenging, because you are asked to follow certain directions within the poem. Look at the example poem to see how to do the Grammar Poems. Then, on a separate sheet of paper, write the three poems as directed.

Example Poem (5 lines)

line 1: participial phrase
line 2: subject of the poem
line 3: two words describing the subject
line 4: verb and a prepositional phrase
line 5: adjective clause that describes the object of the preposition

1. Reaching into his hat,
2. the magician,
3. tall and handsome,
4. pulled out the rabbit
5. that had been hiding inside.

Poem One (4 lines)

line 1: 2 adjectives
line 2: the subject of the poem
line 3: participial phrase describing the poem's subject
line 4: single-word verb followed by a prepositional phrase

Poem Two (4 lines)

line 1: adverb phrase indicating "when"
line 2: subject of the poem
line 3: adjective phrase describing the poem's subject
line 4: verb and direct object

Poem Three (6 lines)

line 1: person's name
line 2: appositive for that person
line 3: conjunction
line 4: another person's name
line 5: appositive for that person
line 6: single-word verb and prepositional phrase

Name_____   Date _____   Period _____

162. FROM ATHENS TO WASHINGTON

Are you ready to travel around the world immediately? Well, if you are, match the underlined portion of each city with its description in Column B. Write the two-letter answer on the line after the number. Then write these two-letter answers, in order, on the line under the columns. One answer has been done for you. If your answers are correct, you will answer the question, "What did you say after you successfully completed this activity?"

COLUMN A	COLUMN B
1. _____ A<u>the</u>ns	af. heavenly messenger
2. _____ Bos<u>ton</u>	~~as.~~ adjective; pronoun; noun; adverb
3. _____ Chic<u>ago</u>	as. verb meaning *to free or clear*
4. _____ C<u>leve</u>land	be. noun for a room
5. _as_ Da<u>lla</u>s	ci. linking verb
6. _____ <u>Den</u>ver	ei. adverb; adjective
7. _____ Hav<u>ana</u>	en. two articles
8. _____ Los <u>An</u>geles	fo. adverb; adjective; noun
9. _____ Mad<u>rid</u>	ip. present participle verb
10. _____ Mi<u>ami</u>	na. adjective; adverb; noun; homo-phone for *film spool*
11. _____ Mont<u>real</u>	ng. conjunction; homophone for *row-boat implement*
12. _____ Phil<u>adel</u>phia	rm. 2000 pounds
13. _____ T<u>oro</u>nto	th. noun; verb; adjective; palindrome
14. _____ War<u>saw</u>	ti. drink; homophone for *help*
15. _____ Wa<u>shin</u>gton	tr. past tense verb

What did you say after you successfully completed this activity? _____

_____

198

© 2001 by The Center for Applied Research in Education

163. FINDING AND SPELLING

Four nouns, four adjectives, four adverbs, four pronouns, four prepositions, and five conjunctions are found in the boxes in this grid. Each box contains both a letter and a word. Find the words that are the same part of speech (they abut one another), and then list them on the appropriate lines beneath the grid. Finally, in the parentheses, write the word that these boxes spell out.

s although	e nor	m and	a or	t for
f lovely	a carpet	r television	e heater	d during
l rude	c ladder	l he	o themselves	l except
e handsome	o very	n now	s itself	o aboard
e wicked	d slowly	e ever	t someone	s under

The four nouns are _____( ).

The four adjectives are _____( ).

The four adverbs are _____( ).

The four pronouns are _____( ).

The four prepositions are _____( ).

The five conjunctions are _____( ).

Name _____   Date _____   Period _____

164. PRONOUNS AND ADJECTIVES ARE GREAT IN 88!

Sixteen clues whose answers are pronouns and adjectives are found below. The first clue is to be placed on boxes 1 through 7. Thus, start with box 1 and place the seven letters of the answers next to the appropriate boxes (1 to 7). Then do the same with the other 15 clues.

Clues

1 – 7   She did it by _____.
7 – 11   weak; not strong
11 – 16   pretty
16 – 18   second person singular or plural pronoun
18 – 21   pretty's opposite
21 – 24   Since it belongs to you, it is _____ bracelet.
24 – 27   poor's opposite
27 – 30   soft's opposite
31 – 34   Since I own it, it is _____.
34 – 37   indefinite pronoun
37 – 43   To lend a hand is to be _____.
43 – 47   fewest
47 – 50   third person plural pronoun objective case
50 – 53   nothing more or other than
53 – 56   not odd but _____
56 – 60   rude

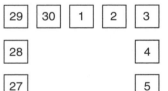

165. NOUNS THROUGHOUT THE ALPHABET

The 26 nouns in these 9 sentences are unique in that each starts with a different letter of the alphabet. Underline these nouns and then write each in the appropriate space after the last sentence.

1. The zebras ate the food quickly.

2. Many historians believe that countries relied upon treaties to promote peace.

3. Georgia is an interesting state for researchers studying economics.

4. Violence, larceny, and arson have unfortunately increased during the last two decades.

5. Warren purchased three xylophones in Yemen.

6. Several mysteries about the queen and the king will help us gain a greater understanding.

7. The bitterness of these medical interns toward their officials is hard to fathom.

8. He selected the joker.

9. Some of the nonconformists felt ostracized there.

Write the noun that starts with each letter.

a	_____	j	_____	t	_____
b	_____	l	_____	u	_____
c	_____	m	_____	v	_____
d	_____	n	_____	w	_____
e	_____	o	_____	x	_____
f	_____	p	_____	y	_____
g	_____	q	_____	z	_____
h	_____	r	_____		
i	_____	s	_____		

166. SENSE BEHIND THE NONSENSE

Each group of words below contains real words and made-up words. Using your knowledge of grammar and word placement, identify each word's part of speech. Read the sentences aloud to help you. Place the following abbreviations above the appropriate words—Noun: n; Pronoun: pn; Verb: v; Adjective: adj; Adverb: advb; Preposition: prep; Conjunction: c; Interjection: i. Be ready to support your answers. On the lines below the last sentence, devise three of your own sentences following the "sense behind the nonsense" idea.

1. A rudtur goked feeg plionts.

2. Eky Marty tuuing digh detrily?

3. The wenb folns ewq the wkiders spoloiply.

4. Ungy oogers raunbly dertted and pouygtred after the woidy, meedy tuighs.

5. During the glout the quafy froin loioded with ghest.

6. Soon my etuits will roppily bax the kjhdans and the ohfos.

7. Will Hutty's irjwe wienwe the kibby asdoijhsa?

_____

_____

_____

© 2001 by The Center for Applied Research in Education

Name_____ Date _____ Period _____

167. FOR STARTERS

Use these letter combinations as the first letters of a word that fits the requirements of the column. Of course, there may be several answers for each blank. The first one is done for you. Share your answers with your classmates.

Letters	Noun	Verb	Adjective
1. psy	psychology	psych	psychic
2. mal			
3. mis			
4. trans			
5. per			
6. sub			
7. cata			
8. cad			
9. grad			
10. por			
11. mem			
12. sen			
13. vac			
14. tele			
15. con			
16. ab			
17. dom			
18. uni			
19. cor			
20. jud			

168. JOURNAL JOTTING

Writing in your journal can teach you much about yourself. Many writers keep a daily journal to record the day's events and thoughts about these events. In this activity, you are asked to keep a mini-journal and do specific tasks. Write your answers on the appropriate lines below.

A. List four actions you witnessed today. Compose a sentence for each of these actions. Then give the present, present participle, past, and past participle tenses for each of these four verbs (actions).

First action: _____

Tenses: (present) _____, (present participle) _____,

(past) _____, (past participle) _____

Second action: _____

Tenses: (present) _____, (present participle) _____,

(past) _____, (past participle) _____

Third action: _____

Tenses: (present) _____, (present participle) _____,

(past) _____, (past participle) _____

Fourth action: _____

Tenses: (present) _____, (present participle) _____,

(past) _____, (past participle) _____

B. List four adjectives to describe people, places, or things you saw today. Then write each adjective's positive, comparative, and superlative degree forms.

First Adjective: _____ (positive) _____

(comparative) _____ (superlative) _____

Second Adjective: _____ (positive) _____

(comparative) _____ (superlative) _____

Third Adjective: _____ (positive) _____

(comparative) _____ (superlative) _____

 Fourth Adjective: _____ (positive) _____

(comparative) _____ (superlative) _____

C. List four words to describe actions that you witnessed today. Each word should end with *-ly*.

_____

_____

_____

_____

169. HI!

Every hidden word in this word-find starts with the letters *hi*. Circle the 30 words and then, next to each word, write its part(s) of speech. Use the abbreviations n (noun), pn (pronoun), v (verb), adj (adjective), advb (adverb), c (conjunction), prep (preposition), and i (interjection). Some words can be used as only one part of speech, some can be used as two parts of speech, and two can be used as three parts of speech. The words are placed horizontally, backward, forward, diagonally, and vertically. Good luck!

```
H  I  C  C  U  P  H  I  A  T  U  S  R  H  H  H  B  N  V  M
I  R  D  P  Q  Y  T  C  M  M  J  Q  R  C  I  Z  I  X  Z  B
L  R  V  H  L  L  R  Q  G  G  G  V  X  V  W  S  S  N  T  B
L  M  P  I  H  L  B  S  F  R  K  D  E  V  W  U  T  Z  D  F
M  T  N  E  H  I  N  D  S  I  G  H  T  J  M  L  S  O  B  I
Z  F  S  R  J  B  N  H  I  D  E  A  W  A  Y  G  H  C  R  K
F  G  X  O  Y  L  Z  G  P  C  J  R  T  X  C  I  I  C  S  Y
G  D  Z  G  L  L  C  Z  E  B  W  O  O  Y  N  R  W  U  R  X
N  N  K  L  C  I  X  S  Y  W  P  T  J  D  O  H  O  N  R  H
L  A  W  Y  W  H  J  S  S  O  R  G  R  T  H  I  J  D  B  J
F  L  M  P  T  I  T  F  P  E  W  A  S  I  R  P  X  T  H  M
H  H  C  H  T  T  V  P  H  H  N  I  G  A  H  P  P  I  G  G
V  G  G  I  Y  C  I  T  I  C  H  H  L  W  H  I  D  C  T  B
H  I  T  C  H  H  I  K  E  T  L  I  H  I  R  E  H  I  P  W
F  H  C  S  H  H  E  T  Y  Y  H  I  N  T  W  Q  H  I  G  H
```

hiatus	hill	hippopotamus
hiccup	hillbilly	hire
hide	hilt	historic
hideaway	Hindi	history
hieroglyphics	hindrance	hit
high	hindsight	hitch
highland	hinge	hitchhike
highly	hint	hither
hike	hip	hitherto
hilarious	hippie	hive

© 2001 by The Center for Applied Research in Education

Name _____ Date _____ Period _____

170. BEWARE THE IDES OF MARCH

Taken from William Shakespeare's full-length play, *Julius Caesar*, "Beware the Ides of March" is one of the most often-quoted lines in *any* play. Yet, you will not have to beware of anything, including the Ides of March, if you know your grammar. Here, 15 famous lines from Shakespearean plays appear, all with two words, a noun and a verb, missing from them. Write the corresponding letter combination next to the quote itself. If your answers are correct, you will spell out five Shakespearean settings. Write those settings in the appropriate lines below.

1. ____ " _____ that _____ must die." (*Hamlet*, Act I, Scene II)

2. ____ "The play's the _____ Wherein I'll _____ the conscience of the king." (*Hamlet*, Act II, Scene II)

3. ____ "He that dies _____ all _____." (*The Tempest*, Act III, Scene II)

4. ____ "The saying is true, 'The empty _____ _____ the greatest sound." (*Henry V*, Act IV, Scene IV)

5. ____ "I will _____ my _____ upon my sleeve." (*Othello*, Act I, Scene I)

6. ____ "The _____ above us _____ our conditions." (*King Lear*, Act IV, Scene III)

7. ____ "_____ truth and shame the _____." (*Henry IV*, Part I, Act II, Scene I)

8. ____ "Journeys _____ in _____ meeting." (*Twelfth Night*, Act II, Scene III)

9. ____ "The devil can _____ _____ for his own purpose." (*The Merchant of Venice*, Act I, Scene III)

10. ____ "There is a way to _____ a _____ with kindness." (*The Taming of the Shrew*, Act IV, Scene I)

11. ____ "She _____, yet she says _____." (*Romeo and Juliet*, Act II, Scene II)

12. ____ "O! _____ not by the moon, the inconstant _____." (*Romeo and Juliet*, Act II, Scene II)

13. ____ "Life's but a walking shadow, a poor player That _____ and frets his hour upon the _____ And then is heard no more:" (*Macbeth*, Act V, Scene V)

14. ____ "I'll not _____ an _____." (*The Taming of the Shrew*, Introduction, I)

15. ____ "The sins of the _____ are to be _____ upon the children." (*The Merchant of Venice*, Act III, Scene V)

AR. speaks, nothing

AT. vessel, makes

DE. cite, Scripture

FO. All, live

HE. wear, heart

KE. swear, moon

LA. budge, inch

ME. end, lovers

ND. father, laid

NG. struts, stage

NM. kill, wife

NS. stars, govern

RE. thing, catch

RO. tell, devil

ST. pays, debts

The five settings are _____, _____, _____,

_____, and _____.

171. FINDING FORTY (OR MORE)

At least 40 words of four or more letters can be formed using the words in the grid below. Start with any letter, and using a letter in a box that touches the original letter's box, move on to the next letter and then another as you spell out a word of four or more letters. Thus, starting with the A in the upper left box, and then moving from box to box, making sure the next box touches the one before it, you can spell the word *afford*. On a separate sheet of paper, list the other words you form.

A	F	F	R	A
D	L	O	O	P
R	L	A	R	K
A	W	O	A	D

172. THE SPORTING LIFE

Thirty words associated with sports are hidden in this puzzle. Circle each word.

```
S U B S T I T U T E Y D N A H E R O F P
L X K C K G X W H P F P N X D L C T F S T
S J K D F G Z V Y V J N B B H I R G Z T S
K Y S X T R Q Y B J B Z R J X F W T T S J
F R K W P L B T S Y Z W S L L I B T J R J
T H A L I S L T K L Z T F A H R F S W J J
K M T J Y T O S M F N V P T T C U Z K P N
D N E F E D C D R I B B L E K A F N P N F
F M V P V O K H R B Z F N R H S U I J T T
C V J S R B W P E J U G I A I D T P J T V
L O S E E S C L P A N W L T O O H S R R B
J A K Z I R F A D T I C T N S P T R W B D
P D I T W B O H A L L T U Q H U F V Z N N
X M C K Q G N W R N G P C Z B T W Z J N S
W Z K D D H B K C F F Q B H B T C N G S
```

block	fake	lose	run	substitute
bunt	forehand	net	sacrifice	switch
cradle	goal	pass	score	tag
defend	hit	pitch	shoot	tie
dribble	kick	punt	skate	tip
dunk	lateral	putt	sprint	win

173. THIS IS NOT A BUM STEER

Creatures—great and small—complete the 20 clues in this crossword. Fill in the blanks and then write the answers in the crossword puzzle's spaces. The expression's meaning is in parentheses after the clue. The clues will help you because we certainly don't want to give you a bum steer!

Down

1. red _____ (deception)
2. meek as a _____ (patient and mild)
4. paper _____ (an ineffective threat)
5. _____ got your tongue (quiet)
6. cart before the _____ (in the wrong order)
7. _____ tears (insincere show of grief)
10. _____ court (unauthorized, irregular court)
11. _____ wrench (tool with one movable jaw to fit various sizes)
15. crazy as a _____ (demented)
16. lame _____ (helpless person or thing)
18. sly as a _____ (very crafty or tricky)

Across

3. bum _____ (bad advice)
5. happy as a _____ (elated)
8. get one's _____ (make one angry)
9. free as a _____ (totally unrestricted)
12. as the _____ flies (directly)
13. take a _____ (look)
14. memory of an _____ (great recall)
17. _____ market (strong stock market)
18. _____ in one's throat (hoarseness)

174. DO YOU HAVE AN IRON WILL?

Call upon that iron will of yours to complete this activity! Start with a two-word adjective-noun term, such as *iron will*, and then think of another two-word adjective-noun term that begins with *will*, the second word of the previous term. Then move on, as we did with *will power*, and add at least three more two-word terms. Three sets of adjective-noun two-word terms are given to you. Write your answers in the space below.

SET ONE	SET TWO	SET THREE
iron will	black magic	cry baby
will power	magic carpet	baby powder
power play	carpet man	powder puff
play toy	man of war	puff ball
toy box	war chest	ballplayer
		player piano

175. THE GREATER WAITER BROUGHT THE CRUDE FOOD

By reading the activity's title, you already have two of the twenty answers. Each answer is two words, an adjective followed by a noun, that rhyme. So *greater waiter* and *crude food*, found in the title, are examples of the answers you will be giving in this activity. Read the clues and fill in the correct answers. Good luck!

1. _____ _____ delayed food for fish

2. _____ _____ larger lever to activate a firearm

3. _____ _____ gloomy father

4. _____ _____ elevated insect

5. _____ _____ better food deliverer

6. _____ _____ plain face indentation

7. _____ _____ intoxicated bushy-tailed carnivore

8. _____ _____ quick acting members of the theatrical production

9. _____ _____ hirsute sprite

10. _____ _____ day before Tuesday soda fountain specialty

11. _____ _____ very untidy perennial plant family

12. _____ _____ not fancy locomotive

13. _____ _____ weird oven

14. _____ _____ broader motorcyclist

15. _____ _____ firm Ace of Spades

16. _____ _____ correct vision

17. _____ _____ circular-shaped pitcher's area

18. _____ _____ coarse matter for nourishment

19. _____ _____ final boom

20. _____ _____ skinny fixer

© 2001 by The Center for Applied Research in Education

Name_____ Date _____ Period _____

176. HAS ANYONE SPOTTED EVE?

Fifteen first names (proper nouns) of people are hidden in these sentences. Underline the letters that make up each person's first name. In the first sentence, *Eve* is found within the word *even*. For the other 14 names, the letters can be found within a single word or can be spread out over two or three words. Disregard internal punctuation when looking for these names.

1. Is the score still even?

2. He seems to be very angry with the group.

3. They did not get involved in much risky behavior.

4. The Smithy family members are rich, ardent people.

5. When in Boston, I visit my relatives.

6. My mom is a committed and avid Mets fan.

7. Try to be the best that you can be.

8. Jodi's has better rye bread than this bakery.

9. You cannot seek revenge or get your way to resolve the situation.

10. This mediator settles terrible disputes.

11. I'd rather study grammar than write another short story.

12. In that region the elk ate those foods most of the time.

13. He often calls us and tells us what problems he encounters.

14. I do it now, or I take a rest.

15. When he came into the parlor, I was introduced to him.

© 2001 by The Center for Applied Research in Education

214

177. WHERE IS MONTANA?

Montana, like the names of 24 other geographical locations, is hidden in this word-find. The names are found below the puzzle. Circle the 25 names, all proper nouns. The words are placed backward, forward, diagonally, and vertically. If you do not know where some of these locations are, look them up in an atlas.

```
C A L G A R Y M P O N T A R I O A L F Y
T S D M N L L S Y O I O A N Y Z L O L H
R W E A A K A M P C R T A S M W G B O Z
E N N A V T T B O A V T B E L P Y E D R Q
N D M I A Q I O B N I B U L O A R T N D H
T E A T H X K I L T D A C G A R T O N D G
O N R O X Z N S T D D N K A N A D B A D S
N P K B X N I E Y A H O F Y J L D B H M
P X J A F F S T R S H E P A G B L Q E C
P B K Q W Q L M Y T F E P A D U B C H C
B K P H G V E L F K F Q J K N B P C E J
V M W F T T H K C M I L W A U K E E N R
F Q Y S W S T A J Y J B V H G E S P A F
J G P X F C J T T X M T P G R F Q F F B
Y D L P H K V N G Z L S Y G C Z F F F T
```

ALBERTA   HAVANA   ONTARIO

BOISE   HELSINKI   OSLO

BUDAPEST   IRELAND   PORTUGAL

CALGARY   ITALY   SPAIN

CANADA   JACKSON   SWEDEN

DENMARK   LONDON   TAMPA

FLORIDA   MANITOBA   TRENTON

FRANCE   MILWAUKEE

GREECE   MONTANA

178. CHARACTERISTICALLY SPEAKING

Select several characters from books, plays, poems, or short stories you have read. You may also select celebrities from the past or the present. For each one you choose, write that person's name, letter by letter, on the lines provided. Then, on the line next to each letter, list two adjectives that describe that person. The adjectives must begin with the letter next to the line. Then be ready to orally explain how those two adjectives befit that character or celebrity. An example is provided for you. You may choose to use the person's first and last names. Use a separate sheet of paper when necessary.

Scout from Harper Lee's *To Kill a Mockingbird*

S   sensitive, smart
C   cheerful, considerate
O   outgoing, optimistic
U   understanding, unsophisticated
T   truthful, trustworthy

_____ (Use as many spaces as necessary.)

— _____

— _____

— _____

— _____

— _____

— _____

— _____

_____ (Use as many spaces as necessary.)

— _____

— _____

— _____

— _____

— _____

— _____

— _____

179. SPELLING IT OUT

Using the names of relatives, friends, celebrities, fictional characters, cities, musical groups, or movie or television titles, write the letters of the name. Then, for each letter, write an adjective to describe that person, place, or thing. After the adjective, write an illustrative example of that adjective. The example below shows you how to do this activity. Your teacher will tell you how many different nouns to describe. Use the space below and other sheets for your answers. Enjoy!

RICHIE

R . . . real . . . He always lets you know what he is feeling.

I . . . interesting . . . He knows much about many things.

C . . . charitable . . . He will always help others.

H . . . humble . . . Never does he brag of his many outstanding accomplishments.

I . . . intelligent . . . He is one of the brightest students in our school.

E . . . energetic . . . He is in several clubs, plays three sports, and has many hobbies.

Name_____   Date _____   Period_____

180. THE PROPER WAY TO DO IT

Twenty proper names are written in a secret code whereby each letter has been substituted with another letter. No letter has been substituted for itself. Start with the clues found on the Substitution Code grid below and then identify these 20 proper names. Write your answers on the spaces provided.

1. HUCDJMDWI _ _ _ _ _ _ _ _ _

2. JURCFW _ _ _ _ _ _

3. CRJUDV _ _ _ _ _ _

4. LFCMSKRX _ _ _ _ _ _ _ _

5. AIBDHF _ _ _ _ _ _

6. ARCDFW _ _ _ _ _ _

7. ARSCIIW _ _ _ _ _ _ _

8. NIWVO _ _ _ _ _

9. ERMI _ _ _ _

10. GXFCDVR _ _ _ _ _ _ _

11. QRAIO _ _ _ _ _

12. RARTFW _ _ _ _ _ _

13. PSIZIH _ _ _ _ _ _

14. VIWYIC _ _ _ _ _ _

15. IVAFWMFW _ _ _ _ _ _ _ _

16. RGCDHR _ _ _ _ _ _

17. ARCOXRWV _ _ _ _ _ _ _ _

18. MDA _ _ _

19. JLRDW _ _ _ _ _

20. ERWJRJ _ _ _ _ _ _

Letter Substitution Code Used:

Letter:	A	B	C	D	E	F	G	H	I	J	K	L	M	N	O	P	Q	R	S	T	U	V	W	X	Y	Z
Code:	R	_	H	_	I	_	_	_	Q	_	_	A	_	_	_	_	_	J	M	_	_	_	_	_	_	_

181. THE NAME GAME

Each of the 30 names below contains words of three or more letters. On the line next to each name, write the word (or words) found within the name and then write that word's part of speech.

1. Charles _____

2. Steven _____

3. Hillary _____

4. Tamien _____

5. Courtney _____

6. Arthur _____

7. Kate _____

8. Andrew _____

9. Sarah _____

10. Seymour _____

11. Warren _____

12. Debbie _____

13. Robert _____

14. Cassandra _____

15. Matthew _____

16. Madeline _____

17. Mildred _____

18. Gerald _____

19. Edward _____

20. Carlotta _____

21. Whitney _____

22. Eleanor _____

23. Angelina _____

24. Winona _____

25. Martha _____

26. Donovan _____

27. Christine _____

28. Frank _____

29. Giovanni _____

30. William _____

Section Eight

FINAL TESTS—
KNOWLEDGE IS POWER!

182. FINAL TEST ON NOUNS AND PRONOUNS

Identify the twenty-five nouns and pronouns found in these six sentences. There are sixteen nouns and ten pronouns. Write your answers, *N* after the nouns and *P* after the pronouns, on the appropriate lines beneath the last sentence. Score 2 points for correctly *identifying* the noun or pronoun and 2 points for correctly *labeling* the noun as a noun or the pronoun as a pronoun.

1. He brought the cans to the house down the block from us.
2. When will they arrive at the airport next Tuesday?
3. You can certainly finish the task by yourself in a few hours, Kyle.
4. The aggravation did not last a long time during the long drive to Tucson.
5. Someone in the group told the others about me.
6. Take this to the booth at the fair, Leo.

Identify and label sentence 1's nouns and pronouns:

_____

Identify and label sentence 2's nouns and pronouns:

_____

Identify and label sentence 3's nouns and pronouns:

_____

Identify and label sentence 4's nouns and pronouns:

_____

Identify and label sentence 5's nouns and pronouns:

_____

Identify and label sentence 6's nouns and pronouns:

_____

Total correct answers _____ × 2 = _____ %

183. FINAL TEST ON THE NOUN AND ITS FUNCTIONS

A word has been underlined in each sentence. On the line before the sentence, tell how the noun functions by writing the function's corresponding letter. The functions and their letters are as follows: (a) subject; (b) direct object; (c) indirect object; (d) object of the preposition; (e) predicate noun; (f) direct address; and (g) appositive. Score 5 points for each correct answer.

1. _____ Our <u>dog</u> chased the truck down the road.

2. _____ <u>Children</u>, please move toward the next door.

3. _____ We handed the <u>packages</u> to the clerk.

4. _____ The salutatorian gave <u>Roberto</u> a sign of approval.

5. _____ Mr. Bauer is our new <u>assemblyman</u>.

6. _____ The Empire State, <u>New York</u>, has several large cities.

7. _____ When are we going to the <u>movies</u>?

8. _____ Joe Josephs passed the <u>ball</u> to his favorite receiver, Phil Phillips.

9. _____ Can you, <u>Bertie</u>, look for my keys in the den?

10. _____ One of the salespeople presented <u>Dad</u> with the required information.

11. _____ A <u>shower</u> of bullets alerted the soldiers of the imminent danger.

12. _____ <u>Tactics</u> such as these will no longer be tolerated.

13. _____ Do you think this can be accomplished sooner, <u>Ed</u>?

14. _____ Lucille is the current <u>champion</u> of the tennis club.

15. _____ The director of the organization is <u>Ricardo Alvarez</u>.

16. _____ None of the tickets had been removed from the <u>bucket</u>.

17. _____ Present the <u>boy</u> with the plaque, Rudy.

18. _____ Take these <u>parts</u> to the front desk.

19. _____ Tina, the team's best <u>player</u>, will be missed next year.

20. _____ We will remember her for a long <u>time</u>.

Number correct _____ × 5 = _____ %

© 2001 by The Center for Applied Research in Education

Name _____ Date _____ Period _____ Score _____%

184. FINAL TEST ON PRONOUNS

Directions: Circle the one pronoun in each sentence and then write that pronoun on the space before the sentence. Do not count pronoun adjectives, such as *other*, as pronouns on this test. Each answer is worth 5 points.

1. _____ Will you please notify the other players?

2. _____ The package next to the cabinet is hers.

3. _____ That is correct, Sid.

4. _____ Needless to say, we will always raise funds for the needy.

5. _____ They wandered throughout the museum without supervision.

6. _____ Which belongs to the woman in the third row?

7. _____ Nobody called to question the Board's most recent decision.

8. _____ Natalie has always pushed herself to work harder.

9. _____ What is your dinner choice, sir?

10. _____ Each has distinct possibilities for success.

11. _____ Does Roberto know who will present the case for the prosecution?

12. _____ Most of the applications have already been reviewed.

13. _____ Without missing an opportunity, the team members questioned us.

14. _____ Everything in her briefcase has been carefully examined.

15. _____ Those are old and virtually worthless.

16. _____ Marge reviewed both of the vacation plans.

17. _____ Have Brenda and Eddie discussed the issues with everyone?

18. _____ Assuredly, Mr Halpin knew whom to select for the task.

19. _____ During the most recent storm, many were stranded in the city.

20. _____ Martina told him to approach the shot more confidently.

Number correct _____ × 5 = _____ %

© 2001 by The Center for Applied Research in Education

225

185. FINAL TEST ON PRONOUN PROBLEMS

Directions: Select the correct pronoun within the parentheses. Write that pronoun on the line next to the sentence. Each correct answer is worth 5 points.

1. _____ Ronnie worked harder than (I, me).

2. _____ To (who, whom) should I address this letter?

3. _____ The man, (who, whom) is my coach, is very intelligent.

4. _____ These players are not as tenacious as (we, us).

5. _____ Please keep this secret between you and (I, me).

6. _____ The champions of the event are Geraldine and (she, her).

7. _____ Some of the tasks were completed by the boys and (she, her).

8. _____ Are you and (he, him) brothers?

9. _____ We transported Frankie and (they, them) to the shopping center.

10. _____ He and (them, they) have been selected to represent this city.

11. _____ It is (I, me) who is knocking.

12. _____ Packages were sent to Helen and (he, him).

13. _____ Can it be (she, her)?

14. _____ (Who, Whom) are your choices for this award?

15. _____ I have decided to buy him and (they, them) separate gifts.

16. _____ Have you spoken to them and (we, us) about it?

17. _____ Next to Christine and (I, me) sat Walt.

18. _____ (He, Him) and his father will travel to San Francisco this summer.

19. _____ Discuss the plans with both her and (he, him).

20. _____ My daughter is a person (who, whom) people admire.

Number correct _____ × 5 = _____ %

186. FINAL TEST ON MAIN AND HELPING VERBS

Directions: Underline the helping and main verbs in each sentence. Helping verbs and main verbs are worth 2 1/2 points each.

1. They will return in a few minutes.

2. Are you going to the bus station soon?

3. Seldom has he heard such caustic remarks.

4. Was this package delivered to your office today?

5. Can you help with the moving tomorrow, Larry?

6. The gardener has planted three beautiful plants.

7. There had been sixteen members in the room next door.

8. Can you take these videotapes there, Charlene?

9. Is he sending in the clowns?

10. Did you forget to mail all the letters?

11. He had sat listening to the CD for over an hour.

12. Growing up in that environment had not been easy.

13. Will you help with these laces, Teddy?

14. They will gladly represent this voting district at next month's meeting.

15. Can it be true?

16. Can they solve this equation in twenty seconds, Cheryl?

17. Deliveries are accepted after four o'clock.

18. Most of the presentations were interesting.

19. Never will I go there again without something to read.

20. Surely she had exercised quite frequently before the accident.

Number correct _____ × 2.5 = _____ %

187. FINAL TEST ON IRREGULAR VERBS

Directions: Each of the underlined words is incorrect. On the line next to each sentence, write the correct form of the irregular verb. Each correct answer is worth 5 points.

1. _____ They had <u>took</u> all the tools to the job site with them.

2. _____ Had you <u>choosed</u> sides much before I arrived at the game?

3. _____ They <u>bringed</u> these pastries with them yesterday.

4. _____ Had she <u>wrote</u> that letter to you before the event occurred?

5. _____ They had <u>eat</u> the sandwiches in the car.

6. _____ We all <u>knewed</u> that it was a closed deal long before it happened.

7. _____ None of us had <u>drove</u> to that mall by ourselves.

8. _____ They <u>rung</u> the bell for dinner ten minutes ago.

9. _____ Monica <u>swimmed</u> in the lake this morning before breakfast.

10. _____ Jasmine had <u>did</u> that activity with the younger students.

11. _____ They had already <u>gaven</u> their donations to the fund.

12. _____ Some of the pipes <u>bursted</u> during the cold snap.

13. _____ These cowboys had <u>rided</u> the broncos skillfully.

14. _____ Several of the garments <u>shrunk</u>.

15. _____ Had they <u>ran</u> all that distance by noon?

16. _____ He <u>stealed</u> second base during the second inning.

17. _____ Many of the politicians had <u>speaked</u> convincingly at the caucus.

18. _____ Sylvia's kittens had <u>went</u> under the shed during the storm.

19. _____ Ulysses had <u>took</u> many soldiers with him on the voyage.

20. _____ It <u>begun</u> to rain around three o'clock.

Number correct _____ × 5 = _____ %

Name _____ Date _____ Period _____ Score _____%

188. FINAL TEST ON VERBAL PHRASES

Directions: Underline the one verbal phrase contained in each sentence. Then, on the line next to the sentence, write whether the phrase is a participle, gerund, or infinitive phrase. Each answer is worth 2 1/2 points.

1. _____ Asking for more food was not impolite.

2. _____ Can you believe they wanted to go there?

3. _____ Investing in the stock market can be quite risky for the common investor.

4. _____ To err is human.

5. _____ The giraffe walking along the stream created little distraction.

6. _____ The giraffe chose to walk along the stream.

7. _____ Walking along the stream was relaxing for the couple.

8. _____ Since he is now in the ninth grade, Steve wants to audition for the school musical.

9. _____ Some of the people reading these magazines are laughing loudly.

10. _____ This is the suit I am going to wear tomorrow night.

11. _____ Brushing the horse down, the trainer thought about the next race.

12. _____ When will we see the ladies wearing their new coats?

13. _____ Do you remember when we used to skate on that lake?

14. _____ A few of the cards dropped on the way to the room are missing.

15. _____ Noticing the difference in the two jars, the scientist made an interesting conclusion.

16. _____ Shuffling along, the man neared the busy street corner.

17. _____ Listing all the club's officials took a few minutes.

18. _____ The bicycle stolen last weekend was recovered by the police.

19. _____ Do you know what we need to do?

20. _____ Found on the shelf, the book will be placed on reserve now.

Number correct _____ × 2.5 = _____ %

189. FINAL TEST ON ADJECTIVES

Directions: Circle the 25 adjectives found in these sentences. Some sentences may contain more than one adjective. Each sentence has at least one adjective. Do not count articles such as *a, an,* or *the* as adjectives. Do not count pronoun adjectives such as *several, you, my, their,* or *these.* Each adjective is worth 4 points.

1. Here are the beautiful paintings.

2. Can these items be sent to the larger office by Wednesday?

3. The old barn stood next to the house.

4. Most of the recent acquisitions were praised by the reporter.

5. Spring has always been my favorite season.

6. The mountain is majestic.

7. She dribbled the soccer ball skillfully.

8. Have your senators heard your legitimate complaints?

9. The overall champion will be honored at the banquet in March.

10. Several huge boulders tumbled down the mountain.

11. The threatening skies did not dampen their spirits.

12. We cautiously removed the glasses from the higher shelves.

13. Wandering through the confusing streets did not help the forgetful man.

14. Warren successfully accomplished the difficult task.

15. Fluffy and warm, the towel was removed from the dryer.

16. I explicitly told him how the old papers should be thrown out.

17. The scary criminal made off with the marked bills.

18. It is difficult to distinguish the humorous pair.

19. Some of the disadvantaged families will receive gifts during the holiday season.

20. Tall and beautiful, the models were loudly applauded.

Number correct _____ × 4 = _____ %

© 2001 by The Center for Applied Research in Education

190. FINAL TEST ON ADVERBS

Directions: Underline the adverb in each sentence. Each sentence contains one adverb. Each correct answer is worth 5 points.

1. The group has consistently tried to monitor the city's accounts.

2. The candidate has been planted squarely in the center.

3. Regina will soon retire from teaching.

4. Other people were still being pursued by the authorities.

5. They have lived in that house forever.

6. The victors hope their platforms will continue to vigorously attract more voters.

7. Producers are increasingly turning their backs on this form of entertainment.

8. Pauline seemed quite confident in her dealings with the company's new president.

9. He is rather tall for his age.

10. The church was first built during the end of the last century.

11. We are often reminded of our responsibilities to our country.

12. Traditionally, we go to my grandmother's house for the holidays.

13. The new owner arrived early.

14. Lately, we have seen a change in the teacher's personality.

15. Trey is always pleasant and cheerful.

16. Some of the choir members rehearsed together last night at Molly's house.

17. The running back fell down at the ten-yard line.

18. They have traveled abroad.

19. There is almost no danger in that experiment.

20. These valuables have been securely locked in the president's safe.

Number correct _____ × 5 = _____ %

191. FINAL TEST ON PARTS OF SPEECH

Directions: Write the part of speech of the underlined word in each sentence on the appropriate line. Each correct answer is worth 5 points.

1. _____ Can he ever <u>win</u> this encounter with this opponent?

2. _____ Warren ran the mile in <u>record</u> time yesterday.

3. _____ <u>This</u> is the easiest puzzle to solve.

4. _____ <u>Unfortunately</u>, these animals are to be moved to another zoo.

5. _____ Evelyn <u>and</u> her sister ventured to Europe several years ago.

6. _____ Will you and she take these <u>cartons</u> downstairs?

7. _____ All <u>of</u> the students attempted the new examination.

8. _____ This example is <u>definitely</u> better than the other one.

9. _____ Rudy had never meant to say <u>that</u> to Patrice.

10. _____ Often these cars are <u>mistaken</u> for one another.

11. _____ <u>Dancing</u> that wildly was fun for the exchange students.

12. _____ The top is about to fall <u>off</u>.

13. _____ These recordings climbed <u>up</u> the charts quite rapidly.

14. _____ He is <u>much</u> like his father in many respects.

15. _____ <u>Wow</u>! My foot is caught under that heavy equipment box.

16. _____ These attractive lamps can be purchased at <u>discount</u> rates.

17. _____ Freedom is one of our country's <u>tenets</u>.

18. _____ <u>Light</u> these candles before the guests arrive.

19. _____ Lorrie left, <u>for</u> she was very disappointed with the results.

20. _____ You will find the solution <u>after</u> a while.

Number correct _____ × 5 = _____ %

© 2001 by The Center for Applied Research in Education

192. FINAL TEST ON SENTENCES, FRAGMENTS, AND RUN-ONS

Directions: Indicate whether each group of words is a sentence (S), fragment (F), or run-on (RO) by writing the correct abbreviation on the appropriate line. Each correct answer is worth 5 points.

1. _____ The couch potato really needs to get more exercise.

2. _____ Near the basket by the gym's exit.

3. _____ Needing to score the goal, the hockey player skated toward the net.

4. _____ These television sets are not inexpensive they are worth the money.

5. _____ Bring the book back with you.

6. _____ Believing that almost anything is possible.

7. _____ Such expeditions bring.

8. _____ It is amazing that the rescuers reached the stranded ice skater.

9. _____ Seeing is believing.

10. _____ The wonder of it all to most of the sightseers.

11. _____ Reach for it.

12. _____ Wish for the best it might come true.

13. _____ Pleased with her choir's performance, Mrs. Blanchard, the veteran director.

14. _____ These radio stations have powerful transmitters that.

15. _____ Please take off your shoes when you enter we are trying to preserve the floors.

16. _____ Underneath all the glitz of the pageant many of the contestants and their families.

17. _____ Anybody wishing to contribute to the cancer research.

18. _____ Our favorite program has yet another rerun scheduled for this evening.

19. _____ Willing but not too able, the boy and his comrades.

20. _____ Typing as rapidly and as accurately as she possibly can.

Number correct _____ × 5 = _____ %

193. FINAL TEST ON PREPOSITIONS

Directions: Circle the preposition (or compound preposition) in each sentence. There is one preposition per sentence. Each correct answer is worth 5 points.

1. My sister has never gone anywhere without her lucky charm.

2. Will they all be there throughout the night?

3. We had found the missing bracelet beneath the pile of papers.

4. Wesley walked around the car to pick up the packages.

5. I have not seen you since that day, Kerry.

6. The children climbed aboard the miniature train.

7. We read another book about the Civil War.

8. Walk around the block several times, and you will feel better.

9. The vice president issued a memo concerning that very matter.

10. The distance runner has succeeded beyond her wildest expectations.

11. We will still try to be there in spite of the inclement weather.

12. They had not heard about the dance.

13. Instead of selecting the pitcher, the manager selected the catcher.

14. That book was written by Mark Twain.

15. Have you gone near the old neighborhood recently?

16. We will start at three o'clock.

17. We will offer extra help sessions because of the test's difficulty.

18. He will travel near that location soon.

19. Did you hear the noises during the concert?

20. It is one of the world's most beautiful buildings.

Number correct _____ × 5 = _____ %

194. FINAL TEST ON COMPLEMENTS

Directions: Indicate whether the underlined complement is a predicate nominate (pn), predicate adjective (pa), direct object (do), or indirect object (io) by writing the complement's abbreviation on the line next to the sentence. Each correct answer is worth 5 points.

1. _____ The cheetah is very <u>fast</u>.

2. _____ Mr. Bloomfield gave us several good test-taking <u>techniques</u>.

3. _____ Our team appeared quite <u>confident</u>.

4. _____ My dad's record collection contains three <u>albums</u> by the Beatles.

5. _____ The principal saw <u>us</u> heading for the exit.

6. _____ The new commander is <u>Paul Repler</u>.

7. _____ That old building was the only <u>school</u> in town in 1940.

8. _____ Several players gave <u>him</u> money.

9. _____ Our newest two-time champion is <u>she</u>.

10. _____ Wendy is her <u>name</u>.

11. _____ Wendy sold her <u>brother</u> the extra concert ticket.

12. _____ His collie looked <u>sick</u>.

13. _____ The horse jumped the <u>hurdle</u> quite easily.

14. _____ Few math problems give <u>Rana</u> any trouble.

15. _____ Her father watered every <u>plant</u> in his beautiful garden.

16. _____ Her favorite author is <u>Jane Austen</u>.

17. _____ My mother gave our <u>pastor</u> good golfing tips.

18. _____ We enjoyed singing <u>carols</u> at the festival.

19. _____ The traffic is too <u>congested</u>.

20. _____ None of the contestants is <u>nervous</u>.

195. FINAL TEST ON SUBORDINATE CLAUSES

Write the underlined subordinate clause's abbreviation on the appropriate line: adjective clause (adj), adverb clause (advb), or noun clause (n). Each correct answer scores 5 points.

1. _____ Whenever the lights flash, the mice react differently.

2. _____ The committee knows what the problem will be.

3. _____ From the moment that we arrived, the atmosphere seemed frightening.

4. _____ Unless he loses the extra pounds, he will not be able to wrestle in that tournament.

5. _____ The four miles that we jogged last night were invigorating.

6. _____ What we did on the trip was memorable.

7. _____ These plants will be there on time if you really want them by Saturday.

8. _____ His cardiologist gave him the pills so that he could live a fuller life.

9. _____ The teacher distributed a review packet to whoever needed one.

10. _____ Did you arrive here before the other bus pulled up?

11. _____ Television sets that were made at that location were recalled.

12. _____ Martha, who sold more than three hundred raffle tickets, was the top salesperson.

13. _____ Morton will send whoever is interested a list of the All-Stars.

14. _____ The radio was turned off because the static from it was annoying.

15. _____ Each candidate whose name appears on the ballot will be present.

16. _____ Whenever the situation is tense, Lara performs well.

17. _____ We assist whoever needs our help.

18. _____ What you say to them has quite an impact.

19. _____ This is the tour guide whom we asked for directions.

20. _____ Reggie walked to the store after he finished his dinner.

Number of correct answers _____ × 5 = _____ %

© 2001 by The Center for Applied Research in Education

196. FINAL TEST ON CLASSIFYING SENTENCES BY PURPOSE

Directions: On the line next to each sentence, indicate whether the group of words is a declarative, imperative, interrogative, or exclamatory sentence. Each correct answer is worth 5 points.

1. _____ Many CDs have been purchased during the last week.

2. _____ Are they moving to Arkansas very soon?

3. _____ Leave the rest to me.

4. _____ What a beautiful dress!

5. _____ Can this be the only way to do the activity?

6. _____ The pitch was definitely in the strike zone.

7. _____ Steady the sails, Ben.

8. _____ These really rock!

9. _____ Here are the capitals of the 50 states.

10. _____ Read what it says under that section.

11. _____ What are the others going to do at that same time?

12. _____ What a sensational party!

13. _____ Be the best that you can be.

14. _____ J.D. Salinger wrote "A Perfect Day for Bananafish."

15. _____ Was that the same man who used to commute with Dad?

16. _____ How beautiful you are!

17. _____ Plenty of spirit was in evidence that night.

18. _____ Will there be enough seats for all of us?

19. _____ These relatives will help you along.

20. _____ Were these stamps part of George's collection?

Number correct _____ × 5 = _____ %

197. FINAL TEST ON AGREEMENT

Directions: Circle the correct word within parentheses, and then write that word in the space provided. Each correct answer is worth 5 points.

1. _____ These books on the shelf (is, are) ready to be removed.

2. _____ Each of the cars (is, are) washed and waxed.

3. _____ These fragrances (was, were) carefully manufactured.

4. _____ Every one of the pens (work, works).

5. _____ Some of the windows (appear, appears) to need a good washing.

6. _____ Bobby, as well as Drew and Juan, (was, were) there yesterday.

7. _____ One shipment of dresses (was, were) received earlier today.

8. _____ The number of passing scores (is, are) commendable.

9. _____ Either the manager or her players (select, selects) the game captain.

10. _____ Both the manager and her players (decide, decides) the issue.

11. _____ There (is, are) several years to review.

12. _____ *The Three Musketeers* by Dumas (has, have) been read by many.

13. _____ Two-thirds of the purchases (has, have) been made by women.

14. _____ Mathematics (is, are) his favorite class this year.

15. _____ All students, teachers, and administrators (has, have) been polled.

16. _____ The most drastic change (is, are) elimination of these classes.

17. _____ Each of the young ladies had (her, their) dress altered.

18. _____ Neither Maurice nor Thomas had (his, their) wallet with him.

19. _____ Rona is one of those students who (is, are) conscientious about every school assignment.

20. _____ Only one of their suggestions (was, were) not approved.

Number correct _____ × 5 = _____ %

198. FINAL TEST ON USAGE

Directions: Underline the correct word within parentheses, and then write the word on the line next to the sentence. Each correct answer is worth 5 points.

1. _____ Nobody will be (accepted, excepted) from the ruling.

2. _____ What (affect, effect) will this mandate have on your group?

3. _____ We have not seen him (anywhere, anywheres) recently.

4. _____ (Beside, Besides) lasagna, what else is available for us?

5. _____ (Bring, Take) the book back to me here.

6. _____ Let us divide the candies (among, between) the three children.

7. _____ How could she (have, of) been there at that time?

8. _____ There were (fewer, less) tickets in that box at the time.

9. _____ The orchestra played (good, well) at the holiday concert in December.

10. _____ Will the commissioner (leave, let) me have a parking sticker?

11. _____ My uncle is taller (than, then) his son, Robbie.

12. _____ (Them, Those) tires need to be filled.

13. _____ (Unless, Without) he can help us there, we probably cannot get the job accomplished.

14. _____ This is the kind of machine (that, who) I like to operate.

15. _____ Perry (can hardly, can't hardly) swim as well as his cousin.

16. _____ Did she (learn, teach) you how to purchase stock on the Internet?

17. _____ The balloon (busted, burst) during Betty's party.

18. _____ How will this (affect, effect) the other candidates?

19. _____ Did Alexander Graham Bell (discover, invent) the telephone?

20. _____ Gladly will the worthy charity (accept, except) your generous donation.

Number correct _____ × 5 = _____ %

199. FINAL TEST ON WORDS OFTEN CONFUSED

Thirty-three words often confused are the answers to this crossword puzzle. Read the clue and then fill in the missing letters. Each correct answer scores 3 points. (You will get the extra point automatically.) Good luck!

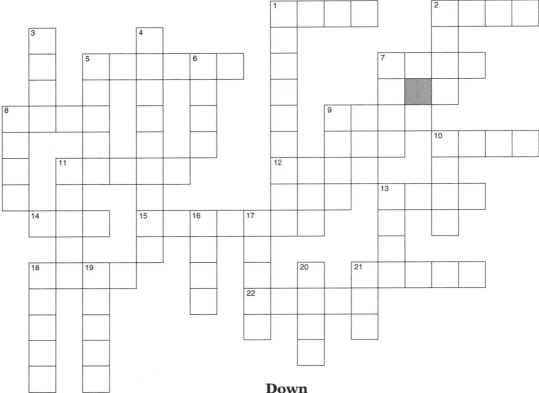

Across
1. window's section
2. to perceive through the ears
5. spirit
7. money paid for transportation; food
8. animals
9. blood vessel or mineral deposit
10. food or flesh
11. open space
12. opposite of pleasure
13. past tense of blow
14. path or route
15. permitted
18. not strong
21. allow to remain behind
22. opposite of tight

Down
1. rule or concept
2. immediate area
3. wind indicator
4. most important; school's administrator
5. what is correct or ethical
6. opposite of win
7. just; celebration
8. expensive; cherished
9. valueless
10. join
11. flat and level
13. a color
16. to misplace
17. entire
18. to measure weight
19. with the normal voice; loudly enough
20. hollow place
21. to permit

© 2001 by The Center for Applied Research in Education

200. FINAL TEST ON WORDS IN CONTEXT

You have worked with parts of speech and anticipating which words belong in specific places within a sentence. Here, 20 words have been deleted from these 10 sentences and are listed below the last sentence. Fill in these words in their *most appropriate* blanks. Each word is used only once. Score 5 points for each correct answer.

1. Several children _____ the playful dog.

2. You are the party's _____ for _____.

3. The _____ headed for the distant _____.

4. A _____ tour guide _____ her group to the restaurant.

5. _____, the _____ engine would not turn over.

6. We could see the _____ with its shining beacon in the _____.

7. A _____ was tied around the _____ of newspapers.

8. The green _____ was _____ _____.

9. Some of the _____ in our football league broke many _____.

10. Did you take the _____ for both _____.

bicycles	island	records
car's	lighthouse	smiling
chased	locks	stack
choice	picturesque	string
distance	president	unfortunately
escorted	quarterbacks	valley
ferry	quite	

Number of correct answers _____ × 5 = ____ %

201. FINAL TEST ON GRAMMAR TERMS

Fill in the letters of these 16 grammar terms. A letter here and there has been given to you to get you started. Each answer counts 6 points. To earn the remaining 4 points, write four prepositions on the reverse side of this paper.

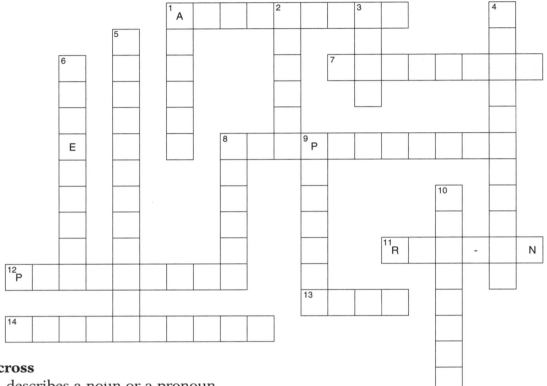

Across

1. describes a noun or a pronoun
7. group of words that does not express a complete thought
8. shows the relation of a noun or pronoun to some other word in the sentence
11. two sentences that are incorrectly joined by a comma
12. another name for a verb
13. name of a person, place, thing, or idea
14. case featuring words such as *he, they,* and *we*

Down

1. modifies a verb, an adjective, or an adverb
2. a group of words that contains a subject and a predicate and is used as part of a sentence
3. action word
4. joins words or groups of words
5. word that expresses emotion and has no grammatical relation to other words in the sentence
6. case featuring words such as *him, them,* and *us*
8. group of words not containing a verb or a subject
9. takes the place of a noun
10. a group of words that expresses a complete thought

202. FINAL TEST ON COMMAS

Insert the 25 commas where they are needed. Each comma scores 4 points. Good luck!

1. Are you going to the fair tomorrow night Jose?

2. Our other car a black Toyota is in the garage.

3. My sister is scheduled to study economics world governments and English literature next semester.

4. No Lou's address is not 417 Smallson Court Ontario Canada.

5. Juan can carry packages and Pedro can load the other cartons now.

6. Mike Rogers who has played in that band for years may go solo next year.

7. Knowing he needed to convince only a few more voters the politician took to the streets again.

8. Since there are so few trains coming home at that late hour we will need to leave the party earlier.

9. Knowledgeable and interesting tonight's guest speaker will captivate all of you.

10. Most people even those who are not that informed have heard of her.

11. Tim would you please check these numbers for me?

12. With due respect I feel Joe that there are better candidates for the position.

13. Her date of birth is May 3 1992 I think.

14. We can submit the application now or we can wait until later this week.

15. Yes Martin Luther King Jr. will always be revered by anyone who cares about human life.

Number of correct commas _____ × 4 = _____ %

Name _____ Date _____ Period _____ Score _____%

203. FINAL TEST ON PUNCTUATION

Insert the required marks of punctuation. This includes end punctuation. Good luck!

1. These are the correct answers Teddy

2. When Natasha studies these folders both she and you will understand the situation more fully Barb

3. This card is quite touching I appreciate your kindness toward our family

4. Please have the following items with you index cards pens and some form of identification

5. Maureen and Tim are headed for the beach today however they will only stay there for a few hours

6. Yes there are many other options available to you Kate but this seems to be the best possible one now

7. The procession will move down the driveway at 1030 or shortly after that

8. Did you enjoy A Christmas Carol by Charles Dickens the British writer

9. There are three es in the word cemetery

10. This is our best chance Jim told Karen his wife

11. *Lord of the Flies* a novel depicting mans inhumanity toward his fellow man was written by William Golding

12. Jasmine announced We need to help these needy people as soon as we can

13. Hurry up Mort George screamed

14. Supper included steak baked potatoes broccoli and gravy

15. John you could certainly borrow our car however we will need it back by this Saturday afternoon

© 2001 by The Center for Applied Research in Education

ANSWER KEYS

SECTION ONE
PARTS OF SPEECH—WORKING WITH WORDS!

1. NOUNS AND NAMES

The nouns are as follows:

1. students, umbrella, Evanston, night
2. opinions, reporters, meeting
3. jury, understanding, acceptance, notification
4. ladies, investigation
5. scientist, acid, microscope, academy
6. research, interest, artifacts
7. There are no nouns in this sentence.
8. radios, October, November
9. dad, entrance
10. bread

The seven first names are Sue, Norm, Juan, Lisa, Maria, Ron, and Deb.

2. IS ... IS NOT ... IS ... IS NOT ... IS ... IS NOT

1. is (p)
2. is (r)
3. is not (m)
4. is (o)
5. is (g)
6. is not (u)
7. is not (l)
8. is not (t)
9. is (r)
10. is not (i)

11. is (a)
12. is (m)
13. is (m)
14. is not (m)
15. is (e)
16. is not (e)
17. is not (d)
18. is not (i)
19. is not (a)
20. is (r)

The "is" answers spell out "programmer." The "is not" answers spell out "multimedia."

3. FOUR-LETTER NOUNS AND VERBS

1. raid
2. note (or tone)
3. find
4. snow
5. joke
6. yell
7. wail
8. dent
9. rent

10. host (or shot)
11. meet
12. rain
13. hand
14. inch (or chin)
15. best (or bets)
16. coat
17. kick
18. stay

19. tilt
20. read (or dare)
21. quiz
22. part (or trap)
23. reel (or leer)
24. arch (or char)
25. loan

4. PRONOUNS ARE IN!

```
H  P  W  Y  M  G  W  E  Y  T  Q  S  C  P  R  Q  Z  X  W  F
W  T  D  X  X  C  N  B  O  Z  D  M  S  Y  S  C  W  X  J  L
C  Q  D  T  P  O  M  D  U  G  V  Q  Y  Z  X  J  Y  T  B  D
H  Z  W  T  Y  T  W  R  X  O  N  L  J  B  T  X  J  T  P  V
D  V  H  H  S  R  H  S  K  F  U  G  C  S  X  J  T  P  K
T  H  E  M  S  E  L  V  E  S  H  E  R  A  N  Y  B  O  D  Y
Z  V  C  K  H  V  X  L  M  P  D  X  S  Z  L  P  N  V  P
E  I  P  T  L  E  A  R  F  S  G  X  H  Y  T  K  H  H  X  P
T  H  I  S  V  R  L  W  E  S  A  N  O  T  H  E  R  K  S  H
W  E  Y  U  Q  A  L  M  I  C  O  H  B  L  M  N  Z  Y  F
N  Q  C  M  D  L  R  H  O  W  Y  M  R  X  H  O  F  G  Z  R
Y  O  U  R  S  E  L  V  E  S  M  X  E  W  B  M  I  N  E  S
F  X  M  G  T  R  K  W  W  P  T  Z  C  O  D  Z  R  P  F  C
R  Y  Z  W  B  W  F  Z  F  M  M  Z  D  M  N  V  D  D  F  C
J  N  G  H  V  L  S  P  V  D  P  Y  K  G  Q  E  V  L  V  K
```

ALL (S/P)
ANOTHER (S)
ANYBODY (S)
EVERYONE (S)
HE (S)
HER (S)
HIS (S)
IT (S)

ME (S)
MINE (S)
MOST (S/P)
NEITHER (S)
NOBODY (S)
OURS (P)
SEVERAL (P)
SOMEONE (S)

THEIR (P)
THEM (P)
THEMSELVES (P)
THIS (S)
US (P)
WE (P)
YOURSELF (S)
YOURSELVES (P)

5. THERE'S SOMETHING VERY DEFINITE ABOUT THESE INDEFINITES!

1. were (sa)
2. is (nt)
3. are (ia)
4. is (go)
5. was (ne)
6. has (wd)
7. knows (el)

8. has (hi)
9. was (he)
10. contain (ls)
11. is (in)
12. had (ki)
13. happen (da)
14. won't (ma)

15. sounds (sc)
16. requests (us)
17. was (ca)
18. needs (nb)
19. were (er)
20. is (ra)

The five capitals are Santiago (Chile), New Delhi (India), Helsinki (Finland), Damascus (Syria), and Canberra (Australia).

6. G(EE), THIS CAN BE FUN!

The verbs are go, grow, growl, grind, gust, grab, give, going, glide, giggle, gaze, and goose. The boxes form the number 14.

7. FINDING THE VERBS ALPHABETICALLY

```
C V M N D C O J H X S M N R Q A K G J F
R S F B P P H X J Q H D E V E R V R P J
E L E C T Z O O M Y H H K N L R L O L L
T T X I R K I Y O S E K F W D I E W I N
U V O R E N M R I Z R E H M N V A L F D
R N P H A J D N Z R S H R M I E R B E D
G U T G Y I R S Y S T A N K G N D L Z
N M T Q L Q P K S Y R Z V I N K N K P C
T B D K L W J U K T S E G N I E S N P G
D P V G N I C G L Z N E X D D P R C G R
G M X Z H N W Z T L B S C X W P R P J G
J M L T G T W D P C V X K J K F D P J P
Q Y Y L L Z L Q C Q Z Q B J F D V S L H
P K R H Z S X W L N D X G D M B D V C V
```

The verbs are arrive, begin, choose, divide, elect, finish, growl, howl, ingest, join, kindle, learn, mend, numb, option, pull, quiz, risk, shatter, treat, utter, void, win, x-ray, yearn, and zoom.

8. VERBS A-PLENTY

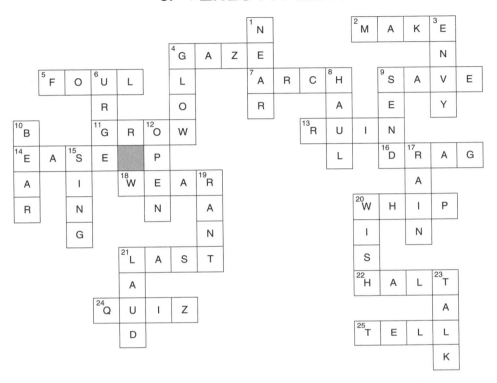

9. CALLING ALL VERBS! CALLING ALL VERBS!

The verbs are underlined. There may be others found by the students.

1. Have you done all of your re<u>search</u> for the pre<u>sent</u>ation?
2. We just loved the holiday dis<u>play</u> in the store <u>window</u>.
3. Another informal <u>meet</u>ing has to be scheduled for next month.
4. He is an inter<u>est</u>ing guy who believes <u>complete</u>ly in our cause.
5. Marion, will you read the para<u>graph</u> from the first <u>chapter</u>?
6. At this stage of your life, you are looking for a more <u>meaningful</u> <u>existence</u>.
7. Do you suppose they can seek in<u>depend</u>ence by <u>them</u>selves?
8. <u>Plenty</u> of res<u>ident</u>s came out to help their neighbors.
9. The curious students looked for sa<u>tell</u>ites and stars with their in<u>strum</u>ents.
10. Those two <u>passengers</u> were discharged from the e<u>merge</u>ncy room.
11. Say "fer<u>vent</u>ly <u>flopping</u>" five times fast.
12. Some of the runners had been wrestling with the op<u>press</u>ive heat.
13. He will be remembered as a cou<u>rage</u>ous and <u>respectable</u> human being.
14. We ask that you <u>please</u> shut off all electronic devices while you are in the <u>theater</u>.
15. It's hard to c<u>hange</u> the basic de<u>sign</u> of the forest.

10. BE ALERT!

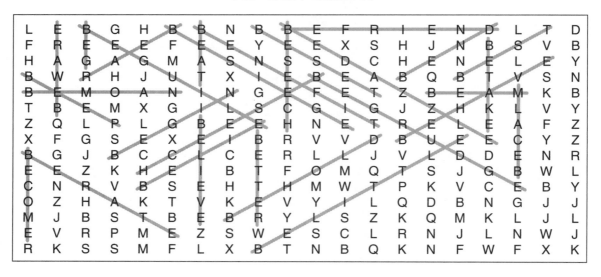

The verbs are be, beam, bear, beat, becalm, become, bedazzle, beep, befriend, beg, begin, begrudge, beguile, behave, behold, belie, believe, belittle, bemoan, bend, benefit, berate, beseech, beset, besiege, best, betake, better, and beware.

11. 26 MINUS X EQUALS 25

12. TAKE TWO MINUTES

Answers will vary.

13. THE LAST BECOMES THE FIRST

Answers will vary.

14. GALLERY OF ADVERBS

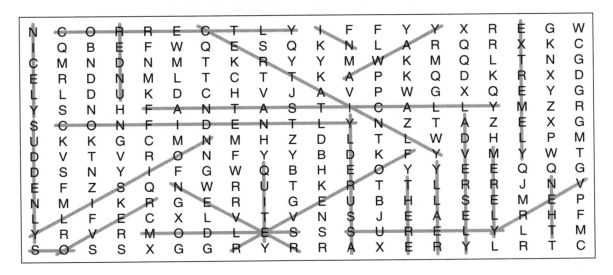

Here are the 25 adverbs.

away	in	seldom
adversely	merely	surely
assuredly	never	suddenly
certainly	nicely	then
correctly	noisily	there
confidently	over	under
extremely	quite	very
forever	really	
fantastically	so	

15. HEY, CONJUNCTION, WE KNOW YOUR FUNCTION!

Answers will vary.

16. BREAKING NORTHWESTERN APART

These are acceptable words. There are other possibilities.

NOUNS	VERBS	ADJECTIVES	CONJUNCTIONS
ether	hewn	short	nor
horn	rent	stern	or
hornet	reset	sterner	when
north	rest	sweet	where
rent	seen	tenth	
rest	sewn	terse	
roster	smart	these	
rower	snow	those	
show	sown	worse	
stew	steer	worst	
store	store		
street	strew		
sweet	strewn		
tern	sworn		
test	test		
thorn	threw		
three	throw		
throne	thrown		
tree	worn		
west	worth		
western	wrest		
worth			

17. END IT CORRECTLY!

1. according <u>to</u>
2. across <u>from</u>
3. alongside <u>of</u>
4. along <u>with</u>
5. apart <u>from</u>
6. aside <u>from</u>
7. because <u>of</u>
8. by means <u>of</u>
9. except <u>from</u>
10. in addition <u>to</u>
11. from <u>among</u>
12. in place <u>of</u>
13. inside <u>of</u>
14. on account <u>of</u>
15. round <u>about</u>
16. subsequent <u>to</u>
17. together <u>with</u>
18. down <u>from</u>
19. instead <u>of</u>
20. on top <u>of</u>

18. TOP TWENTY-FIVE

Here are suggested answers. There may be others.

1. bake or bike
2. inspiration
3. herself
4. about
5. between
6. shortly
7. already
8. several
9. eager

10. for
11. interest
12. hello
13. itself
14. splendid
15. heaven
16. imitate
17. country
18. mention

19. gratify
20. hefty
21. great
22. during
23. within
24. lawn
25. should

19. PARTS OF SPEECH MAGIC SQUARE

A=11	B=13	C=8	D=2
E=4	F=6	G=15	H=9
I=5	J=3	K=10	L=16
M=14	N=12	O=1	P=7

20. NURSERY RHYME TIME

Jack and Jill

noun – conjunction – noun – verb – preposition – article – noun
preposition – verb – article – noun – preposition – noun.
noun – verb – adverb – conjunction – verb – pronoun/adjective – noun
conjunction – noun – verb – adjective – preposition
adverb – noun – verb – conjunction – noun – verb – verb
conjunction – adverb – conjunction – pronoun – verb – verb.
pronoun – verb – preposition – noun – preposition – verb – pronoun/adjective – noun
preposition – noun – conjunction – adjective – noun.

There Was an Old Woman

adverb – verb – article – adjective – noun — pronoun – verb – preposition – article – noun;

pronoun – verb – adverb – adjective – noun – pronoun – (verb/adverb) – verb – pronoun – verb – verb;

pronoun – verb – pronoun – pronoun/adjective – noun – preposition – pronoun/adjective – noun;

pronoun – verb – pronoun – pronoun – adverb – conjunction – verb – pronoun – preposition – noun;

21. YOU DO PARTS OF SPEECH RIGHT!

1. pro – v – n – advb!
2. pro/adj – n – v – advb!
3. art – adj – n – prep – n!
4. n – art – adj – n!
5. art – n – pro/v – prep – v!
6. pro – v – pro – prep – pro – prep – n!
7. v – prep – v – advb!
8. pro – v – art – n – advb – prep – pro/adj – n!
9. n – prep – n!
10. adj – n – prep – pro!
11. adj – n!
12. n – prep – pro – prep – art – n!
13. art – n – pro – advb – v!
14. n – advb – prep – pro/adj – n!
15. pro – verb – verb – pro – prep – art – n – prep – n!

22. BULL'S-EYE

1. forward
2. heave
3. Canada
4. but
5. occasional
6. ion
7. litigate
8. into
9. herself
10. down
11. hah
12. rush
13. queue
14. wrought
15. khan

23. TWICE EACH

1. adjective
2. noun/adverb
3. noun
4. conjunction/ preposition
5. pronoun

6. adverb
7. preposition
8. adjective
9. conjunction
10. interjection
11. pronoun

12. preposition
13. adverb
14. verb
15. interjection
16. verb

24. TEN AND TEN AND TEN AND TEN AND TEN (AND THEN FIVE)

These are possible answers. There may be others.

GROUP A	GROUP B	GROUP C	GROUP D
attractive	charge	apartment	define
beautiful	dance	building	note
cute	jog	cabin	read
dashing	meander	chateau	recall
exotic	plod	hovel	review
gorgeous	prance	hut	peruse
handsome	run	igloo	reread
lovely	saunter	mansion	study
striking	sprint	palace	test
tall	trudge	teepee	write

GROUP E	GROUP F	GROUP G
drastically	cans	Great!
elegantly	float	Hurrah!
frantically	lifeguard	Super!
gradually	rocks	Yeah!
haphazardly	sand	Yippee!
intelligently	shovel	
jokingly	surfers	
kinetically	swimmers	
laboriously	umbrella	
maliciously	waves	

25. FOLLOWING DIRECTIONS

Here are possible sentences. There are other possibilities.

1. Geraldo is the champion.
2. John approached Marty.
3. She is beautiful.
4. The talented dancer performed for two hours.
5. Did they forget to wash the car?

6. Turn the dial slowly.
7. Juanita and I will help now.
8. We have not seen him.
9. With your help, I can do it.
10. Listen carefully.

26. MORE THAN ONE

```
R  P  P  M  G  J  S  Q  D  M  F  K  W  K  T  R  W  C  J  P
V  G  T  N  I  A  P  W  R  O  L  I  G  H  T  R  O  H  S  N
K  C  V  V  M  R  M  T  R  E  W  J  B  R  O  L  L  S  F  P
L  J  Y  L  M  F  R  E  N  N  S  N  A  F  P  M  G  I  X  P
R  S  N  O  W  O  C  O  F  S  Z  P  I  H  S  W  T  D  M  K
J  E  R  W  K  L  H  Q  R  N  T  E  R  X  Z  L  R  P  G
S  Y  C  K  T  L  D  Y  D  M  K  Q  V  C  S  T  A  X  C  B
F  W  G  O  V  O  F  J  X  K  K  J  F  R  T  H  T  N  G  W
K  Q  U  K  R  W  W  R  L  F  Z  Y  G  N  X  C  R  P  M  J
Q  X  A  H  S  D  Y  M  O  Y  B  D  Y  Q  I  J  J  D  N  M
G  B  R  N  L  J  L  S  Y  S  S  R  M  L  Q  T  D  G  J  K
Z  F  D  D  F  Z  B  V  R  C  T  H  F  Z  L  C  R  N  N  X
W  Y  N  M  J  X  P  M  B  Z  R  N  B  M  Y  L  S  R  X  Y
D  Q  L  F  J  G  S  F  Y  H  O  L  G  Z  V  H  Y  X  Q  K
H  G  B  Y  C  G  Y  L  P  C  F  W  Y  Q  V  W  N  J  F  Q
```

by—preposition, adverb

conflict—noun, verb

dish—noun, verb

down—noun, verb, adjective, adverb, preposition

follow—noun, verb

frost—noun, verb

game—noun, verb, adjective

glow—noun, verb

guard—noun, verb

harm—noun, verb

light—noun, verb, adjective, adverb

mirror—noun, verb

paint—noun, verb

part—noun, verb, adjective

record—noun, verb

respect—noun, verb

ship—noun, verb

short—noun, verb, adjective, adverb

snow—noun, verb

top – noun, verb, adjective

SECTION TWO
PHRASES AND CLAUSES—WORD WEAVERS!

27. GETTING THE GIST OF GRAMMAR

1. GR
2. AM
3. MA
4. RE

5. XE
6. RC
7. IS
8. ES

9. CA
10. NB
11. EC
12. HA

13. LL
14. EN
15. GI
16. NG

The sentence reads: Grammar exercises can be challenging.

28. NO FRAGMENTED THOUGHTS HERE!

A=4	B=15	C=10	D=5
E=6	F=9	G=16	H=3
I=13	J=2	K=7	L=12
M=11	N=8	O=1	P=14

29. U CAN DO IT!

These are acceptable answers. There are others.

1. umbrella
2. understand
3. us
4. undaunted
5. unfairly
6. unless
7. Ugh!

8. underneath
9. <u>Unless he sees the signal</u>, he will not react.
10. <u>Unraveling the knot</u> was not hard for Susie.
11. <u>Unfazed by the crowd's boos</u>, the player still hit a home run.
12. Urchins play a big role in that drama, Hank.
13. You will see the blanket <u>under the shelf</u>.
14. The blanket <u>under the shelf</u> is the one we need now.
15. <u>Until he transferred to another school</u>, Charles was not very involved in extracurricular activities.

30. THE *GETTYSBURG ADDRESS*

1. upon this continent
2. adjective
3. equal
4. verb
5. to dedicate
6. adjective
7. here, altogether
8. their, this
9. fitting, proper
10. conjunction
11. who struggled here
12. adverb
13. The
14. verb
15. they

31. DISSECTING THE SENTENCE

1. match
2. momentarily
3. After the long match
4. rested
5. before
6. to sign autographs
7. they
8. players
9. before they began to sign autographs
10. autographs
11. adjective
12. players
13. began
14. plural
15. complex

32. SEEING *ROMEO AND JULIET* GRAMMATICALLY

1. in dignity
2. adverb
3. grudge
4. adjective
5. of these two foes
6. overthrows
7. verb
8. noun
9. love
10. noun
11. nought
12. now
13. if
14. verb
15. to mend

33. WHAT EXACTLY IS A TUFFET?

These are possible answers. There are others.

1. The spider frightened Miss Muffet.
2. Little Miss Muffet ate curds and whey.
3. Little Miss Muffet sat on a tuffet.
4. Because the spider sat down beside Little Miss Muffet, she was frightened.
5. The spider frightened Little Miss Muffet.
6. The spider came along and frightened Little Miss Muffet.
7. Eating her curds and whey, Little Miss Muffet sat on a tuffet.
8. The spider that sat down beside Little Miss Muffet frightened her away.
9. Little Miss Muffet was frightened by the spider.
10. Sitting on a tuffet was what Little Miss Muffet was doing when a spider came along.

34. WALKING WEARILY

The following are possible answers.

acting avidly	maligning madly
betting boldly	negotiating noisily
checking casually	opining openly
driving dangerously	parading proudly
eating eagerly	questioning quietly
finding fortuitously	reading rapidly
greeting graciously	serving speedily
helping heartily	talking thoughtfully
inquiring interestingly	uttering understandingly
joking jovially	violating viciously
kissing kindly	walking wearily
laughing loudly	zooming zealously

35. PARTICIPLES AND VERBS

These are acceptable participles. There are others.

REGULAR VERBS

a.	annoyed	q.	quizzed
b.	battered	r.	resigned
c.	contented	s.	signaled
d.	dedicated	t.	troubled
e.	embarrassed	u.	unfazed
f.	frightened	v.	vindicated
g.	glued	w.	washed
h.	hurried	x.	x-rayed
i.	irritated	y.	yanked
j.	joined	z.	zippered
k.	kicked		
l.	loosened		
m.	maneuvered		
n.	named		
o.	outsmarted		
p.	puzzled		

IRREGULAR VERBS

b.	broken
c.	chosen
d.	driven
e.	eaten
f.	fallen
g.	grown
h.	hung
k.	known
l.	lied
r.	ridden
s.	stolen
t.	taken
w.	written

36. DO YOU NOTICE THIS?

These are acceptable answers. There are many other possibilities.

1. The notice arrived shortly after you left.
2. Did the class members notice the noise coming from the other room?
3. This is your last notice.
4. The director gave the notice to the actors.
5. Helena trudged into the room without the notice.
6. After she received the notice, the apartment owner spoke with the authorities.
7. The renter who received the notice spoke with the landlord.
8. All the apartment residents wanted to read the notice.
9. Reading the notice, the residents were stunned by the landlord's words.
10. Reading the landlord's notice was not a pleasant experience for the renters.
11. The landlord with the notice is Mr. Loweree.
12. Our landlord walked in with the notice.

37. THERE ARE NO OPPOSING APPOSITIVES HERE

1. el
2. vi
3. sp
4. re
5. sl

6. ey
7. ar
8. oc
9. ka
10. nd

11. ro
12. ll
13. le
14. ge
15. nd

The two-letter answers spell out <u>Elvis Presley, a rock and roll legend</u>.

38. FINDING THOSE SIXTEEN PREPOSITIONAL PHRASES

```
P  U  B  E  S  I  D  E  S  T  H  A  T  R  S  H  E  W  S  Y
B  A  N  B  E  Y  O  N  D  T  H  E  L  A  S  T  H  I  L  L
Y  P  S  D  A  B  O  U  T  S  I  X  Y  E  A  R  S  T  F  V
H  Q  T  T  E  D  R  Y  V  Q  D  N  F  N  B  Q  U  H  B  V
I  T  X  L  H  R  X  X  C  R  E  H  T  M  N  N  K  O  B  D
M  F  N  I  V  E  N  J  N  Q  K  Z  M  H  T  T  W  N  Y  X
S  F  O  K  T  F  R  E  V  F  A  X  G  I  E  G  N  D  G  V
E  T  E  C  Y  R  E  A  Z  B  L  R  Z  P  S  D  H  J  R  R
L  C  N  Y  K  N  M  L  R  T  E  T  D  X  G  S  A  E  N  Y
F  V  T  O  W  A  R  D  M  Y  H  O  U  S  E  N  J  R  N  T
F  L  A  U  R  W  C  V  F  E  T  M  F  Y  M  B  B  X  K  P
Z  P  R  D  D  Z  Y  K  N  P  Y  D  Y  C  L  G  T  M  F  M
O  N  T  H  E  A  I  R  D  D  B  Q  B  B  T  R  S  C  T  L
F  Z  F  H  X  K  Y  T  N  E  A  R  T  H  E  R  O  A  D  K
W  I  T  H  I  N  T  H  E  C  A  V  I  T  Y  D  W  X  W  V
```

39. DON'T LET THESE PHRASES FAZE YOU!

1. s
2. n
3. o
4. w
5. r

6. a
7. i
8. n
9. h
10. a

11. i
12. l
13. m
14. i
15. s

16. t
17. h
18. a
19. z
20. e

The five four-letter words associated with weather are <u>snow</u> (1 to 4), <u>rain</u> (5 to 8), <u>hail</u> (9 to 12), <u>mist</u> (13 to 16), and <u>haze</u> (17 to 20).

40. PHRASES AND SCIENTISTS

1. NE	6. AR	11. EI
2. WT	7. TE	12. NG
3. ON	8. SE	13. AL
4. DE	9. IN	14. IL
5. SC	10. ST	15. EO

The scientists are Newton, Descartes, Einstein, and Galileo.

41. GERUNDS

1. cooking for the event—(do)
2. Blaine's decorating—(s)
3. scratching on the screen door—(op)
4. Diving to such depths—(s)
5. accounting—(pn)
6. Researching her family's history—(s)
7. Nancy's running the New York City Marathon last fall—(s)
8. their telling us—(op)
9. Turning on the lights too early—(s)
10. alerting her readers to the potential problem—(pn)
11. skiing the slopes—(do)
12. seeing your relatives so often—(op)
13. rowing against a mild wind—(do)
14. fishing with Uncle Ted—(do)
15. collecting canned goods—(op)
16. finding enough interested donors—(pn)
17. photographing sunsets—(pn)
18. bowling and golfing—(op)
19. reading *A Tale of Two Cities*—(do)
20. feeding the newborn—(pn)

42. TO BE OR NOT TO BE

Answers will vary.

43. LUCKY SEVEN

1. s	4. s	7. s	10. pn	13. pn	16. pn	19. s
2. o	5. o	8. s	11. o	14. pn	17. pn	20. o
3. o	6. pn	9. pn	12. o	15. s	18. s	21. o

44. COMPLETING THE IDEA

Answers will vary.

45. BECAUSE OF THE CLAUSE

1. E	5. H	9. I
2. J	6. A	10. C
3. G	7. B	
4. D	8. F	

46. PHRASE AND CLAUSE INDICATORS

1. prepositional phrase and subordinate clause
2. prepositional phrase
3. verbal phrase (gerund phrase and participial phrase)
4. verbal phrase (infinitive phrase) and prepositional phrase
5. prepositional phrase
6. prepositional phrase and subordinate clause
7. verb phrase
8. verbal phrase (participial phrase) and verb phrase
9. subordinate clause
10. verb phrase
11. subordinate clause
12. prepositional phrase
13. subordinate clause
14. subordinate clause and prepositional phrase
15. prepositional phrase
16. verbal phrase (participial phrase and gerund phrase)
17. verb phrase and verbal phrase (participial)
18. verb phrase
19. verbal phrase (participial phrase)
20. verb phrase

47. STARTING AND ENDING

Answers will vary.

48. PHRASES AND CLAUSES AND MORE

1.	C.	Infinitive Phrase
2.	A.	Sentence
3.	D.	Participial Phrase
4.	B.	Gerund Phrase
5.	D.	Participial Phrase
6.	E.	Subordinate or Dependent Clause
7.	E.	Subordinate or Dependent Clause
8.	B.	Gerund Phrase
9.	D.	Participial Phrase
10.	C.	Infinitive Phrase
11.	A.	Sentence
12.	F.	Run-On
13.	E.	Subordinate or Dependent Clause
14.	B.	Gerund Phrase
15.	C.	Infinitive Phrase
16.	A.	Sentence
17.	F.	Run-On
18.	F.	Run-On

49. WIN'S NINE LIVES

Here are acceptable sentences. There are other possibilities.

1. (verb phrase) The current tennis champion has won four straight sets.
2. (gerund phrase) Winning the championship was not easy for our squad.
3. (participial phrase) Winning the second game, the New York Mets were on a hot streak.
4. (infinitive phrase) She certainly wanted to win the big contest.
5. (adverb phrase) The champion was serving for the win.
6. (adjective phrase) His point for the win was very exciting.
7. (adverb clause) Because she was able to win, Brianne advanced to the next round.
8. (adjective clause) This was the game that they had to win.
9. (noun clause) The champion will be whoever notches the next win.

50. WEATHERING THESE PHRASES, CLAUSES, AND SENTENCES

The *phrases* are: after the hurricane (S), before the flood (T), during the summer months (O), in the beginning (R), and since the morning show (M).

The *clauses* are: after all the papers are delivered (W), after the storm subsided (I), as soon as the moon wanes (N), unless you find a better way to do it (D), and when these cars make the turn (Y).

The *sentences* are: if you fix the cabinet, I can help you reinstall it (S), it is raining now (L), let us mend the fences (E), when you see her, tell her I miss her (E), and you should read more magazines (T).

The three words related to weather are *storm*, *windy*, and *sleet*.

51. FILLING IN THE BLANKS

These are possible answers.

1. He went slowly.
2. Cheryl received an award.
3. Is this your shoe?
4. Bring it here.
5. She and I will go with you.
6. Never do that again.
7. Stacey looked curiously at me.
8. When she sings, we listen.
9. The small package arrived in the morning.
10. I was shocked to hear the news.
11. As soon as it occurred, we reacted intelligently.
12. The picture that Hector purchased was in great condition.
13. I often remember what you told me.
14. They are the happiest members of the club.
15. After the concert, we went to eat.

52. COMBATING THIRTEEN

1. ar	4. ts	7. an	10. ck	12. en
2. ab	5. fo	8. da	11. yp	13. ny
3. bi	6. ot	9. lu		

<u>A rabbit's foot and a lucky penny</u> help to combat 13, a number some people think is unlucky.

53. WHY?

1. It begins with a preposition and ends with a noun; it is not a sentence.
2. It is a prepositional phrase; it modifies the noun *desk*.
3. It is a prepositional phrase; it tells *where* they walked.
4. It is not a complete thought; it begins with a subordinating conjunction and has a subject and a verb.
5. It depends on the independent clause to complete the thought; it begins with a subordinating conjunction and has a subject and a verb.
6. It is not a complete thought; it does not have a subject.
7. A comma has been incorrectly inserted between the independent clauses; a semicolon should join these two independent clauses.
8. It issues a command; it is a complete thought with a subject and verb (*you understood*) included.
9. It has a subject and a verb, but it is not a complete thought; it begins with a relative pronoun.
10. There are two complete sentences; a punctuation mark should be inserted between them.

54. SINGING ALONG

1. Sentence (S)
2. Phrase (P)
3. Clause (C)
4. Sentence (S)
5. Sentence (S)
6. Phrase (P)
7. Sentence (S)
8. Phrase (P)
9. Phrase (P)
10. Clause (C)
11. Clause (C)
12. Sentence (S)
13. Sentence (S)
14. Clause (C)
15. Sentence (S)
16. Sentence (S)
17. Phrase (P)
18. Clause (C)
19. Sentence (S)
20. Sentence (S)

55. TWO SENTENCES TELL IT ALL!

1. the
2. cat
3. our
4. constantly
5. into our yard
6. adjective
7. that constantly comes into our yard
8. since the Smiths went skiing in Colorado
9. skiing
10. Smiths
11. past
12. verb
13. not
14. prepositional
15. adverbial

SECTION THREE
SENTENCES—GRAMMAR'S GALAXY!

56. THE COMMON WORD

Answers will vary.

57. ODD ONE OUT

1. O	5. E	9. E
2. F	6. A	10. I
3. F	7. T	11. R
4. B	8. W	12. D

The two words associated with odd are *offbeat* and *weird*.

58. UNSCRAMBLING THE SENTENCES

These are possible sentences. There could be others.

1. Take a rest.
2. Can you finish the test?
3. This is a beautiful day!
4. Some of them will be there.
5. Tom has been awarded a scholarship.
6. If you can help him, please do so.
7. The bracelet that you found is pretty.
8. She wrote her dad an interesting note.
9. Paula and he will represent our group.
10. My car has been in the repair shop for the past two days.
11. When you decide to go to the meeting, I want to go with you.
12. After you complete this sentence, take a break.

59. MAKING SENSE

These are acceptable sentences. There may be others.

1. Bring it here.
2. Do you see it?
3. He enjoys eating ravioli.
4. They will recharge their batteries.
5. Scientists have already researched the situation.
6. NASA is under pressure to succeed.
7. Did they hear anything about it?
8. It is time to talk about the weather.
9. The humidity is slowly increasing.
10. We have read most of Bernard Malamud's stories.
11. You will not understand all of it.
12. Call me when you hear the radio announcement.

60. SOME GOOD ADVICE

      v   adj n prep n c p v   v prep v p/a   n
1. "Destroy the seed of evil or it will grow to be your ruin."

      adj   n   v adj n
2. "Clumsy jesting is no joke."

       p advb   v   p v advb adj prep p
3. "We often despise what is most useful to us."

      adj   n   v adj   p/a   n v adj
4. "Every ruler is harsh whose rule is new."

      advb   v   adj   n   prep adj n prep   n
5. "Never trust the advice of a man in difficulties."

61. LET'S GET SOME ORDER HERE!

There may be other ways to reconstruct these sentences.

1. We went to the store yesterday.
2. This is the best reason!
3. Can they play these video games now?
4. Since she is so tall, she will play center.
5. Keep in touch with one another.

6. The wind continued to blow the leaves around the yard.
7. Jim's valise was left near the front door.
8. Yesterday the sun was roasting the picnickers.
9. Will you return my book to the library?
10. Please forgive and forget.
11. You know you make me laugh when you say that.
12. This is a very typical family.
13. Push the button, and your change will drop down.
14. They charged us extra for the mashed potatoes.
15. Can you remember when that event occurred?

62. CONSECUTIVE LETTERS

These are acceptable answers. There may be others.

1. Brad called Debbie excitedly.
2. Lately my niece opines pretty quickly.
3. King Leo made nothing official.
4. Since Ted understand violins well,
5. Because children do enjoy friends,
6. Although bees can dart easily,
7. If Joe kids Linda,
8. is thinking this through
9. had irritated kids
10. Selling ten umbrellas,

63. FIRST AND FOREMOST

These are possible sentences.

1. (w) We wondered when we would walk with Wally.
2. (f) Freddie found five fantastic films.
3. (t) The tremendous tournament topped the television tonight.
4. (o) Only ordinary officers obey occasionally.
5. (c) Can Chester choose certain choice clusters?
6. (s) Surely servants seek such solutions.
7. (b) Brilliant Barbara bought bright bulbs.
8. (g) Glad girls gave gorgeous George gifts.
9. (h) Has Hank had his host hoist his heirloom?
10. (p) Perhaps pretty pictures pervade Paul's private palace.

64. STEP BY STEP

These are acceptable sentences. There can be others.

1. Rob ran swiftly.

   During the race Rob ran swiftly.

   During the race Rob and Dan ran swiftly.

   During the race at Morris High School, Rob and Dan ran swiftly.

2. You sang.

   You and Gary sang.

   You and Gary sang nightly.

   During that time you and Gary sang nightly.

3. They gave Tom a present.

   They gave Tom a present with little fanfare.

   For his birthday they gave Tom a present with little fanfare.

   Did they, with little fanfare, give Tom a present for his birthday?

4. Liz fell accidentally.

   Liz fell accidentally on the dance floor.

   When she was at her prom, Liz fell accidentally on the dance floor.

65. THE STUFF OF SENTENCES

These are sample answers.

1. I drive
2. I will drive
3. I will drive slowly
4. I will drive slowly and
5. I will drive slowly, and
6. I will drive slowly, and she will
7. I will drive slowly, and she will run
8. I will drive slowly, and she will run quickly
9. I will drive slowly in my new car, and she will run quickly
10. I will drive slowly in my new car, and she will run quickly on the sidewalk.

66. DOING WHAT'S REQUIRED

These are acceptable sentences.

1. The car in the parking lot is white.
2. Are you removing the paint from the can now?
3. I am your partner.
4. It is Friday, and tomorrow we will go to the amusement park.
5. Once they moved from here, the neighborhood changed.
6. I am who I am.
7. The painting that you bought is priceless.
8. When did Christine start the project?
9. Do it now!
10. She turned and looked at the new arrivals.

67. TIME AND TIDE WAIT FOR NO MAN! (SO MANY A PHILOSOPHER HAS SAID)

These are acceptable sentences. There are others.

1. Time seems to agree with you.
2. Regina is both creative and wise.
3. The tide made it almost impossible for us to use our sailboat.
4. Wait for the handsome and interesting guide to show us how to get there.
5. For us to feel safe, we needed to contact the police.
6. No official spoke candidly or realistically about the dilemma.
7. A man saw a woman.

A. So that she could be in the ballet company, Cathy practiced very hard.
B. Many people love to go skiing here.
C. A tiger is a feared and interesting creature.
D. Justin often spent Tuesdays and Fridays in the library studying the life of his favorite philosopher.
E. Has the movie begun?
F. "I really think that this is the house we want to buy," Martina said to Larry.

68. IN THE BEGINNING AND AT THE END

These are possible sentences. There may be others.

1. After the game, the players rested comfortably.
2. When the sun came out again, the children went swimming.
3. Sitting in the bleachers, the fans cheered for their team.
4. You are my best friend.
5. They are beautiful.
6. Carole was certainly dancing beautifully.
7. Carlos was running because he was late for English class.
8. Whether you stay or go, we will be shopping in the mall.
9. Roberta and Helena were talking and laughing.
10. Venice is a city that I would like to visit soon.
11. Skiing in those particular mountains was exciting for our family members.
12. To win these matches was important for the young contestant.
13. After the show we went into the kitchen.
14. Inaction can be quite upsetting.
15. Bravely, Kim moved the children away from the rabid dog.

69. SOPHISTICATION IS IN

These are acceptable sentences. There are, of course, many other ways to combine these groups of sentences.

1. The girl who has two sisters is tall and smart.
2. The movie star in his sports car waved to us.
3. My mother bought a new, red, oval rug for $300.
4. Tonight, for about 45 minutes in my bedroom, I will read our English class assignment, three chapters from *The Adventures of Tom Sawyer*.
5. Since it is sunny today, we will go to the beach this afternoon and take our supper.
6. Because my other CD player broke last month, I hope that my brother, who went shopping for my birthday present today, bought me a new CD player.
7. The police searched for the Kenson's missing car, a new Chrysler.
8. Our family physician told my dad to get more exercise, reduce his cholesterol, and improve his eating habits.
9. Yesterday, after oil was spilled on the road near our house, we called the hazardous materials bureau workers who took care of the problem immediately.
10. My cousin and her husband, a man she had dated for three years, recently married and spent their week-long honeymoon in South America.

70. SHOWING YOUR BUILDING SKILLS

Answers will vary.

71. TWO (OR MORE) INTO ONE

These are acceptable sentences. Of course, there are many other ways to combine these sentences.

1. Now that I am eighteen, I can drive.
2. Geraldo, a talented, professional magician, can perform many interesting tricks.
3. When Marina heard a knock at the door, she went to answer it.
4. The sun was shining, the wind was blowing, and the children were playing in the fields.
5. She drove her car, a new convertible.
6. My father spends much time working in our garden full of beautiful plants and flowers.
7. New photographs hang on the walls of their newly decorated bedroom.
8. I will have to go to the library to get more information for our seven-page English assignment focusing on Mark Twain.
9. Because the Taggert family had to put their old cat to sleep, Nancy was especially saddened.
10. She brought her computer that needed costly repairs to the local computer store.

72. PUTTING THE WORDS IN THEIR PLACES

The six original sentences are:

We read two newspapers carefully.
Her watch needed to be repaired.
It has been raining throughout the day.
Did you fix the living room light?
The heavy snow caused many traffic problems.
Some of the town's residents opposed the new plan.

73. I LOVE TO COMB YOUR HAIR, JOE!

These are possible sentences. There are others.
1. Remember to comb your hair, Joe.
2. He will remember the way to comb your hair.
3. I love to remember your usual way.
4. Then you will never cut hair!
5. Then you can lose a car, Joe!
6. Never can he remember the usual way.
7. You can lose your way in a car.
8. I will cut and comb your hair.
9. Then remember the car on your way.
10. Can you remember your way to the car, Joe?

74. WRITING A SHORT, SHORT STORY

Answers will vary.

75. ARE YOU UP TO THE CHALLENGE?

1. com   interrogative
2. pet   complex
3. iti   complex
4. onb   exclamatory
5. rin   complex
6. gso   complex
7. utt   compound
8. heb   simple
9. est   complex
10. (an   compound
11. dwo   imperative
12. rst   imperative
13.)in   compound-complex
14. peo   declarative
15. ple   simple

The correct choices spell out "Competition brings out the best (and worst) in people."

76. WHAT TYPE OF SENTENCE IS THIS?

1. simple
2. complex
3. compound
4. complex
5. compound

6. compound-complex
7. simple
8. simple
9. compound-complex
10. compound

11. compound
12. compound-complex
13. simple
14. complex
15. compound

77. DOING THE DIAGRAMMING

1.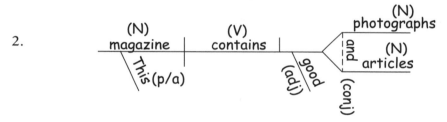

2.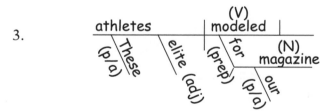

3.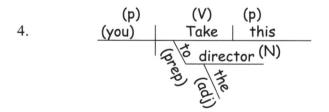

4.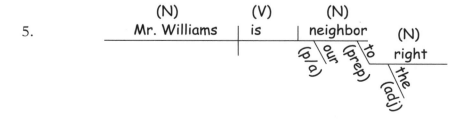

5.

78. DECIPHERING THE DIAGRAMMING

    adj   adj   n   v advb   v
1. The fancy clothes were not purchased.

    adj advb   adj   n   advb   v
2. A very intelligent student usually excels.

    adj   n   v advb
3. Both recordings sold well.

    Adj adj c   adj   n   v   c   v   advb
4. The tall and handsome models spoke and walked gracefully.

79. MATCHING THE DIAGRAMS

A. (4)

B. (1)

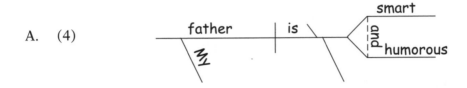

C. (3)

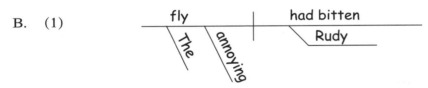

D. (5)

E. (2)

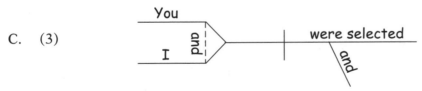

80. TO SPLICE IS NOT SO NICE

The comma splices are numbers 2, 5, 7, 8, 13, 14, 15, 17, and 19.

81. THE SENTENCE POEM

Answers will vary.

SECTION FOUR
USAGE—A WAY WITH WORDS!

82. GRAMMAR VOCABULARY

A=13	B=3	C=6	D=12
E=8	F=10	G=15	H=1
I=11	J=5	K=4	L=14
M=2	N=16	O=9	P=7

83. GRAMMAR SPANNING

A=7	B=11	C=6	D=10
E=14	F=2	G=15	H=3
I=12	J=8	K=9	L=5
M=1	N=13	O=4	P=16

84. JUGGLING THE IRREGULARS

Present	Past	Past Participle	Present	Past	Past Participle
1. go	went	gone	11. speak	spoke	spoken
2. eat	ate	eaten	12. choose	chose	chosen
3. know	knew	known	13. write	wrote	written
4. swim	swam	swum	14. ring	rang	rung
5. begin	began	begun	15. do	did	done
6. freeze	froze	frozen	16. put	put	put
7. bring	brought	brought	17. shrink	shrank	shrunk
8. break	broke	broken	18. take	took	taken
9. burst	burst	burst	19. throw	threw	thrown
10. give	gave	given	20. steal	stole	stolen

85. A PRO WITH PRONOUNS

The number after each pronoun indicates the number of letters in that pronoun.

GROUP 1

1. I (1)
2. her (3)
3. he (2)
4. We (2)
5. he (2)
6. me (2)
7. me (2)
8. who (3)
9. Who (3)
10. I (1)

GROUP 2

11. me (2)
12. she (3)
13. Who (3)
14. whom (4)
15. whom (4)
16. He (2)
17. him (3)
18. are (3)
19. who (3)
20. it (2)

The Group 1 total is 21.

The Group 2 total is 29.

86. HOW IRREGULAR!

1. chosen	6. know	11. say	16. spoken
2. grown	7. driven	12. eaten	17. swum
3. led	8. begun	13. crept	18. sung
4. seen	9. burst	14. come	19. written
5. rode	10. borne	15. broke	20. swore

87. THE SUBJECTS OF SCIENCE

1. days	6. Annapolis	11. Part	16. regulars
2. Interest	7. machine	12. Halloween	17. toddler
3. All	8. graduation	13. Children	18. Many
4. Georgia	9. regiment	14. hound	19. activity
5. realization	10. attorney	15. album	20. Protocol

The four words you hear in science class are <u>diagram</u>, <u>graph</u>, <u>chart</u>, and <u>map</u>.

88. BROADWAY BOUND

The subject is listed first; the main verb follows.

1. We enter	8. Everything sold
2. Several tried	9. Much includes
3. Suicide is	10. search entered
4. delicacies enjoyed	11. Raymond acted
5. Some tossed	12. bundle left
6. others restore	13. Each serve
7. You lose	

The two Broadway plays are *West Side Story* and *Les Miserables*.

89. THINKING ABOUT THE PAST

The correct form of each incorrect past tense verb is as follows.

2. burst	13. ran
3. chose	14. shook
5. drew	16. shrank
6. drank	18. tore
9. gave	19. wore

90. FIVE ADJECTIVES

1. scientist	6. intelligence	11. anybody	16. beautiful
2. like	7. cautious	12. deer	17. beautician
3. ornery	8. heart	13. noticed	18. ordered
4. Wendy	9. groaned	14. umbrella	19. lease
5. radios	10. letter	15. member	20. ditch

The five adjectives are <u>slow</u>, <u>rich</u>, <u>glad</u>, <u>numb</u>, and <u>bold</u>.

91. MUSICALLY INCLINED

The ten words are: actually, aimlessly, entirely, eventually, hoisted, loosely, my, tremendously, very, and youthfully. Their first letters spell out Heavy Metal.

92. YOU RAISE A SON, BUT A SUN RISES

1. choose	6. burst	11. taken
2. begun	7. torn	12. flown
3. rose	8. risen	13. used
4. set	9. lying	14. asked
5. sitting	10. laid	15. made

The words are <u>sure</u>, <u>turn</u>, <u>yak</u>, and <u>weed</u>.

93. GETTING PERSONAL

A=7	B=11	C=6	D=10
E=14	F=2	G=15	H=3
I=12	J=8	K=9	L=5
M=1	N=13	O=4	P=16

94. SOMETHING'S WRONG HERE—HALF THE TIME

3. buy
6. knew
7. too
9. heel
10. affect

13. scene
14. whether
16. You're
17. then
19. number (not amount)

The saying is, "Rome wasn't built in a day."

95. JUST IN CASE

Numbers 2, 5, and 6 are nominative and spell *Mark Twain*.
Numbers 1, 8, and 9 are objective and spell *Judy Blume*.
Numbers 3, 4, 7, and 10 are possessive and spell *Thomas Edison*.

96. LET'S EXAMINE THOSE CASES!

The Ns are sentence numbers 5, 8, 12, and 15. The Os are sentence numbers 4, 9, 16, 17, and 19. The Ps are sentence numbers 1, 3, 7, 10, 11, 13, 14, 18, and 20. The NOs are sentence numbers 2 and 6.

97. CASING OUT THE PUZZLE

```
L  H  D  H  I  X  Y  P  P  H  T  H  H  E  R  S  P  X  B  V
J  S  X  B  Z  T  D  Q  C  X  P  H  S  X  T  C  B  P  J  H
P  P  S  N  S  S  K  C  X  C  P  N  E  R  R  V  P  V  S  B
M  X  G  Q  M  T  K  H  R  G  W  P  T  I  R  Z  F  B  W  Z
D  D  K  R  R  F  D  F  L  V  M  H  H  Z  R  K  Q  L  N  Q
M  W  F  T  X  S  X  F  C  X  H  F  P  W  G  S  F  N  K  G
L  B  M  K  W  R  L  V  Y  Z  Z  R  F  R  J  D  W  L  Z  C
Z  Y  M  M  C  J  J  R  W  O  G  F  O  C  K  V  K  S  J  E
Z  W  H  L  B  N  B  R  T  N  U  W  U  N  Y  S  H  L  N  K
Q  Q  P  I  S  V  W  M  H  J  R  R  R  D  O  H  Y  I  W  G
Z  W  D  U  S  X  S  Q  E  R  B  S  S  X  U  E  M  E  M  T
V  Q  M  C  D  K  S  H  Y  H  T  Z  D  Z  P  E  W  V  H  H
Z  M  S  H  M  V  S  J  M  I  J  P  L  Z  H  N  M  C  Q  N
K  Q  C  N  S  G  F  J  K  R  Y  B  X  T  Y  M  V  B  X  F
X  B  T  D  X  N  C  Q  C  W  D  F  J  H  X  L  K  K  V
```

The strictly nominative case pronouns are *he, she, they,* and *we.*

The strictly objective case pronouns are *him, me, them,* and *us.*

The strictly possessive case pronouns are *his, its, mine, my, ours, theirs,* and *yours.*

Her is both objective and possessive. *You* and *it* are both nominative and objective.

98. DON'T OBJECT TO THESE THIRTY OBJECTS!

              OP
1. Many prizes were given to the children.

          IO   DO
2. My sister and he gave them another present.

              DO   OP
3. When will the director post the list of characters?

          DO   OP
4. John delivered his speeches to small crowds.

         IO   DO   OP
5. His psychiatrist wrote him a prescription for a new medication.

                                       DO   OP

6. This Chicago highway always offers an interesting view of the city's skyline.

            IO   DO   OP   OP

7. Give Serena the list of books to borrow from the library.

                  OP   OP

8. Some of these grapes were bought at this store.

            IO   DO   OP

9. Mike lent Sam twenty dollars for the tickets.

                         DO

10. Have these activities inspired Brett?

                     DO   OP

11. You have yet to submit a poor excuse to the teacher.

                  IO   DO

12. The DVD player gave the family another electronic device.

          DO

13. See no evil.

             DO   OP

14. Dad has cooked salmon for you.

               DO

15. An apple a day keeps the doctor away.

99. IS THAT OBJECT A SIGN?

1. yes A	6. no O	11. no C	16. yes G
2. yes R	7. yes E	12. yes I	17. no P
3. no L	8. yes S	13. yes R	18. yes O
4. yes I	9. yes V	14. no O	19. no I
5. no E	10. no S	15. no R	20. no O

The Yes line spells out Aries and Virgo.

The No line spells out Leo and Scorpio.

All four are astrological *signs*.

100. THE FARMER GREW MY YOUNGER BROTHER?

The correct sentences are numbers 3, 4, 6, 7, 13, 14, 15, and 17. The following are acceptable corrected sentences. There are other ways to correct the misplaced modifier problem in each sentence.

2. The view was enjoyed by my sister sitting on the dock.
5. My gym teacher, nearing the end of the marathon, spotted the finish line.
8. The accident was seen by the young girl looking out the window.
9. Having finished her term paper, Darlene walked the dog.
10. My family, visiting New York City for the first time, saw the Statue of Liberty, a popular attraction.
11. Looking for Commerce Street, his wife perused the map.
12. The sun was too bright for me relaxing on the beach chair.
16. Burnt in the oven, the charred bread was taken out by the chef.
18. Jasmine, yawning from the long day, spotted the moon.

101. WHEN TOO MUCH IS TOO MUCH!

These are acceptable answers. There may be others.

1. Her beautiful hair was brown.
2. Presently, there are no plans to construct another bridge to the island.
3. The bank robber was later murdered by the guard.
4. If you open an account in our bank, you will receive a gift.
5. What will be the result of all these arguments about the budget?
6. The characters made me laugh throughout the novel.
7. Let's study all the history about that war now.
8. Since our treasury is almost depleted, we need to think of ways to raise money.
9. Those basketball players are tall.
10. Most of these models are quite handsome.
11. Here is a check for $350.
12. I would like to reflect on the old days.
13. I do not think we had received notice.
14. Do you want me to repeat the directions?
15. This gift is for my parents' thirty-fifth anniversary.
16. Kenny really has no use for those imports.
17. The police think that it was an accident.
18. How many innovations made that big a difference this decade?
19. This day marks the end of our time together.
20. This is the start of the novel.

102. IT'S ALL HAPPENING AT THE ZOO

The correct answers spell out "These Are a Few of My Favorite Things."
The incorrect answers spell out "Climb Every Mountain."
The corrections are as follows:

2. *their* should be *his (or hers)*
8. *tiger's* should be *tigers'*
9. *ate* should be *eaten*
11. *Less* should be *Fewer*
12. *Everywheres* should be *Everywhere*
13. *guides'* should be *guides*
14. *was* should be *were*; *then* should be *than*
15. *besides* should be *beside*

103. MAKING CHANGES

Though there are other possibilities, these are acceptable changes.

1. A toy was found under the shelf.
2. Both of the choices are good ones.
3. Persons (People) are not expected to tolerate such rude behavior from their friends.
4. Hank is quite happy to see you.
5. One of the animals built his (or her) home across the river.
6. Here are some notes for you.
7. Five dollars is not a high asking price for that.
8. Jane is the better of those two dancers.
9. There was much philosophical disagreement among the four states.
10. Why doesn't this driver change his (or her) schedule?
11. All the tires in this store are on sale today.
12. I know that Jamey and Kate are at the store.
13. The gifts are these cards.
14. Edie devised her own skit.
15. Were any of the breads eaten?

104. HOW AGREEABLE!

The sentences that display correct subject–verb agreement are numbers 1, 3, 4, 6, 8, 9, 10, 11, and 14. These total 66.

105. DON'T GET NONE OF THESE QUESTIONS WRONG!

Though there may be other ways to correct the double negative problems in these sentences, these are acceptable corrections.

1. We do not need any education.
2. I cannot get any satisfaction.
3. They can hardly run the required distance.
4. Harry does not have any reason to complain.
5. These seagulls never resist the waste receptacles at the beach.
6. Our choir members can scarcely hear the director's cue.
7. It really does not make any difference to them.
8. When we looked for disposable razors on the shelf in the drugstore, we found that there were none.
9. Unfortunately, the search party has found none of the missing airplane parts.
10. My mother couldn't locate any of the other Web sites.
11. After doing so many pushups, Benny could hardly lift his arms.
12. Our treasurer reported that we have but fifty dollars left in our account.
13. You do not need any fancy tools to do that job, Martin.
14. Some of the bird watchers haven't spotted any of the orioles.
15. There is no way that I am going to fall for his silly tricks!

106. EXPLAIN WHY!

1. The correct verb should be _was_ since _Each_ is a singular subject.
2. The correct word is _way_, not _weigh_.
3. _I_ should be replaced by _me_ since _me_ is in the objective case.
4. The word _ain't_ is slang. Replace it with _isn't_ or _is not_.
5. The correct adverb is _really_, not _real_.
6. Replace _better_ with _best_ since _best_ is the superlative degree.
7. There is a verb tense problem. The word _traveled_ is correct since it is a past tense verb.
8. _Block_ is not the correct word. A group is a _bloc_.
9. Use _visiting the Caribbean_ since parallel structure (all _-ing_ endings) is needed.
10. The correct form is different _from_, not different _than_.
11. _Morale_ means spirit, as in a team's morale. A _moral_ is an intended message.
12. _He_ is the needed nominative case word. _Him_ is in the objective case. A subject must be a nominative word.
13. The restrictive clause should begin with _that_ and not _who_.

14. This is a misplaced modifier problem. It should read, "Burning in the oven, the chicken was taken out by the man."

15. This is a conjunction problem. The correlative conjunction that teams with *neither* is *nor*, not *or*.

107. THE OLD "WHO VERSUS WHOM" PROBLEM

The *who* answers are numbers 1, 2, 3, 6, 8, 9, 11, and 13.
The *whom* answers are numbers 4, 5, 7, 10, 12, 14, and 15.

108. WHAT ON EARTH?

1. E us	6. H her	11. H she
2. A me	7. A whom	12. E I
3. R whom	8. T she	13. A me
4. T We	9. E he	14. R me
5. H she	10. R he	15. T she

These three words are <u>earth</u>, <u>hater</u>, and <u>heart</u>. All three words are composed of the exact same five letters.

SECTION FIVE
MECHANICS—THE TOOLS OF THE TRADE!

109. IS THAT WHAT IT IS?

A=1	B=15	C=8	D=10
E=4	F=14	G=5	H=11
I=13	J=3	K=12	L=6
M=16	N=2	O=9	P=7

110. TELEPHONE SPELLING

Answers will vary.

111. A CAPITAL OFFENSE . . . NOT GETTING 37!

1. I am going to go to Shea Stadium with my family this Saturday night.
2. Do you think that geometry is harder than English?
3. Her favorite musical group is playing at Radio City Music Hall in February.
4. The people who come over the Canadian border are stopped by the police officials there.
5. Clinton County in New York is a beautiful upstate area.
6. Did you study the debates between Kennedy and Nixon?
7. Maurice Richard was an outstanding hockey player years ago.
8. *The Last of the Mohicans* was written by Cooper.
9. We visited several Japanese and Chinese restaurants on our vacation.
10. We love to celebrate Mother's Day in May and Father's Day in June each year.

112. SPELLING MNEMONICS (PART ONE)

Here are possible mnemonics. Of course, students can devise others.

1. all right: all right is better than all wrong
2. amiable: Ami is very aMIAble.
3. beginning: Beg to start the inning in the BEGINNING.
4. buoyant A buoy is BUOYant.
5. cadence: We heard the caDENce in the DEN.
6. charlatan: The charlaTAN had a tan.
7. clientele: The Brit saw his clienTELE on the tele.
8. collaborate: When we collaborATEd, first we did the labor, and then we ate.
9. competent: A pet is usually comPETent.
10. controversy: In a contROVERSy no e follows the ROVERS.
11. denounce: Do you DENOUNCE the OUNCE after the DEN?
12. dissect: Slice the 2 s's when you diSSect.
13. gallery: There is GALL in the GALLery.
14. indomitable: Can you OMIT those who are ABLE , those indOMITABLE ones?
15. navigator: The naviGATOR had a GATOR in him.

113. SPELLING MNEMONICS (PART TWO)

Here are possible mnemonics. Of course, students can devise others.

1. optimistic: TIM is always opTIMistic.
2. paramount: PA and RA on the MOUNT thought they were PARAMOUNT.
3. pessimistic: Try to be LESS pESSimistic.
4. promenade: The PRO MEN drink ADE while they promenade.
5. protagonist: A proTAGONist loves to TAG ON.
6. reprimand: RE is PRIM and loves to REPRIMAND others.
7. sedentary: A seDENTary person might DENT the cushion.
8. separate: We will use par to sePARate the golfers.
9. submission: The SUB was on a MISSION to deliver her submission.
10. tantalize: TANTALI loves to ZING with his not so tantalizing remarks.
11. tutor: Either King TUT OR his tutor will be remembered.
12. veneer: E's are the only vowels that appear in vEnEEr.
13. villain: A villAIN ends the same as the rAIN.
14. volatile: VOLA knew that TILE was not volatile.
15. wrangle: What is the best ANGLE to wrANGLE?

114. MUSICALLY SPEAKING

1. lady's (O)	6. hers (U)	11. aren't (T)
2. theirs (I)	7. Tom and Lucy's (D)	12. e's (P)
3. Whose (M)	8. Sherry's (R)	13. Someone's (A)
4. Everybody's (A)	9. else's (N)	14. Chris's (R)
5. bosses' (I)	10. years' (U)	15. Sheep's (G)

The three musical instruments are <u>piano</u>, <u>drum</u>, and <u>guitar</u>.

115. UNLUCKY SEVEN

Numbers, 2, 3, 5, 8, 9, 16, and 17 are incorrect. Here are the correct versions.

2. students' records
3. druggist's lotion
5. radios' sounds
8. your bicycle

9. women's room
16. box's side
17. four cents' worth

116. GETTING TECHNICAL AND STAYING EVEN

The titles that require italics, bold letters, or underlining (and have been assigned the number 1 for this activity) are numbers 1, 2, 4, 7, 9, 11, 12, and 13.

The titles that require quotation marks (and have been assigned the number 2 for this activity) are numbers 3, 5, 6, 8, 10, 14, 15, and 16.

117. THE COMMA COUNT IS THIRTY-TWO

1. Murray, will you please send this letter to Duluth, Minnesota?
2. To tell you the truth, you really should have made the team.
3. The couple married on Saturday, August 25, 1973, on Long Island, New York.
4. Our chef considered roast beef, veal, chicken, and steak as possible entrees.
5. When you reach the department store on the corner of Main Street and Hudson Avenue, turn left.
6. Jesse is a warm, playful puppy.
7. Irene left the game, but we decided to stay until it was over.
8. I am sure that I can go to the movies, but I question whether they will decide to go.
9. Marcia Smithers, who is a television news personality, has a great delivery.
10. *Oliver Twist*, written by Charles Dickens, is a popular read for English majors during their college years.
11. Selecting the smaller home, the family members knew that they could be happy there.
12. By the stream behind our junior high school, our science class conducted several experiments.
13. Yes, the correct answer is letter A!
14. Until the rowdy neighbors choose to act differently, others will be adversely affected.
15. Jeremiah, of course, was a bullfrog.
16. My dad, however, does not see it the same way as I do.
17. Mark, I assume, will go along with the new arrangements.
18. This political candidate is, in one man's opinion, the best qualified.
19. Please send the announcement to Seaford, Delaware.
20. Her birth date was March 24, 1980.

118. COMING ALONG WITH COMMAS

1. D March 24, 1980, was a very special day.
2. A Do you remember Artie Sherwood, the former mayor?
3. C Roberto, will you help with these packages?
4. E Most sincerely,
5. F The relentless, aggressive defense continued to hound the quarterback.
6. B Mickey Mantle, I think, was one of the most popular players of his day.
7. F Here are the priceless, oft-talked about diamonds.
8. E Yours truly,
9. B In truth, the essential question was not asked.
10. B They did not, however, remember to close the door behind them.
11. A The subject of last night's program, obesity, has become a major concern.
12. D Do you remember how important July 31, 1977, was for all of us?
13. C There are many reasons why you should be there, Juan and Carlos.
14. A Jaspers, the nickname of the Manhattan College teams, was written on the poster.
15. C The reason, my friends, is easy for all of us to see.
16. E Dearest Grandmother,
17. F This is certainly a beautiful, engaging poem.
18. D The family has moved to 65443 Georgetown Boulevard, Wesleyville, Ohio.

119. THE VERSATILE COMMA

1. E Well, is this your final answer?
2. G In her depiction of young children, the author displays great sensitivity.
3. A I would like to ask her to the prom, and I hope she will accept.
4. B While the doctor reviewed the patient's records, the nurse helped explain the options.
5. D Mitch Carter, who won the tennis tournament last year, has moved to Seattle.
6. F Reset by the doctor, Karen's forearm mended well.
7. C Her birthday presents included a bracelet, CD player, and a trip to Holland.
8. G Over the river and through the woods, the children ran to grandmother's house.
9. G Near the door to the smaller gym, I left my equipment.
10. C The test was long, boring, and very difficult.
11. B Unless these dinners are not reheated, they will not be very tasty.
12. B As soon as the tree was cut down, the workers began to chop it up.
13. E Why, I did not know that!
14. E No, this is not the best way to the highway.
15. A This is a beautiful painting, but I think it is overpriced.

16. F Drafted by Vancouver, the basketball player was later traded to Houston.
17. F Purchased last year, Dad's car already has 20,400 miles on it.
18. A Either you can drive there yourself, or we can arrange to have you driven.
19. C He called upon his friends, his teachers, and even his enemies for help in the trying situation.
20. D Edison, who invented many useful products, is known as The Wizard of Menlo Park.
21. D *An American Tragedy*, written by Theodore Dreiser, depicts the problems inherent in the American Dream.

Note: The comma after the second item in numbers 7, 10, and 19 does not have to be included.

120. IS A SEMICOLON HALF A COLON?

1. Initially, I was going to memorize my speech; then I decided to read it.
2. The first five answers are as follows: A, B, B, D, and C.
3. Mr. Pryal, our English teacher, said that we must read the following books: *Ethan Frome, Catcher in the Rye,* and *I Know Why the Caged Bird Sings.*
4. This is a great location; moreover, the price is also quite agreeable.
5. Please meet her by the ticket station no later than 6:30 A.M.
6. These boxes should be enough for now; however, we do need to order more of them immediately.
7. I chose not to apply for the summer camp position; instead, I will work in the carpenter shop with my uncle.
8. We discussed Genesis 26:20-25 in class today.
9. You have done extremely well on your state tests; consequently, you have earned a noteworthy citation.
10. Our treasury needs replenishing; furthermore, we must decide to do that immediately.
11. Two of the vans need repair; therefore, the principal has decided to rent a bus for the trip.
12. The mail arrived at exactly 9:30 A.M.
13. We will select a new representative; accordingly, we will need to have names submitted by the people.
14. Our plumbing problem has been repaired; hence, we can start to fill the swimming pool.
15. Our teacher described the various parts of the plot: background, initial incident, rising action, climax, falling action, and denouement.

Semicolons (1, 4, 6, 7, 9, 10, 11, 13, and 14): "You should always practice what you preach."

Colons (2, 3, 5, 8, 12, and 15): "Seize the great times in life."

121. HALF A HUNDRED AND YOU'RE HOME!

1. Have you ever heard Mariah Carey sing "Love Takes Time" or Spin Doctors sing "Two Princes?"
2. What do the members of the Veterans of Foreign War group intend to do for the Fourth of July?
3. When Fordham University plays Manhattan College, there is much excitement.
4. *Time* and *Fortune* are two magazines that Mr. Jackson reads each weekend.
5. *The New York Times* is an outstanding daily newspaper.
6. Edgar Allan Poe's short story, "The Fall of the House of Usher," is more than interesting.
7. At the Denver conference we met people of many different religions.
8. Los Angeles and Vancouver are two beautiful cities near the Pacific Ocean.
9. How far south of New Jersey is Georgia?
10. Officer Thompson and Officer Goodren responded immediately to the call.

122. PUNCTUATING DIALOGUE

"I haven't had time to call you," Steve said to Maria. "What has been happening with you?"

"Nothing much. Same old, same old."

"What are your plans for this summer? Will you be going away to Nova Scotia again?" Jane asked as she opened her pocketbook.

"My entire family will be going to Vermont this July, " Steve said. "I think we will be there for the whole month. We will probably be staying with my father's sister's family, the Robertsons."

With a questioning look, Jane asked," Do you think you will be home in time to try out for the school's soccer team? If you are not there for the week's tryout, you cannot be on the team. Do you think you should speak to Coach Butler before you go away?"

"That's not a bad idea, Jane. I hadn't even thought about that. This could really be a problem, I guess. There's no way my parents will let me stay home by myself though."

With a helpful gesture, Jane asked, "Steve, why don't you have your parents talk to the coach? That might solve the problem."

Steve quickly replied, "

123. PUNCTUATING PROPERLY AND PURPOSEFULLY (PART ONE)

1. After she finished reading the newspaper, Marlene washed the breakfast dishes.
2. These are the U.S. states we will study this month: Nebraska, Kansas, Missouri, and Wisconsin.
3. It's about 12:30 so we should be heading for the fire department's picnic.

4. The best years of Mitch's life were from 1980–1995.
5. Softball tryouts will be held from 10–2:30.
6. We told them that they could stay for one week—and one week only!
7. The house on Webster Street, the one owned by the Murphy family, is quite beautiful.
8. Our family firmly believes in this commandment: Do unto others as you would have them do unto you.
9. Heads up, everybody!
10. But can we believe him?
11. Serena's serve is equal to her sister's serve.
12. The magician worked with the following props: rabbits, handkerchiefs, wands, and hats.
13. Since we were sitting in traffic for over two hours, we arrived home at 11:30.
14. Barbara, the following are the cars that my dad has owned: a 1992 Toyota, a 1995 Cadillac, and a 1998 Dodge.
15. Jill will be moving to Milwaukee, Wisconsin, at the end of August.

124. PUNCTUATING PROPERLY AND PURPOSEFULLY (PART TWO)

1. Billy Joel loves to sing his hit song, "Piano Man."
2. "When," Sylvia asked, "are they going on vacation?"
3. "Molly," Mrs. Glynn, our English teacher, asked, "did Robert Frost write 'And that has made all the difference'?"
4. We shipped out two hundred (200) packages of books, Joe.
5. The evening's main speaker [Donald Trump] was quite informative.
6. "How do the British pronounce the word 'schedule'?" Tim asked.
7. When will they resume the tennis match, Dottie?
8. Please shut the window, Tawana; it is getting cold in here.
9. I like her plan better; furthermore, it will be the more efficient as well.
10. Franco, are you and Pedro, the other assigned officer, patrolling both parades next weekend?
11. The tilde (~) is found on the left side of the keyboard.
12. Unfortunately, this medication did not work; nevertheless, we will continue to pursue other, more effective medications.
13. My mom often tells me, "These are the best times of your life, Christine."
14. James was born on August 27, 1977, in Topeka, Kansas.
15. Our invitees include Dr. William Brennan, chiropractor; Professor Martha Gavigan, literature enthusiast; and Dr. David Gilliam, our keynote speaker.

125. FITTING THEM IN PROPERLY

1. Herman Hesse wrote those two novels, *Siddhartha* and *Steppenwolf*.
2. "Are you," James asked Emma, "going to the playground later?"
3. "Is this the movie guide you misplaced, Sharon?"
4. Was it Shakespeare who wrote, ". . . a pair of star-crossed lovers take their lives"?
5. Almost all the water has evaporated, but I still feel the area is quite slippery.
6. Wishing and hoping, the cheerleaders did their best to remain calm as the judges tallied their votes.
7. The day trader purchased stocks mostly in technology, health care, and farm products.
8. Ryan Smythe is a cordial, warm-hearted employer.
9. Our humble home, located on the corner of Clendon Street and Stuart Road, is 20 years old.
10. These problems that challenged most of my classmates were designed by the college professor.
11. The beach, with its 500 acres and beautiful shoreline, is a valuable tourist attraction for our county.
12. Herman Melville's most successful novel, *Moby Dick*, was published in 1851.
13. Our family's Thanksgiving plans were changed due to the day's inclement weather.
14. Both ambassadors' papers had been reviewed by the mediator.
15. Have you listened to everybody's suggestions?

126. HOW BAD CAN IT GET?

1. Roberto's wallet was found near the sofa.
2. Betty and Lucy's new bedroom set was delivered yesterday.
3. Stu's and Brad's wardrobes show their exquisite tastes in clothing.
4. Has anybody seen the town's financial records lately?
5. Because the concert has been rescheduled, the promoted groups will have to reset the date.
6. Art Carney, the actor who starred in the movie *Harry and Tonto*, is a versatile performer.
7. Our dog did not hear the whistle; moreover, she did not even hear our calls.
8. Basketball, as most fans recall, was invented by Dr. James Naismith.

9. Remember, folks, to take off your shoes upon entering the house.

10. Although he seldom speaks out of turn, Gerald let us all know what he felt.

11. We'll discuss the careers of the following celebrities: Jay Leno, Marlon Brando, and Chevy Chase.

12. Also, the studios are set up in those three locations.

13. He doesn't realize that everybody's opinion is important, Robbie.

14. Obviously, it was a careless, immature thing to do.

15. Behind the barn near the stream, the artist often achieved his greatest work.

16. "Why can't they pick us up here?" Susan asked. "It won't be a major problem."

17. Please adjust the mirror; the sun's glare is too much for me.

18. A great deal of effort went into decorating the gymnasium for the dance; the band, however, did not meet our expectations.

19. The seven packages have arrived, and you can now distribute them.

20. Don't leave the car unlocked; this is a tough neighborhood.

127. PITY THIS POOR PRINTER!

1. Tina doesn't know where she'd be without her parents' help in this matter.

2. It's beginning to look as if they'll be moving within two months' time.

3. How many 8's and how many 12's should I add to this total?

4. He's a fixin' to carry out his daddy's plans to expand the farm.

5. There are many children's books that Mike's great- grandmother has passed down to the family.

6. Mr. Williams will deliver the two families' gifts to you.

7. The men's department, and not the women's department, has the sale now.

8. My boss's car was purchased at Ben London's All- Star Automotive.

9. We love to listen to Crosby, Stills, and Nash's old hit songs.

10. Because Jane's so understanding, she'll listen to almost anyone's sad story.

11. Larry's sister-in-law's job is both interesting and stressful.

12. Do you think you had taken somebody else's jacket by mistake?

13. Our class studied Theodore Roosevelt's, Franklin Roosevelt's, and Dwight Eisenhower's speeches.

14. You have earned how many A's and how many B's this semester?

15. Wasn't it Pink Floyd's lyric that stated, "We don't need no education"?

128. PRETTY BAD PUNCTUATION

A. This is probably the last time our entire class will be together. In a few months we will be moving on to different colleges and jobs. Let's make the most of our last weeks together.

B. My next-door neighbors own a dog that barks throughout the day. Since the neighbors, Alice and Tom, work long hours, the dog receives little attention. Wow! This noise has really become a major annoyance to my family and other families in the neighborhood.

C. After we have our holiday dinners together, either I will drive my grandparents home, or my parents will. When Mom and Dad are too tired to do it, I will still volunteer my services because I love to listen to my grandparents' stories of the past.

SECTION SIX
GRAMMAR'S HELPERS—TAKING CARE OF BUSINESS!

129. THEY SOUND THE SAME BUT . . .

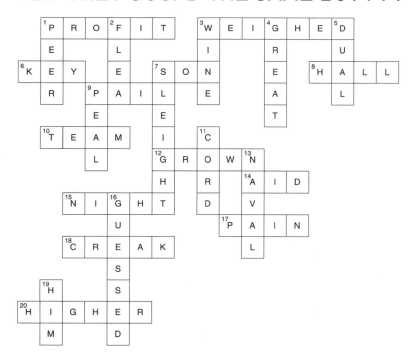

130. THE PRINCIPAL GAVE ME DESSERT AND QUITE A COMPLIMENT!

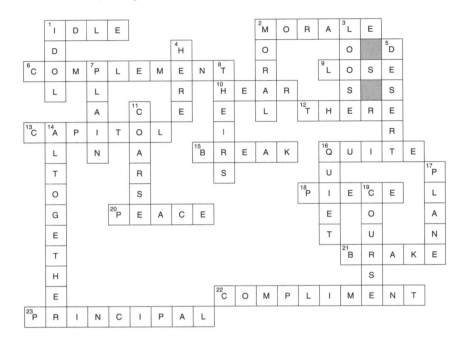

131. ACCEPT A WEAK MINER

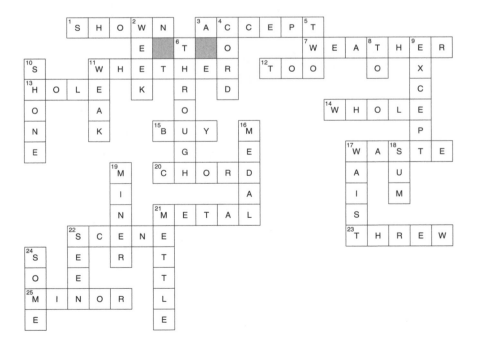

132. HOMOPHONES CROSSWORD PUZZLE

```
          ¹B                  ²S E N T          ³R Y E
  ⁴M   ⁵R E ⁶A D              O                O
  ⁷E W E     L               M                D
  A    A   ⁸T H ⁹Y M E              ¹⁰S E ¹¹E
  N    K   O     O             ¹²F I    ¹³H
    ¹⁴C     G     U             L  G    I
  ¹⁵L O O S E     '          O ¹⁶H I G H E R
  A     E  T      L   ¹⁷A ¹⁸C C E P T    H
  R     H         L        O
  ¹⁹S L O E          ²⁰W O U L D
  E       ²¹R O L E        N
          T               C
               ²²S I G H T
               L
```

133. DEFINING THE CONFUSING

A=2	B=15	C=17	D=23	E=8
F=10	G=22	H=1	I=20	J=12
K=21	L=19	M=13	N=7	O=5
P=14	Q=6	R=25	S=4	T=16
U=18	V=3	W=9	X=11	Y=24

134. HOMOPHONES WORD FIND

```
H  C  I  H  W  V  Z  R  W  W  Z  T  B  B  G  W  H  T  M  J
X  D  G  H  E  Q  Z  S  P  F  G  Y  W  E  S  R  C  A  R  J
M  D  Z  R  G  A  X  T  C  J  F  Y  D  N  R  P  T  A  I  J  G
S  L  N  S  T  Z  H  M  R  W  N  D  D  P  L  R  A  G  R  N  G  R
M  V  C  J  H  X  V  R  W  Y  J  T  V  J  L  R  J  R  E  Q  C  C
L  Y  S  T  Z  K  N  B  T  F  R  Y  R  Q  S  C  K  B  B  L  P  C
B  T  L  Z  R  L  T  J  F  Y  Z  C  Q  H  T  T  Z  B  K  D  T  T
X  L  K  Q  Z  Q  L  L  Q  R  S  J  Z  L  T  B  B  D  B  X  H  Y
G  V  H  K  D  H  J  W  W  C  W  D  L  K  W  S  T  B  K  N  H  B
H  Z  F  G  P  C  T  B  L  L  S  M  F  Y  N  E  X  C  R  R  R  R
K  K  H  G  P  B  T  H  B  E  M  T  V  J  N  X  V  I  B  E  R  D  T
K  N  N  F  C  D  T  M  E  M  A  V  I  N  D  S  C  B  N  G  T  E
L  K  O  V  D  O  F  V  A  I  R  E  H  A  T  A  P  I  L  T  N  G  E  W
T     O  N  I  A  P  E  P  D  S  U  N  M  R  Z  W        L  S  E  W
```

135. TOOOOOOOOO GENERAL

Answers will vary.

136. IT'S THE END THAT COUNTS

1. adjective	6. verb	11. verb
2. adjective	7. adjective	12. adjective
3. noun	8. noun	13. verb
4. noun	9. noun	14. verb
5. adverb	10. adjective	15. adjective

137. SWEET SIXTEEN

GROUP ONE	GROUP TWO	GROUP THREE
A. 6	F. 4	K. 3
B. 2	G. 5	L. 2
C. 3	H. 2	M. 9
D. 3	I. 1	N. 1
E. 2	J. 4	O. 1

138. THE PLURALS PUZZLE

					¹B	R	U	N	²C	H	³E	S				⁵T		⁶M
			⁴D	A	T	A			U		C					R		O
	⁷P			O		B		⁸F		P	H		⁹C			I		N
¹⁰O	X	E	N		¹¹M	I	C	E		F	O		H			E		K
	T		K			E		N		U	E		I			K		E
¹²C	A	L	V	E	S			C		L		¹³S	O	L	O	S		Y
	T		Y			¹⁴G	E	E	S	E			D					
¹⁵R	O	O	¹⁶F	S				S			¹⁷A	E	R	I	A	L	S
	E		L								N		E					
	¹⁸S	K	I	E	S						A		N					
			E		¹⁹M	O	U	²⁰T	H	F	U	L	S				
²¹C	R	I	S	E	S			E			Y						
					²²W	I	V	E	S		S						
								T			E						
								H			S						

139. WHEN Y SOUNDS LIKE A AND I

```
P  J  J  V  M  H  B  Y  N  R  X  Y  F  V  T  J  R  N  K  L
Z  H  V  M  C  K  C  F  H  M  B  Q  N  Q  F  Q  R  X  Q  S
T  S  Q  M  K  V  N  Q  M  F  R  L  L  S  X  R  Q  C  N  X
Y  F  J  D  D  F  T  Z  K  P  A  D  F  R  S  X  B  N  R  N
A  F  H  W  F  M  J  D  E  N  L  G  T  D  B  M  P  L  F  C
L  J  O  C  W  C  M  K  S  N  L  V  Y  R  U  R  Z  K  W  Y
F  L  Y  R  Z  A  C  Q  T  R  L  A  Y  S  K  A  C  E  D  P
S  N  D  Z  A  Q  Q  S  R  G  L  D  Y  L  A  Z  E  V  V  V
P  W  V  B  C  F  Y  P  N  E  C  W  P  T  S  T  S  G  J  J
R  Q  X  V  F  D  Y  R  R  V  H  A  L  V  A  Q  F  P  N  Q
A  E  S  P  Y  Y  H  A  W  S  B  A  F  R  Y  C  W  Y  N  Q
Y  F  Z  K  J  H  Q  Y  D  S  S  K  K  F  Y  Q  S  L  R  W
G  Z  P  B  D  K  Q  Z  H  W  L  R  W  L  P  J  J  X  N  H
J  Y  T  K  N  S  J  G  B  G  B  Y  Y  F  C  J  Y  K  K  V
Y  L  Z  G  N  Y  P  W  Z  K  X  G  C  R  F  P  G  Y  J  J
```

140. LET'S GO TO THE MOVIES!

1. (T) tomorrow

2. (O) squirrel

3. (M) allowed

4. (O) interrupt

5. (R) forfeit

6. (R) cashier

7. (O) exercise

8. (W) burglar

9. (I) colossal

10. (S) condemn

11. (A) laboratory

12. (N) desirable

13. (O) cemetery

14. (T) boundary

15. (H) guardian

16. (E) lightning

17. (R) persuade

18. (D) preferred

19. (A) impossible

20. (Y) professor

The movie quote is, "Tomorrow is another day," from *Gone with the Wind*.

141. DIVIDED DESCRIBERS

blossoming

evasive

embellished

grateful

intellectual

indomitable

intelligent

opportune

perceptible

premature

predatory

reluctant

stupendous

stylistic

turbulent

142. DARING? TIMID? OPTIMISTIC? WHAT ARE YOU?

1. chamber (noun): apartment, room, stall

2. daring (noun): boldness, bravery, courage

3. grab (noun or verb): clutch, grasp, snatch

4. improper (adjective): erroneous, incorrect, mistaken

5. lawless (adjective): disobedient, insurgent, rebellious

6. lenient (adjective): easygoing, liberal, permissive

7. optimistic (adjective): assured, expectant, hopeful

8. promote (verb): boost, encourage, hearten

9. timid (adjective): afraid, fearful, frightened

10. undecided (adjective): debatable, unresolved, unsettled

143. "ROMAN" AROUND

A=1	B=15	C=8	D=10
E=4	F=14	G=5	H=11
I=13	J=3	K=12	L=6
M=16	N=2	O=9	P=7

144. THE PREFIXES AND ROOTS MAGIC SQUARE

A=2	B=15	C=17	D=23	E=8
F=10	G=22	H=1	I=20	J=12
K=21	L=19	M=13	N=7	O=5
P=14	Q=6	R=25	S=4	T=16
U=18	V=3	W=9	X=11	Y=24

equi : equilateral and equilibrium
hetero : heterodox and heterogeneous
jur : jury and jurisdiction
hyper : hypertension and hypertext
cred : credible and credulous
deca : decade and decathlon
non : nonessential and nondescript
clud : include and preclude
omni : omnipresent and omnibus
multi : multitalented and multifaceted
pre : prevent and pretest
spec : spectacular and spectacle
biblio : bibliography and bibliophile
di : divert and divide
vert : invert and subvert
oct : octagon and octopus
morph : morphology and endomorph
phil : philosophy and philology
mono : monogram and monolith
bene : benevolent and beneficial
graph : autograph and graphics
fid : fidelity and confidence
anti : antidepressant and antiwar
hypo : hypochondriac and hypodermic
penta : pentagon and pentathlon

145. IT'S GREEK (AND ROMAN) TO ME!

1. ou	6. la	11. es	16. sl	21. re
2. re	7. ng	12. mu	17. at	22. ek
3. ng	8. ua	13. ch	18. in	23. ro
4. li	9. ge	14. to	19. an	24. ot
5. sh	10. ow	15. it	20. dg	25. s!

The sentence reads, "Our English language owes much to its Latin and Greek roots!"

146. SOME FOOD FOR THOUGHT

1. eggs	6. apple	11. herring
2. bacon	7. mackerel	12. salt
3. beans	8. mustard	13. fruitcake
4. cake	9. dough	14. bananas
5. clam	10. potatoes	15. oats

147. IGNORANCE IS NOT BLISS!!!

1. f	6. a	11. n	16. t
2. l	7. c	12. y	17. h
3. e	8. k	13. m	18. u
4. d	9. b	14. i	19. g
5. p	10. o	15. s	20. e

The 5 four-letter words are fled (1 to 4), pack (5 to 8), bony (9 to 12), mist (13 to 16), and huge (17 to 20).

148. PULLING OUT THE STOPS

Answers will vary.

149. COMPLETING THE APHORISMS

1. (al) If at first you don't succeed, try, try again.
2. (oa) If the shoe fits, wear it.
3. (fe) These are the times that try men's souls.
4. (ra) Be the best that you can be.

5. (lw) If he hollers, let him go.
6. (ay) Eat, drink, and be merry for tomorrow we may die.
7. (sh) Great riches have sold more men than they have bought.
8. (as) The artist doesn't see things as they are, but as he is.
9. (th) Grace is to the body what clear thinking is to the mind.
10. (ec) What does not destroy me, makes me stronger.
11. (or) Necessity poisons wounds which it cannot heal.
12. (re) Whenever I feel afraid, I whistle a happy tune.
13. (ct) When gossip grows old, it becomes myth.
14. (ti) Blessed are the meek for they shall inherit the earth.
15. (me) The worst cliques are those which consist of one man.

A loafer always has the correct time. (Kin Hubbard)

150. DON'T BE DOWN IN THE DUMPS

1. down
2. make
3. raise
4. cast
5. break

6. stern
7. means
8. wrench
9. envy
10. head

11. fist
12. nose
13. airs
14. hook
15. champ

16. midstream
17. jump
18. heart
19. cheek
20. arms

151. ST WI TH TW LE

Answers will vary.

152. THE TERMS OF GRAMMAR

A=4	B=15	C=10	D=5
E=6	F=9	G=16	H=3
I=13	J=2	K=7	L=12
M=11	N=8	O=1	P=14

SECTION SEVEN
GRAMMAR GAMES—AND AWAY WE GO!

153. ENGLO

To the teacher: Direct the students to fill in their ENGLO cards as follows: For the E column, they should place any 5 numbers from 1 to 10 in the E column, 11 to 20 in the N column, 21 to 30 in the G column, 31 to 40 in the L column, and 41 to 50 in the O column. The free space is just that—free. Thus, a student could have numbers 2, 4, 5, 7, and 10 in the E column. When you dictate the word, the student will write that word in the appropriate space and then also write the word's part of speech in the same box. After you have dictated all 50 words, then give the 50 answers. The students will check their own ENGLO cards and see who has ENGLO!

1.	happy	adjective	26.	activate	verb
2.	bring	verb	27.	active	adjective
3.	window	noun	28.	activity	noun
4.	slender	adjective	29.	casually	adverb
5.	carefully	adverb	30.	lend	verb
6.	televise	verb	31.	telepathy	noun
7.	friend	noun	32.	happiness	noun
8.	stapler	noun	33.	befriend	verb
9.	simple	adjective	34.	very	adverb
10.	recount	verb/noun	35.	thin	adjective
11.	practical	adjective	36.	into	preposition
12.	camera	noun	37.	a	adjective
13.	without	preposition	38.	agility	noun
14.	and	conjunction	39.	brought	verb
15.	or	conjunction	40.	ouch	interjection
16.	agile	adjective	41.	they	pronoun
17.	them	pronoun	42.	we	pronoun
18.	is	verb	43.	nobody	pronoun
19.	slipping	adjective/verb	44.	did	verb
20.	she	pronoun	45.	crafty	adjective
21.	hurrah	interjection	46.	winless	adjective
22.	swift	adjective	47.	casual	adjective
23.	Helena	noun	48.	James	noun
24.	lose	verb	49.	yippee	interjection
25.	abruptly	adverb	50.	itself	pronoun

154. THE ALPHABET GAME

Answers will vary.

155. SCORING WITH SENTENCES

These are possible answers. There are others.

       pro   v
1. (7) He resigned.

       pro   v   advb
2. (10) You run slowly.

       v prep pro   advb
3. (12) Talk to them immediately.

       v   n   v   adv
4. (13) Can Bob go now?

       pro   v   v   pro
5. (14) She will help you.

       adj   n   v   v   pro
6. (16) The data has helped us.

       pro con pro   v adj   n
7. (18) He and she are best friends.

        pro v adj   n prep   n
8. (19) They are the heroes of yesterday.

       adj   n   v   v   v   prep   n
9. (21) The building had been abandoned for years.

         n   conj   n   v advb v prep pro
10. (24) Stavros and Mark can never go with you again.

156. ROLL THE DICE!

Answers will vary.

157. TIMING IS EVERYTHING!

Answers will vary.

158. THE GENERATING WHEEL

The following words can be formed. There may be others.

age	noun, verb		get	verb
agent	noun		green	noun, adjective
agree	verb		net	noun, verb
ate	verb		rage	noun, verb
eager	adjective		range	noun, verb
eat	verb		rate	noun, verb
eaten	verb		rent	noun, verb, adjective
eater	noun		tea	noun, adjective
enter	verb		tear	noun, verb
erg	noun		tee	noun, verb
gate	noun		teen	noun
gear	noun, verb		ten	noun, adjective
gee	interjection		tern	noun
genre	noun		tree	noun
gent	noun			

159. THE LAST AND THE FIRST

These are possible answers. Others are possible.

COLUMN A (NOUNS)	COLUMN B (VERBS)
beach	wash
charcoal	shatter
altitude	erase
devil	secede
illustrator	debate
oracle	teach
lemur	char
uranium	arraign
umbrella	gnaw
ladder	await
erasure	itemize
resemblance	zero
certainty	roast
tyro	stare
rocket	reposition

160. I'LL TAKE THE FIFTH

These are possible answers. There can be others.

1. The minister wanted his *congregation* to pray for the flood victims.
2. John could not ask *her* for the manuscript.
3. Run the distance and *set* the school record.
4. Do you think these *tall* women are models?
5. Yvonne had never walked *so* quickly as she did that frightful night.
6. Forget about the past *and* concentrate on the future, Lyle.
7. Some monkeys have crawled *into* the other cage.
8. We could easily see *John* as he signaled to the traffic officials.
9. Yesterday the intelligent man *answered* the forty questions without the least hesitation.
10. We heard the music *during* our meeting.
11. Can she cope with *frustration* as well as her mother can?
12. It is understood that *we* are willing to help you make the payments.
13. You should watch these *large* animals perform such challenging tricks.
14. Jamey, watch the show *since* your hometown is the topic of the presentation.
15. The school's orchestra played *there* last winter

161. GRAMMAR POEMS

These are acceptable poems that follow the directions.

Poem One:
1. Swift and agile,
2. the cheetah,
3. chased by the other animals
4. ran into the distance.

Poem Two:
1. On a dark and stormy night,
2. a knocking
3. at our cabin's front door
4. frightened us.

Poem Three:
1. Lucille,
2. the most talented player
3. and
4. Belinda,
5. nearly her equal,
6. sprinted after the ball.

162. FROM ATHENS TO WASHINGTON

1. fo	6. be	11. na
2. rm	7. en	12. ti
3. ei	8. af	13. ng
4 . th	9. as	14. tr
5. as	10. ci	15. ip

What did you say after you successfully completed this activity? "For me, it has been a fascinating trip."

163. FINDING AND SPELLING

The four nouns are: ladder, carpet, television, and heater. (care or race)
The four adjectives are: lovely, rude, handsome, and wicked. (flee)
The four adverbs are: slowly, very, now, and ever. (done or node)
The four pronouns are: he, themselves, itself, and someone. (lost)
The four prepositions are: under, aboard, except, and during. (sold)
The five conjunctions are: for, or, and, nor, and although. (tames or steam)

164. PRONOUNS AND ADJECTIVES ARE GREAT IN 88!

1 – 7	herself
7 – 11	frail
11 – 16	lovely
16 – 18	you
18 – 21	ugly
21 – 24	your
24 – 27	rich
27 – 30	hard
31 – 34	mine
34 – 37	each
37 – 43	helpful
43 – 47	least
47 – 50	them
50 – 53	mere
53 – 56	even
56 – 60	nasty

165. NOUNS THROUGHOUT THE ALPHABET

The number following each noun indicates the sentence in which the noun is found.

arson (4)

bitterness (7)

countries (2)

decades (4)

economics (3)

food (1)

Georgia (3)

historians (2)

interns (7)

joker (8)

king (6)

larceny (4)

mysteries (6)

nonconformists (9)

officials (7)

peace (2)

queen (6)

researchers (3)

state (3)

treaties (2)

understanding (6)

violence (4)

Warren (5)

xylophones (5)

Yemen (5)

zebras (1)

166. SENSE BEHIND THE NONSENSE

These are possible answers.

    adj n   v   adj   n
1. A rudtur goked feeg plionts.

    v   n   v   adj   n
2. Eky Marty tuuing digh detrily?

    adj adj n v adj n   advb
3. The wenb folns ewq the wkiders sploiply.

    adj   n advb   v c   v   prep adj adj   adj   n
4. Ungy oogers raunbly dertted and pouygtred after the woidy, meedy tuighs.

    prep   adj n adj adj   n   v   prep n
5. During the glout the quafy froin loioded with ghest.

    Advb pro/adj   n   v   advb v adj   n   c adj   n
6. Surely my   etuits will roppily bax the kjhdans and the ohfos.

    v   n   n   v adj adj   n
7. Will Hutty's irjwe wienwe the kibby asdoijhsa?

167. FOR STARTERS

These are acceptable answers.

Letters	Noun	Verb	Adjective
1. psy	psychology	psych	psychic
2. mal	malnutrition	malign	malicious
3. mis	mistake	mistreat	misshapen
4. trans	transit	transport	transcontinental
5. per	permission	permit	permissible
6. sub	substance	substitute	substandard
7. cata	catapult	catalogue	catalytic
8. cad	cadaver	cadge	cadaverous
9. grad	gradation	graduate	gradual
10. por	portfolio	pore	portly
11. mem	member	memorize	memorable
12. sen	sensation	sense	sensory
13. vac	vacation	vacuum	vacuous
14. tele	telephone	televise	telescopic
15. con	condemnation	confess	congratulatory
16. ab	absence	abstain	absolute
17. dom	domicile	dominate	domineering
18. uni	unicorn	unite	universal
19. cor	cord	correct	corporal
20. jud	judgment	judge	judicial

168. JOURNAL JOTTING

Answers will vary.

169. HI!

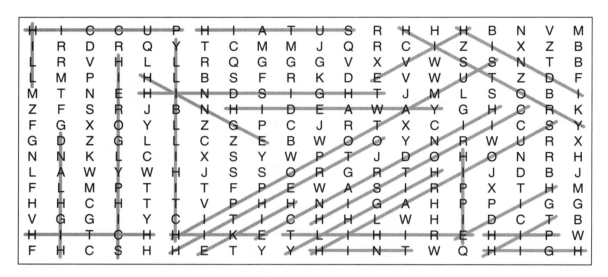

hiatus (n)	hill (n)	hippopotamus (n)
hiccup (n, v)	hillbilly (n)	hire (n, v)
hide (n, v)	hilt (n)	historic (adj)
hideaway (n)	Hindi (n, adj)	history (n)
hieroglyphics (n)	hindrance (n)	hit (n, v)
high (n, adj, advb)	hindsight (n)	hitch (n, v)
highland (n, adj)	hinge (n, v)	hitchhike (v)
highly (advb)	hint (n, v)	hither (advb)
hike (n, adj)	hip (n, adj, i)	hitherto (advb)
hilarious (adj)	hippie (n)	hive (n,v)

170. BEWARE THE IDES OF MARCH

1. FO
2. RE
3. ST
4. AT
5. HE
6. NS
7. RO
8. ME
9. DE
10. NM
11. AR
12. KE
13. NG
14. LA
15. ND

The five settings are forest, Athens, Rome, Denmark, and England.

171. FINDING FORTY (OR MORE)

These are possible answers. There may be additional words.

afford	floral	look	prowl
award	foal	loop	road
dark	fold	lord	roar
draw	follow	papa	roll
drawl	fool	pool	roof
drop	ford	poor	wall
fall	fork	pork	ward
fallow	koala	proof	warp
flaw	lard	prop	word
floor	lark	prow	work

172. THE SPORTING LIFE

```
S U B S T I T U T E Y D N A H E R O F P
L X K C K G X W H P F P X D L C T F S T
S J K D F G Z V Y V J N B B H I R G Z S
K Y S X T R Q Y B J B Z R J X F W T Z J
F R K W P L B T S Y Z W S F L L I B T J R
T H A L I S L T K L Z T F A H I F S W J
K M T J Y T O S M F N V P T T C U Z K N
D N E F E D C D R I B B L E K A F N P F
F M V P V O K H R B Z F N R H S F T P J T
C V J S R B W P E J U G I A L D T P V D
L O S E W E S C A P A N W T O O H S R
J A K Z I R F O H T I C T N S P T H R W B
P D I T W B O H A L L T U Q H B F V Z D
X M C K Q G N W R N G P C Z B T W Z J N
W Z K D D H B K C F F Q B H B T C N G S
```

173. THIS IS NOT A BUM STEER

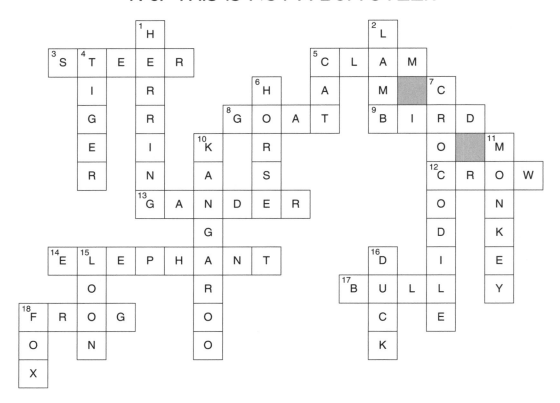

174. DO YOU HAVE AN IRON WILL?

Answers will vary.

175. THE GREATER WAITER BROUGHT THE CRUDE FOOD

1. late bait
2. bigger trigger
3. sad dad
4. high fly
5. greater waiter
6. simple dimple
7. drunk skunk
8. fast cast
9. hairy fairy
10. Monday sundae
11. sloppy poppy
12. plain train
13. strange range
14. wider rider
15. hard card
16. right sight
17. round mound
18. crude food
19. last blast
20. slender mender

176. HAS ANYONE SPOTTED EVE?

1. Is the score still <u>even</u>? (Eve)
2. He seems to be ve<u>ry ang</u>ry with the group. (Ryan)
3. They did not get involved in mu<u>ch ris</u>ky behavior. (Chris)
4. The Smithy family members are <u>rich, ard</u>ent people. (Richard)
5. When in Bos<u>ton, I</u> visit my relatives. (Toni)
6. My mom is a committed an<u>d avid</u> Mets fan. (David)
7. Try to <u>be th</u>e best that you can be. (Beth)
8. Jodi's has bet<u>ter rye</u> bread than this bakery. (Terry)
9. You cannot seek reven<u>ge or ge</u>t your way to resolve the situation. (George)
10. This mediator sett<u>les ter</u>rible disputes. (Lester)
11. I'd rather study gram<u>mar than</u> write another short story. (Martha)
12. In that region the el<u>k ate</u> those foods most of the time. (Kate)
13. He often call<u>s us and</u> tells us what problems he encounters. (Susan)
14. I do it now, o<u>r I take</u> a rest. (Rita)
15. When he came into the par<u>lor, I</u> was introduced to him. (Lori)

177. WHERE IS MONTANA?

```
C A L G A R Y   M   P O N T A R I O   A L F Y
T S D M N L L A   S Y O I O A N Y Z L O L H
R W E A K T A T I B P C R R S M W G Y B N O Z
E E N N V T I K B O A V T E L P Y E D R I Q
N D M I Q X N I O B N I B U L Q A R O N I H
T E A H X Z N S L A T N T G A T N D H G
O N R X X N I E L T D D A C K A N A R A S
N P K B X N T Y A H D N Y J L D B B D M
P X J A F F S R S H O F A G B L Q H C
P B K Q W Q L M Y T S E P A D U B C C
B K P H G V E L F K F Q J K N B P C C J
V M W F T T H K C M I L W A U K E E N R
F Q Y S W S T A J Y J B V H G E S P A F
J G P X F C J T T X M T P G R F Q F F B
Y D L P H K V N G Z L S Y G C Z F F F T
```

178. CHARACTERISTICALLY SPEAKING

Answers will vary.

179. SPELLING IT OUT

Answers will vary.

180. THE PROPER WAY TO DO IT

1. Christine	11. Jamey
2. Sharon	12. Amazon
3. Rashid	13. Quebec
4. Portugal	14. Denver
5. Mexico	15. Edmonton
6. Marion	16. Africa
7. Maureen	17. Maryland
8. Wendy	18. Tim
9. Kate	19. Spain
10. Florida	20. Kansas

Letter: A B C D E F G H I J K L M N O P Q R S T U V W X Y Z
Code: R Z H V I G K U D Q E X A W F L P C J M S Y N B O T

181. THE NAME GAME

These are possible answers. There may be others.

1. Charles char (noun and verb)
2. Steven even (adjective, adverb, verb, and noun)
3. Hillary ill (adjective)
4. Tamien mien (noun)
5. Courtney court (noun and verb); our (pronoun)
6. Arthur art (noun)
7. Kate ate (verb)
8. Andrew and (conjunction); drew (verb)
9. Sarah rah (interjection)
10. Seymour our (pronoun)
11. Warren war (noun and verb)
12. Debbie ebb (noun and verb)

13. Robert rob (verb); robe (noun and verb)
14. Cassandra and (conjunction); sand (noun and verb)
15. Matthew mat (noun); the (adjective); hew (verb)
16. Madeline made (verb); line (noun and verb); mad (adjective, verb, and noun)
17. Mildred mild (adjective)
18. Gerald era (noun)
19. Edward war (noun and verb); ward (noun)
20. Carlotta car (noun); lot (noun, verb, and adverb)
21. Whitney whit (noun); hit (noun and verb)
22. Eleanor lea (noun); lean (noun, verb, and adjective)
23. Angelina angel (noun); gel (noun and verb)
24. Winona win (noun and verb)
25. Martha mar (verb); mart (noun)
26. Donovan don (verb); nova (noun); van (noun)
27. Christine tine (noun)
28. Frank ran (verb); rank (noun, verb, and adjective)
29. Giovanni van (noun)
30. William will (noun and verb); ill (noun)

SECTION EIGHT
FINAL TESTS—KNOWLEDGE IS POWER!

182. FINAL TEST ON NOUNS AND PRONOUNS

1. He (P); cans (N); house (N); block (N); us (P)
2. they (P); airport (N); Tuesday (N)
3. You (P); task (N); yourself (P); hours (N); Kyle (N)
4. aggravation (N); time (N); drive (N); Tucson (N)
5. Someone (P); group (N); others (P); me (P)
6. this (P); booth (N); fair (N); Leo (N)

183. FINAL TEST ON THE NOUN AND ITS FUNCTIONS

1. (a) subject
2. (f) direct address
3. (b) direct object
4. (c) indirect object
5. (e) predicate noun
6. (g) appositive
7. (d) object of the preposition
8. (b) direct object
9. (f) direct address
10. (c) indirect object
11. (a) subject
12. (a) subject
13. (f) direct address
14. (e) predicate noun
15. (e) predicate noun
16. (d) object of the preposition
17. (c) indirect object
18. (b) direct object
19. (g) appositive
20. (d) object of the preposition

184. FINAL TEST ON PRONOUNS

1. you
2. hers
3. That
4. we
5. They
6. Which
7. Nobody
8. herself
9. What
10. Each
11. who
12. Most
13. us
14. Everything
15. Those
16. both
17. everyone
18. whom
19. many
20. him

185. FINAL TEST ON PRONOUN PROBLEMS

1. I
2. whom
3. who
4. we
5. me
6. she
7. her
8. he
9. them
10. they
11. I
12. him
13. she
14. Who
15. them
16. us
17. me
18. He
19. him
20. whom

186. FINAL TEST ON MAIN AND HELPING VERBS

The helping verb is listed first, and the main verb is listed second.

1. will return
2. Are going
3. has heard
4. Was delivered
5. Can help
6. has planted
7. had been
8. Can take
9. Is sending
10. Did forget
11. had sat
12. had been
13. Will help
14. will represent
15. Can be
16. Can solve
17. are accepted
18. were interesting
19. will go
20. had exercised

187. FINAL TEST ON IRREGULAR VERBS

1. taken
2. chosen
3. brought
4. written
5. eaten
6. knew
7. driven
8. rang
9. swam
10. done
11. given
12. burst
13. ridden
14. shrank
15. run
16. stole
17. spoken
18. gone
19. taken
20. began

188. FINAL TEST ON VERBAL PHRASES

1. Asking for more food—gerund
2. to go there—infinitive
3. Investing in the stock market—gerund
4. To err—infinitive
5. walking along the stream—participle
6. to walk along the stream—infinitive
7. Walking along the stream—gerund
8. to audition for the school musical—infinitive

9. reading these magazines—participle
10. to wear tomorrow night—infinitive
11. Brushing the horse down—participle
12. wearing their new coats—participle
13. to skate on that lake—infinitive
14. dropped on the way to the room—participle
15. Noticing the difference in the two jars—participle
16. Shuffling along—participle
17. Listing all the club's officials—gerund
18. stolen last weekend—participle
19. to do—infinitive
20. Found on the shelf—participle

189. FINAL TEST ON ADJECTIVES

1. beautiful
2. larger
3. old
4. recent
5. favorite
6. majestic
7. soccer
8. legitimate
9. overall
10. huge
11. threatening
12. higher
13. confusing, forgetful
14. difficult
15. Fluffy, warm
16. old
17. scary, marked
18. humorous
19. disadvantaged, holiday
20. Tall, beautiful

190. FINAL TEST ON ADVERBS

1. consistently
2. squarely
3. soon
4. still
5. forever
6. vigorously
7. increasingly
8. quite
9. rather
10. first
11. often
12. Traditionally
13. early
14. Lately
15. always
16. together
17. down
18. abroad
19. almost
20. securely

191. FINAL TEST ON PARTS OF SPEECH

1. verb
2. adjective
3. pronoun
4. adverb
5. conjunction
6. noun
7. preposition
8. adverb
9. pronoun
10. verb
11. noun
12. adverb
13. preposition
14. adverb
15. interjection
16. adjective
17. noun
18. verb
19. conjunction
20. preposition

192. FINAL TEST ON SENTENCES, FRAGMENTS, AND RUN-ONS

Numbers 1, 3, 5, 8, 9, 11, and 18 are sentences (S).
Numbers 2, 6, 7, 10, 13, 14, 16, 17, 19, and 20 are fragments (F).
Numbers 4, 12, and 15 are run-ons (RO).

193. FINAL TEST ON PREPOSITIONS

1. without
2. throughout
3. beneath
4. around
5. since
6. aboard
7. about
8. around
9. concerning
10. beyond
11. in spite of
12. about
13. Instead of
14. by
15. near
16. At
17. because of
18. near
19. during
20. of

194. FINAL TEST ON COMPLEMENTS

For numbers 1, 3, 12,19, and 20, the answer is pa.
For numbers 8, 11,14, and 17, the answer is io.
For numbers 2, 4, 5, 13, 15, and18, the answer is do.
For numbers 6, 7, 9, 10, and16, the answer is pn.

195. FINAL TEST ON SUBORDINATE CLAUSES

1. adverb
2. noun
3. adjective
4. adverb
5. adjective
6. noun
7. adverb
8. adverb
9. noun
10. adverb
11. adjective
12. adjective
13. noun
14. adverb
15. adjective
16. adverb
17. noun
18. noun
19. adjective
20. adverb

196. FINAL TEST ON CLASSIFYING SENTENCES BY PURPOSE

1. declarative
2. interrogative
3. imperative
4. exclamatory
5. interrogative
6. declarative
7. imperative
8. exclamatory
9. declarative
10. imperative
11. interrogative
12. exclamatory
13. imperative
14. declarative
15. interrogative
16. exclamatory
17. declarative
18. interrogative
19. declarative
20. interrogative

197. FINAL TEST ON AGREEMENT

1. are
2. is
3. were
4. works
5. appear
6. was
7. was
8. is
9. select
10. decide
11. are
12. has
13. have
14. is
15. have
16. is
17. her
18. his
19. are
20. was

198. FINAL TEST ON USAGE

1. excepted
2. effect
3. anywhere
4. Besides
5. Bring
6. among
7. have
8. fewer
9. well
10. let

11. than
12. Those
13. Unless
14. that
15. can hardly
16. teach
17. burst
18. affect
19. invent
20. accept

199. FINAL TEST ON WORDS OFTEN CONFUSED

200. FINAL TEST ON WORDS IN CONTEXT

1. Several children <u>chased</u> the playful dog.
2. You are the party's <u>choice</u> for <u>president</u>.
3. The <u>ferry</u> headed for the distant <u>island</u>.
4. A <u>smiling</u> and friendly tour guide <u>escorted</u> her group to the restaurant.
5. <u>Unfortunately</u>, the <u>car's</u> engine would not turn over.
6. We could see the <u>lighthouse</u> with its shining beacon in the <u>distance</u>.
7. A <u>string</u> was tied around the <u>stack</u> of newspapers.
8. The green <u>valley</u> was <u>quite picturesque</u>.
9. Some of the <u>quarterbacks</u> in our football league broke many <u>records</u>.
10. Did you take the <u>locks</u> for both <u>bicycles</u>?

201. FINAL TEST ON GRAMMAR TERMS

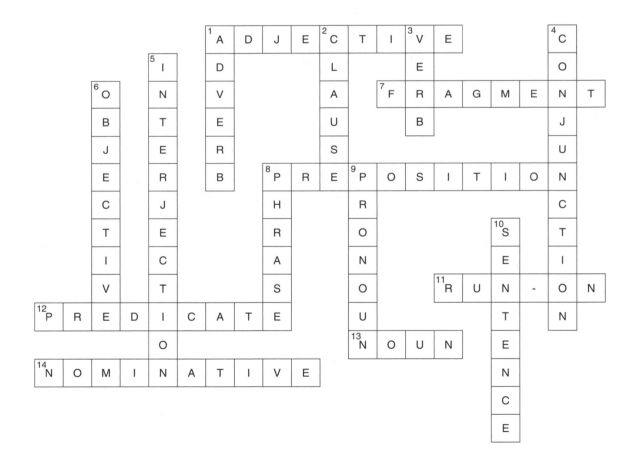

202. FINAL TEST ON COMMAS

1. Are you going to the fair tomorrow night, Jose?

2. Our other car, a black Toyota, is in the garage.

3. My sister is scheduled to study economics, world governments, and English literature next semester.

4. No, Lou's address is not 417 Smallson Court, Ontario, Canada.

5. Juan can carry packages, and Pedro can load the other cartons now.

6. Mike Rogers, who has played in that band for years, may go solo next year.

7. Knowing he needed to convince only a few more voters, the politician took to the streets again.

8. Since there are so few trains coming home at that late hour, we will need to leave the party earlier.

9. Knowledgeable and interesting, tonight's guest speaker will captivate all of you.

10. Most people, even those who are not that informed, have heard of her.

11. Tim, would you please check these numbers for me?

12. With due respect, I feel, Joe, that there are better candidates for the position.

13. Her date of birth is May 3, 1992, I think.

14. We can submit the application now, or we can wait until later this week.

15. Yes, Martin Luther King, Jr. will always be revered by anyone who cares about human life.

203. FINAL TEST ON PUNCTUATION

To the teacher: You can decide how to score this Final Test. Including a pair of quotation marks as one mark of punctuation (sentences 8, 10, 12, and 13), and inserting the commas following *pens* in sentence 4 and *broccoli* in sentence 14, there are 50 marks of punctuation.

1. These are the correct answers, Teddy.

2. When Natasha studies these folders, both she and you will understand the situation more fully, Barb.

3. This card is quite touching; I appreciate your kindness toward our family.

4. Please have the following items with you: index cards, pens, and some form of identification.

5. Maureen and Tim are headed for the beach today; however, they will only stay there for a few hours.

6. Yes, there are many other options available to you, Kate, but this seems to be the best possible one now.

7. The procession will move down the driveway at 10:30 or shortly after that.

8. Did you enjoy "A Christmas Carol" by Charles Dickens, the British writer?

9. There are three e's in the word <u>cemetery</u>.

10. "This is our best chance," Jim told Karen, his wife.

11. *Lord of the Flies*, a novel depicting man's inhumanity toward his fellow man, was written by William Golding.

12. Jasmine announced, "We need to help these needy people as soon as we can."

13. "Hurry up, Mort!" George screamed.

14. Supper included steak, baked potatoes, broccoli, and gravy.

15. John, you could certainly borrow our car; however, we will need it back by this Saturday afternoon.

NOTES

NOTES

NOTES

NOTES

NOTES